INSTITUTE OF INTERNATIONAL STUDIES
YALE UNIVERSITY

Congress and Foreign Policy

The Yale Institute of International Studies was organized in 1935 for the purpose of promoting research and training in the field of international relations. Although concerned with all aspects of international affairs, its studies have been primarily devoted to clarifying contemporary problems in the foreign policy of the United States. The members of the Institute work at all times in close association, but each member is free to formulate his research projects in his own way and each published study represents an individual analysis of a problem.

Publications of the Institute include: A. Whitney Griswold's "Far Eastern Policy of the United States," George T. Davis' "A Navy Second to None," Arnold Wolfers' "Britain and France between Two Wars," Nicholas John Spykman's "America's Strategy in World Politics" and "The Geography of the Peace," and Samuel Flagg Bemis' "The Latin-American Policy of the United States."

Other publications have been William T. R. Fox's "The Super-Powers," David Nelson Rowe's "China among the Powers," and Percy E. Corbett's "Britain: Partner for Peace." "The Absolute Weapon," written by members of the Institute and edited by Bernard Brodie, was a collaborative analysis of atomic power. The most recent volumes are William Reitzel's "The Mediterranean: Its Role in America's Foreign Policy," Annette Baker Fox's "Freedom and Welfare in the Caribbean," and Gabriel A. Almond's "The American People and Foreign Policy."

Frederick S. Dunn, Director

Congress and Foreign Policy

Robert A. Dahl

New York

HARCOURT, BRACE AND COMPANY

TO MY PARENTS

Contents

PART THREE

A NEW PATTERN OF POLICY-MAKING

Acknowledgments

I AM particularly indebted to Frederick S. Dunn and the Yale Institute of International Studies for having made this study possible. In addition to Mr. Dunn, a number of colleagues at Yale and elsewhere have read parts or all of the manuscript: William T. R. Fox, Willmoore Kendall, Gabriel A. Almond, Francis W. Coker, V. O. Key, Charles Hyneman, Ernest S. Griffith, William Y. Elliott, and Elmer E. Schattschneider. Numerous improvements in the book were made as a result of their criticisms and suggestions.

Many people in government service made helpful suggestions while I was preparing the manuscript. I am obliged to Secretary of State Dean Acheson for an interview held during the interim between his two periods of service as Under Secretary and Secretary of State, and I am grateful for discussions with Senators Elbert D. Thomas, Raymond E. Baldwin, and Brien McMahon; Representatives Sam Rayburn, Christian A. Herter, Karl Stefan, Mike Mansfield, John McCormack, A. S. Mike Monroney, and Henry M. Jackson; Delegate E. L. Bartlett; Leslie L. Biffle, then Executive Director of the Democratic Policy Committee; George H. E. Smith, then Staff Director of the Republican Policy Committee; Robert E. Lee, Chief Investigator, House Committee on Appropriations; Francis O. Wilcox, Chief of Staff of the Senate Committee on Foreign Relations; Lewis Deschler, Parliamentarian of the House; and Miss Florence Kirlin, Special Assistant to the Counselor, Department of State.

By the efforts of Karl Cerny, Karl Hochschwender, and Duane Lockard, I was relieved of much of the drudgery of accumulating the data on which the tables in this volume are based. Mrs. Alvin Johnson has provided a patient and sympathetic editing of the manuscript.

The usual caveat is in order. None of the people I have named necessarily agrees with any particular statement of fact or value in this book; some of them will disagree with my conclusions.

For permission to quote from works published by them I am indebted to Cambridge University Press, Columbia University Press, Committee on Public Administration Cases, Doubleday and Company, Inc., Harper and Brothers, Henry Holt and Company, Inc., The Macmillan Company, G. P. Putnam's Sons, and the publishers of *The Public Opinion Quarterly*.

Bibliographical notes are to be found on pages 265-79.

ROBERT A. DAHL

Congress and Foreign Policy

Introduction

MODERN international politics is a rigorous testing ground for the classic instruments of government in a democratic society. Of such extraordinary rigor is the test, indeed, that one can make an impressive case for the proposition that the democratic legislature is an anachronistic survival of a bygone epoch.

Ours is the era of permanent crisis: crisis at home, crisis abroad. So universal and commonplace a fact renders the very word a cliché. Ours is the electric atmosphere favorable to the appearance of the "leader"—not, certainly, the calm environment congenial to discussion, debate, and orderly agreement.

And yet despite these grounds for pessimism, the Congress of the United States has far from taken the Jeremiahs to heart. Its vigor and liveliness often seem more like the boisterous demands of a contentious youngster than "the petty tyrannies of an already close-to-powerless old man" (as one of the Jeremiahs, James Burnham, described it a few years ago). In either case, however, the analogy is inaccurate; for Congress is not an organism of fixed life span. It is an institution whose fate may be influenced to some extent by rational calculation.

Yet if one scrutinizes Congress with some care, the conclusion is unavoidable that the national legislature, as it now plays its exacting role on the political stage, is remarkably ill-suited to exercise a wise control over the nation's foreign policy. To anyone who values the democratic process on the one side and ponders the desperate urgencies of international politics on the other, this conclusion, however little novelty it may possess, is bound to be profoundly disturbing. For the conclusion raises some fundamental questions about American political institutions and values.

There are three useful criteria for evaluating the method by which decisions about public policy (including foreign policy) are made: criteria, I hasten to point out, relevant in their entirety only in a democratic society.

1. To what extent does the decision-making process provide for *responsible leadership*? Leadership may be regarded as responsible to the extent that it selects policies based upon the preferences of the citizens. Where members of the community disagree, as of course they commonly do, responsible leadership reflects the preferences of the greatest number of citizens. That leadership should be fully responsible is, I take it, an elemental prerequisite to democracy.

2. To what extent does the decision-making process facilitate *agreement* among citizens of the community? How successfully does the process provide for discussion directed toward a clarification of ends, the means to those ends, and the possibility of agreement on means and ends? Like responsibility, opportunity for reaching agreement, particularly by amicable and informed discussion, is one of the fundamental values of a democratic order. This is not to say that when discussion is terminated and the time for decision arrives, everyone in the national community must be satisfied with the decision. But it is to say that the preferences of no substantial minority should be *unnecessarily* ignored by a majority. Particularly in the field of foreign policy great advantages will be derived from any method that maximizes agreement. The effectiveness of foreign policy today rests in substantial measure upon the capacity of a nation for undertaking sacrifices and, when the last card has been played, for waging war. For a democratic nation—and particularly perhaps for the United States—to impose sacri-

fices upon itself with substantial success requires a very considerable amount of agreement on the policies that presuppose the sacrifices.

3. To what extent does the method of decision-making lead to *rational* policies—to policies, that is to say, best designed to achieve the purposes agreed on? It is one thing to have responsible leadership and a substantial area of agreement; but it is quite another to abstract out of that agreement policies that are rational—that are, in other words, best calculated to satisfy, in the real world of international politics, the desires and aspirations underlying the agreement. To put it somewhat differently, it is by no means impossible that a policy could be completely "democratic" and at the same time quite suicidal. No doubt few citizens would consciously seek the self-destruction of their country. But out of confusion about the issues, lack of information, or widespread irrationality they might be party to the selection of such a policy—one, surely, they would not have chosen had they possessed a clear understanding of its consequences.

In the American democracy, as indeed in any other, much of the burden for securing responsible leadership, for maximizing agreement, and for developing a more rational understanding among the electorate ought to fall upon the legislative body. Yet the plain and ominous fact is that Congress faces tremendous difficulties in discharging this burden. Such an observation might suggest that one should explore ways of dealing with foreign policy that would relieve Congress wholly or in part of its responsibilities; some of the more important of these alternatives will be considered in Part Two. There it will appear that most such proposals are, if desirable, unattainable; and if attainable, undesirable. In Part Three, therefore, I shall turn to some proposals for building into our political framework a kind of policy-making process in foreign affairs that would offer somewhat better chances for the survival of democracy during the present period of bitter and sustained international conflict. We may say "survival of democracy," for in the present state of the world powers it seems likely that the disappearance of American democracy would bring about elsewhere an extinction of that lengthy experiment in freedom and equality.

PART ONE

FOREIGN POLICY AND THE INFLUENCES ON CONGRESS

I. The Congressman and His Beliefs

TO understand the vast difficulties Congress faces in wielding an intelligent and responsible control over American foreign policy, you have only to do two things. First, look at the influences acting upon the Congressman as he arrives at a decision. And second, ask yourself this single question: To what extent do these influences foster responsibility, agreement, and rationality?

One cannot talk about influences, to be sure, without abstracting somewhat from reality. In real life situations the "influences" not only overlap one another but vary in intensity and importance. They vary, for example, from issue to issue. Constituents are sometimes aroused, sometimes passive; pressure groups are activated by some issues and not by others; the President may bring all the power and authority of his great office to bear, or he may deliberately choose to remain aloof. The influences vary, too, from Congressman to Congressman. Representative X lends a willing ear to private pressure groups; his colleague Y relies heavily on expert testimony. Senator Jones tries desperately to adjust his vote to the attitudes of a few influential groups among his constituents; Senator Brown prides himself, with some justification, on holding fast to his "principles."

To speak of influences is even more of an abstraction from reality because Congressmen themselves often arrive at decisions without quite knowing how or why they do so.[1] Like the soldier on the battlefield, the Congressman does not always know why he made the move he did, and even later casualty lists will not always tell whether his move, for him, was the right one.

His Private Preferences *

The Congressman is a rather ordinary person in some respects, not much wiser than the average small town lawyer, banker, doctor, or bartender, frequently confused, almost always harassed, excessively overworked, busy with an enormous variety of problems presented by his constituents, and sometimes called upon to make decisions on foreign policy that will affect man and his institutions over a large part of the earth's surface for generations to come.

All too often, those who see him as *homo politicus* (rather than the small town lawyer turned *homo politicus*) hold him to be animated by nothing more than the drive ascribed to him by Hobbes: ". . . I put for a general inclination of all mankind a perpetual and restless desire of power after power, that ceaseth only in death." From this assumption it is easy to pass on to a simplified, mechanistic interpretation of the politician, pressed relentlessly by his dominant drive for power, with an ear cocked only to the main chance.

But this is oversimple and overgeneralized. Politicians are complicated human beings with a considerable repertory of motivations. Doubtless one of the most important of these motivations is a desire for power or influence. But such a statement tells us very little as to *why* a politician desires power. To the understanding of his behavior, this "why" is crucial.

---

* By *private* preferences I mean his inner, highly subjective feelings of what he regards as desirable for self and others, as distinguished from his publicly articulated and discussed preferences. The two may coincide; they also may not.

It may be that he seeks power only under conditions acceptable to his "principles" (or if one prefers, acceptable to the demands of his super-ego). In this case his behavior may be quite different from that of a colleague whose imperious needs for deference and prestige are allayed by the simple act of holding public office. To say this is to say nothing more than what newspaper reporters at the state and national capitols have long recognized: how a legislator votes is partly determined by "what kind of a person he is."

Now if we were to observe *homo politicus* carefully and were to speculate about our observations, probably we should find it useful to distinguish between his personality, his character, his preferences, and his picture of reality. Let me say here a word about each of these except the last, which will be dealt with in the following section.

About the relationship between personality and character on the one side and political behavior on the other, very little is known even today, and I do not propose to speculate about this relationship in Congressmen.[2] It is, to be sure, a plausible hypothesis that some kinds of personality types find certain kinds of political behavior and attitudes more satisfying than others. And yet it is highly improbable that there is any simple one-to-one relationship between a Congressman's attitudes on foreign policy and his basic personality pattern, or that Congressmen with similar attitudes about foreign affairs tend to have similar kinds of personalities.

This terra incognita may be left, however, for exploration by others, while we advance to the slightly more accessible terrain referred to as the Congressman's "preferences." By his preferences, I mean his sense of what he would like to have happen as distinct—when it is distinct—from his sense of what is in fact happening in the world, which may be called his picture of reality. That is to say, his preferences govern the manner in which he tries to adapt his conduct to the world he discerns about him, and conversely, to adapt the world about him to his purposes.

The Congressman's preferences are shaped by his loyalties, his attitudes of deference and respect, his view of a desired future for himself and for those with whom he identifies himself, for his constituency, for his society, his country, the world, posterity.*

A recent study of the events surrounding passage of the Foreign Service Act of 1946 suggests the variety of private preferences that may go into a Congressional decision:

> Personal factors . . . played some part in the Subcommittee acceptance of the basic structure and character of the draft bill. To Judge Kee it was an administration measure sponsored by a member of the President's cabinet; as such it deserved his support. To Mr. Richards it was a favored project of two fellow South Carolinians, Mr. Byrnes and Mr. Russell. As for Mr. Vorys, his interest in the Foreign Service and his conviction of the need for a non-patronage career service dated back to his work with the Disarmament Conference in 1922. At that time he had found a higher level of competence and devotion among the career diplomats and officials than among the patronage appointees on the staff of the U.S. delegation, even though he was himself a patronage appointee. To him, therefore, the Rogers Act and this proposed revision of it seemed wise.[3]

The influence of the legislator's private preferences is magnified whenever the other influences playing upon him are weak. Among the most important of these other influences

---

* To describe the individual's evaluations I use the word "preferences" rather than the older term "interests" or the newer term "values." On occasion, where the reference is to widely shared preferences of "basic" importance, the word "value" will be used; and because the phrase "interest group" has wide acceptability among political scientists, it is sometimes employed here.

are political parties and pressure groups. To the extent that party influence is weak, there is greater room for the expression of the legislator's private preferences as to the kind of foreign policy he would like the nation to have. At the very least, the limited force of party means that the private, nonparty preferences of the legislator influence his choice of the particular pressures to which he defers. When pressure groups are active, they can be extraordinarily effective. But on many issues of foreign policy they are not mobilized, or they cancel one another. On vital foreign policies, therefore, the Congressman is sometimes virtually a free agent.

Many Congressmen enjoy this role. They like to think of themselves as relying on their private preferences, which they call "principles," rather than on the "dictates" of party leaders, or the party program, or pressure groups, or occasionally even constituents. They call this "independence," and "independence" is highly regarded not only in Congress but evidently among the electorate. A high place is reserved in the American political tradition for the insurgents—Theodore Roosevelt, the La Follettes, George Norris, and the like. In emphasizing the supreme importance of one's own private conscience, the independent simply expresses in politics the religious attitudes of the Protestant sects that have so much shaped the American temper.

Not long after his election in 1948, Senator Paul Douglas expressed this set of attitudes thus: "Support one's party in all procedural matters everywhere. Argue substantive programs within party councils in the hope of gaining a majority within the party. But when the chips are down in the Senate, a Senator should vote his profound individual convictions on substantive matters regardless of who is with or against him." [4]

An observer who interviewed thirteen Congressmen to discover how they made up their minds on the repeal of the arms embargo during the special session in the fall of 1939 reported that twelve of them put their own "independent judgment" in first place. Only two listed "party considerations"—and these two put this influence in third place.[5] These Congressmen were, no doubt, grossly exaggerating their "independence." But what is significant is their evident agreement that "independent judgment" is a highly respectable influence in Congress.

If the Congressman likes to think of himself as "independent" of party and other pressures, why does Congress not break up into a multiplicity of different groups, shifting and reforming on every issue? How can we explain such homogeneity and consistency of voting groups as do exist? The answer is, in part, that Congress *does* tend to break up into voting groups that change from issue to issue. The historic weakness of the American party system is precisely that it has been unable to prevent this occurrence. Although we often pride ourselves on our two-party system in Congress, in some respects we have little more than a system of multiple parties operating under two labels.

The functioning of a two-party system is helped, however, because influences often tend to enlist in two camps. They polarize. What party loyalty by itself cannot accomplish is achieved by a rather formidable combination. Supporting one side, for example, one may find these allies: the President; executive experts interpreting and communicating events, who in turn may influence the views of newspaper editors and other publicists; party leaders in Congress; and possibly executive-stimulated pressures among constituents or private pressure groups. Lined up on the other side may be a variety of influences working together: hostility toward the President; interpretation and communication of events by newspapers and party staffs; party loyalty and leadership; and possibly pressure induced by important opinion leaders.

Thus in the period 1932-48, the accumulation of executive and party influences helped to produce a certain unity and consistency in Democratic voting on foreign policy issues. A lesser but nonetheless significant unity and consistency in Republican voting also resulted from the tendency for various influences to coincide, such as party, anti-presidential hostility, and judgment as to constituent opinion. (See Tables IV and V on pages 46 and 47.)

Finally, foreign policy is only a part of a general Weltanschauung. Preferences about policy tend to be *persistent, consistent,* and *shared.* Attitudes that cause Senator Jones to vote in a particular way on one issue persist into subsequent issues. Likewise, Jones strives for a behavior that is internally consistent from his own point of view: he tries to bring his attitudes on domestic issues into some kind of subjective harmony with his attitudes on foreign issues; his various attitudes on foreign issues also tend to take on a certain subjective consistency. And because Jones is a product of a cultural milieu shared by others, his views, too, tend to be shared by others.

Thus, if one were to observe Congressional voting on foreign policy issues over a period of time, one might detect a number of different "clusters" of more or less persistent attitudes, held by groups frequently cutting across the more obvious lines of party and region. It seems likely, for example, that in the years 1933-48, at least three critical sets of attitudes underlay the activities of many Congressmen. These were: attitudes toward international violence; attitudes concerning collaboration of the United States with other nations or international organizations; and attitudes toward the domestic status quo. There were, to be sure, many minor variations, but for schematic purposes one might divide the attitudes toward vio-

lence into pacifist (rejection of violence) and militant (acceptance of violence); attitudes toward collaboration into isolationist (rejection) and internationalist (acceptance); and attitudes
toward the domestic status quo into reformist (rejection) and
conservative (acceptance). Given the various possible combinations, it is easy to see why, indeed, politics does make strange
bedfellows:

While it would be tedious to explore all the permutations
of these six key preferences, three combinations may be taken
for illustrative purposes: the pacifist-isolationist-reformist, the
pacifist-internationalist-reformist, and the militant-internation-
alist-reformist. Congressional supporters of the New Deal were
largely drawn from these three groups, operating in an un-
easy alliance with militant-internationalist-conservatives from
the South. These New Deal groups tended to vote together
on questions of domestic reforms. But on international questions they often tended to fall apart, even under the meticulous
guidance of party leaders in Congress and the White House.

The first group was isolationist because of its pacifism; its
members looked upon war as a destroyer of life and welfare;
isolationism in foreign affairs and social security at home were
both devices for protecting the welfare of the "victims" of
modern social arrangements. The second group, unlike the first,
was internationalist because it was pacifist; it looked upon international collaboration as a way of avoiding violence. Its
members therefore tended to break away from support for
"internationalist" action whenever such a commitment might
involve violence. This in turn would tend to foster an alliance
between the militant internationalists, both reformist and conservative. It was this alliance that President Roosevelt increasingly relied upon as, after 1937, he moved toward foreign policies of the militant-internationalist type.

Thus we see how the persistency, consistency, and sharing of attitudes about certain broad classes of issues helped to create clusters in Congress much more inclusive than the individual Congressman, but less inclusive than the party.

So far, the Congressman's preferences have been treated as if they were something detached from his view of reality. Such a sharp delineation, if insisted upon, would almost certainly be nonsense. For it is highly probable that the Congressman, like most other mortals, in some degree adapts his view of what *ought* to be to his view of what *is;* and conversely, he adapts his view of what *is,* albeit unconsciously, to his view of what *ought* to be. For example, Congressman Vorys supported the Foreign Service Act of 1946 because he valued competence and devotion in the public service—and also because his view of reality, shaped by his experience at the Disarmament Conference in 1922, seemed to confirm his belief that the principles of the Act were likely to produce the competent and devoted public servants he desired.

The Pictures in His Head

Congressman X is a small town lawyer who originally went into politics in Illinois in the well-founded hope that a little campaigning would build up his clientele. He was sent to a small rural grade school, attended a high school in a nearby town, studied at a denominational college in Ohio, and earned his law degree by correspondence. He was a little too young for service in the First World War; his brother, a sergeant in the infantry, was killed three days after arriving at the front. Most of his life, Congressman X has read little other than small town newspapers and the Chicago *Tribune*. His personal experiences, his relationships with people, his cultural milieu, the images that have stuck in his mind from reading the newspapers—all these have given him what I have called his view of reality.

These "pictures in his head," to use Walter Lippmann's graphic expression of two decades ago,[6] he now summons up in what he finds is a confused and yet familiar kind of intellectual newsreel, as he ponders how he is to vote on the first European recovery bill. He finally votes against the bill, as he had voted against proposals of a similar stripe ever since the bill to repeal the arms embargo at the special session of Congress in 1939. He is no longer so sure as he once was of the validity of the old familiar jumble of snapshots in his mind that represent "England," "Europe," "Socialism," "Allies." Radio commentators he has sometimes listened to, his reading of the New York *Times* (which he felt it his duty to begin perusing during the war as events were happening he felt he ought to know more about), the speeches of some of his acquaintances on the Foreign Affairs Committee, and the evident discontent of many of his constituents in the last campaign have all combined to give him doubts. But the familiar snapshots are the only ones that hang together in some kind of sense-making arrangement. So he votes against the bill.

Congressman Y grew up in South Carolina, the son of a cotton exporter. Like John C. Calhoun before him, he went North to Yale College; he took his law degree at Harvard just before the First World War, worshiped Wilson, enlisted in the Air Corps but missed going overseas, developed a furious youthful hatred for Senator Lodge, and during his years as a small town lawyer in his home state discovered in his local library the books provided by the Carnegie Endowment for International Peace, which confirmed his feeling that American rejection of the League was a tragic blow to world unity. Elected to the House, he supported "internationalism" on those infrequent occasions when the House debated subjects relevant to such an issue. During the recent war he spoke frequently for a permanent United Nations and was overjoyed upon American entry. In Washington he has consistently read the New York *Times* and the Washington *Post*. The "pictures in his head" under the caption "foreign affairs" were most neatly arranged, perhaps, shortly after the end of the war in Europe. Since that time they have become somewhat jumbled and indistinct. He is not without serious doubts about ERP. But after a five-minute speech in which he parades the same set of familiar word pictures he has employed on previous occasions, he casts his vote in favor of the bill.*

Now it is not too much to say that whoever, or whatever, put the pictures in the heads of Congressman X or Congressman Y substantially determined his decision about ERP. To be sure, if other pressures—the President, the party leaders in Congress, his constituents—pile up sufficiently, the Congressman, despite his private view of reality and the policy consequences that seem to flow from that view, may support a policy contrary to the one suggested by his own view of reality. But unless these pressures overwhelm him (and whether they do so is, in the last analysis, a matter of his own preferences) he will try to achieve some kind of adjustment between his private preferences, public policy, and the pictures in his head. For his concept of reality—his idea of what is happening, what is likely to happen, what is capable of happening—indicates to him what policies will help him to achieve his preferences, given the "objective" situation as he sees it.

The importance of these pictures in determining foreign policy can scarcely be overestimated. If the pictures in the heads of leaders and a working majority of Congressmen are "correct,"—which is to say, if they accurately reflect what is happening, what is likely to happen, and what is capable of happening in the real world of international politics—a fair chance exists that foreign policy will be realistically designed to achieve

* Y, like his colleague X, is purely fictional.

the most for whatever set of preferences the leaders and a working majority of Congressmen can agree on. But if the pictures are distorted, out of focus, hazy in important details, it is possible that the foreign policy decided on will not in fact achieve its intended goals. In a period like the present, the accuracy or falsity of the pictures may well determine for many generations the boundary lines of popular government.

Who, then, supplies these pictures? It is not enough simply to say, "Events themselves." For events—the First World War, Wilson's activities, the League of Nations, Hitler's rise —must be *observed*. They must be *reported*. And they must be *interpreted*.

Almost never does a Congressman (or for that matter a State Department official, a newspaper correspondent, or any other observer) physically witness the "events" that inspire policy. Time-space limitations alone make such observations improbable. But even more important, the significant problem-making "events" in international politics usually include a number of interconnected happenings, taking place at different times and places. The event is understandable only when it is seen in some kind of totality and arranged in a pattern. Anyone who has ever seen a battle will understand that the map at headquarters, when it is not too far out of touch with events, will often reveal more meaningfully "what is happening"—so far as the fate of the battle is concerned—than will any foxhole view.

Interpretation is necessary to the understanding of an event. Indeed, the event often cannot even be observed and reported unless it is first interpreted. What was happening on August 31, 1939 would not have been clear to a man from Mars who witnessed some soldiers in gray-green uniforms deploying eastward through the woods at the Polish border. And even the "event" of December 7, 1941 was of such complexity that some years later, members of a Congressional committee, not to say several historians, provided with enough facts, inferences, and assertions to fill thousands of pages, were unable to agree on "what happened at Pearl Harbor."

X's picture of the stream of events—"what is happening"— is produced by the interplay between his own attitudes and mind-set and what is reported to him, or between what he brings to the issue and what is brought to him. Our Congressman X, to suppose an extreme but not wholly improbable case, is a xenophobe; as long as he can remember he has distrusted strangers, and since late childhood he has classified foreigners into the simple categories: dirty, lazy, dangerous. The pictures that come to him, therefore, are really not so much snapshots as they are wet clay models which are altered and remolded by his own mind-set and attitudes. No single report (nor perhaps many reports) describing clean, ambitious, and pacific foreigners is likely to change fundamentally the pictures in X's mind. For in the last analysis, if it is true that the reports he hears and reads help determine his view of reality, it is equally true that his fundamental view of reality determines the meaning of reports given to him.

Nevertheless, it would be wrong to say that reports and their interpretations by others have no influence, or even that their influence is altogether slight. To the extent that one's view of reality is not quite so compulsive as we have supposed that of our friend X to be, it is susceptible of some measure of adjustment to new reports of reality. People possess different capacities for rational behavior. The inward concepts of many people change as events take place and are reported to them. "Nazi aggression" implies one thing in 1939, something else in 1941. "Japanese expansion" takes on new meaning after Pearl Harbor. "Russia" evidently symbolized one thing to many Americans at the time of Stalingrad, and something quite different by the time of the Foreign Ministers' Conference at Paris in 1949.

The variation among different individuals in capacity for "rational" adaptation to reality, as against compulsive behavior, indicates a problem of crucial importance to the role of Congress in foreign policy, but one which can only be alluded to here. A solution of the problem of how Congress is to act rationally on foreign policy questions must finally depend upon the extent to which the American political process recruits the more rational, noncompulsive personality types into Congress, rather than the more compulsive, irrational types. I am inclined to believe, however, that this problem of recruiting the right personality types involves a social process so complex and comprehensive that it is doubtful, paradoxically enough, whether it can be solved at present by any *rational* prescriptions a social scientist can offer, and I do not intend to deal further with it here.[7] I shall simply assume we are going to have Congressmen with a moderate *capacity* for rational behavior.

With such Congressmen—and for our purposes this is the critical point—those who report and interpret events are in positions of tremendous power. Their power is threefold:

1. The power to influence the Congressman's *view of reality*, the pictures in his mind. ("French Communists, sinister and grim-visaged, marched a hundred thousand strong in Paris today.")

2. The power to influence the Congressman's preferences, private and public. ("Last week there were signs over the nation that Americans were at last firmly committed to the preservation of their freedom against Communist aggression.")

3. The power to influence the Congressman's support for certain specific *means*, or *policies*, by which it is alleged reality may be brought into better adjustment with preferences. ("The

world situation seems to offer only these two alternatives: aid to western Europe, or the destruction of free societies.")

The strategic importance of this power may be summed up as follows:

First, unless the system by which international events are communicated to the Congressman provides adequate guarantees that the "realities" are conveyed to him, there can be little hope for rationality in foreign policy. It must never be forgotten that a decision is produced in Congress not by what the event "actually" is but by what it is believed to be by those who make the decision.

Second, unless the political system provides adequate guarantees that the preferences on which the Congressman acts are those shared by the community, there can be no effectively responsible leadership.

Third, unless the political system provides a process of exploring the widest possible consensus on preferences in the community, there may be but limited agreement to the foreign policies on which the leadership embarks.

How, then, do the influences "outside" the Congressman operate on foreign policy questions?

II. The Congressman and His Public

IN 1937, international violence tended to produce in Congress the responses of pacifist-isolationism. That was the year when Representative Ludlow was pressing for his constitutional amendment requiring a popular referendum prior to a declaration of war. For several months he had been unable to persuade a majority of the House to sign a petition to discharge his proposed amendment from the House committee where it was bottled up. Then one day an American gunboat, the *Panay*, was sunk in Chinese waters by a Japanese attack. Within two days, Representative Ludlow had all the signatures he needed.[1]

In 1940, the responses to violence were often those of militant-isolationism. James Byrnes writes of a Senatorial experience:

> Early in the spring we had completed hearings on the Naval Appropriation Bill, providing for construction of additional battleships and cruisers. Conversation with my Senate colleagues forced me to conclude that passage of the bill without destructive amendments was very doubtful, so I deliberately delayed consideration of it in the Senate. . . . From statements made by our Intelligence officers and from the opinions of our military leaders, I was convinced that with the coming of spring the Nazis would attack on the western front. They did. And when they did I brought up the Naval Bill in the Senate. It passed in three hours.[2]

In 1948, the responses were those of militant-internationalism. Late in the previous year, Senator Kenneth McKellar of

Tennessee had voted with five others in the Senate against "interim aid" to western Europe. Here is what he said on the Senate floor in March 1948:

> Mr. President, when the Marshall plan was first announced and I read it, I tried to read it with some care. After reflection I rather came to the conclusion, because of the enormous loans, or gifts involved, and especially after we had made so many already, that I would vote against it when it came up for a vote in the Senate.
>
> In the last few weeks, however, conditions have arisen which have caused me to reconsider the opinion I then reached on the European recovery program, or Vandenberg bill, S. 2202, and I am obliged to say that a careful reconsideration in connection with facts that have developed in Europe since that time and the specific fact of Russia taking over Czechoslovakia last week or week before last, and her efforts to take in Finland last week and this week, have caused me to change my mind. At this time I believe that I should vote for the Vandenberg bill, putting into effect the Marshall plan.[3]

Each of these instances seems to be characterized merely by the occurrence of an event and a response. But why the particular response to the particular event? In the case of the *Panay*, why not a joint resolution asking the President to dispatch the American fleet to China? If we were to look at the instances more carefully, we would see that these instances were composed of several factors: (1) events; (2) one or more reports of the event; (3) one or more interpretations of the event in the light of some conception of international reality; (4) appraisals of the events by Congressmen from the standpoint of some set of preferences; and (5) some conclusions by Congressmen about policies for dealing with the events in the light of this set of preferences.

This is, of course, entirely an analytical breakdown. Probably no Congressman considered the situation in these steps, nor was he aware of anything more than a supposed event and his reaction to certain policy proposals. But the key question—Why the particular response to the particular event?—could only be answered in terms of the influences at work along the entire chain, from events to policy conclusions. Keeping in mind the problems presented by our three criteria (responsible leadership, agreement, rationality), what can we say about such influences?

Unofficial Sources of Information and Opinion

One of the basic characteristics of Congress as it now operates is this: on foreign policy, in contrast with domestic, for the most part Congress must arrive at its policy conclusions on the basis of information provided by individuals over whom it has little or no control.

There are five principal sources on which the Congressman relies for his pictures of international reality: (1) "private reports"; (2) commercial media—the newspapers, magazines, books, radio; (3) overlapping these commercial media, various unofficial "opinion leaders"; (4) sources in, and generally speaking under the control of, the executive; * (5) sources in, and generally speaking under the control of, the Congress.

The fifth set of sources, as will be seen later, is to a large degree forced to derive its information from the others. And the first is of limited importance, particularly after Senator Borah's reliance on "private sources" for his ill-famed prediction in the

---

* In this book "the executive" refers to the President and his relevant policy advisers. "President" or "Presidency" refers to the individual or the office. "The administrative branch" refers to those who nominally carry out policy laid down by Congress and/or the executive. Following a suggestion of Professor Charles Hyneman, executive and administrative taken together will be referred to as the executive-administrative (branch).

spring of 1939 that there would be no war in Europe that year.[4] To a very significant extent, therefore, Congressmen must fall back on information provided either by the executive-administrative branch or by commercial sources and "opinion leaders" of various sorts—columnists, leading businessmen, radio commentators, religious leaders, and the like.

As a consequence, commercial publications, chiefly the press, play a role of enormous importance in shaping Congressional opinions about foreign policy. For not only do they influence the Congressman *directly*, by providing him the daily fare of reports and interpretations on which his idea of international reality is fed, and by reiterating, frankly or through innuendo, the policies appropriate to this idea; they also perform a similar function for the Congressman's constituents, whose responses in turn act upon the Congressman's preferences (for example, his desire for re-election).

The Congressman, unlike the President, has no consistent and regular source for examining the accuracy of the press in its reporting of international events. If press accounts differ, he has no ready instrument for judging among them. If accounts furnished by the executive and its intelligence agencies conflict with press reports, his decision as to authenticity must be largely a matter of faith. And yet, decide he must. He cannot, like the social scientist, suspend judgment until the facts are in. In ignorance or enlightenment, he must cast his vote upon the issues before him. Strengthening Congress' capacity for securing accurate and timely reports on international events and expert interpretations of the meaning of those events is an indispensable prerequisite to the existence of a Congress capable of acting with speed and competence on issues of foreign policy.*

But even if means can be devised for insuring a flow of ac-

---

* As used in this book "competence" means the capacity for rational judgment in a given policy situation or policy sector.

curate information—for bringing the pictures in Congressmen's heads more nearly into accord with the realities of international events—it is still by no means certain that Congressmen will act upon this information in order to support the kinds of policies desired by their constituents. For one thing, the view of reality held by the constituents may differ from that of the Congressman. What is crucially difficult for the Congressman —adjusting the pictures in his head to reality—is an even greater difficulty for most private citizens, who generally lack even the Congressman's facilities for validating the reports that they read and hear. This is a point I shall return to in a later chapter.

But even assuming that both citizens and Congressmen agree on their pictures of international reality, it is far from a necessary result that the Congressman will adopt policies desired by the citizens. For the preferences of Congressmen and citizens may differ. "Practical-minded" people, snug in their faith that conflicts over policy would cease if only there were enough "facts" at hand, customarily overlook what is perhaps the most important political fact of all: that people have different and often conflicting preferences. Which is to say, the Smiths and the Browns simply do not want the same things out of life. Now, if one of the Smiths happens to be a Congressman representing a constituency made up of people like the Browns, if Congressman Smith decides on policy according to his private preferences, and if, out of apathy, ignorance, or inadequate political techniques, his constituents cannot bring him to account, they have, for all practical purposes, no responsible representation in Congress.[5]

In practice, then, what role do constituents actually play in the process by which Congressman Smith and his colleagues make up their minds on a question of foreign policy?

Constituents: Limits

The problem arising out of the relation between the Congressman and his unofficial sources of information and opinion is essentially that of rationality and competence. But the chief problem arising out of the relation between the Congressman and his constituents is that of *responsibility*.

There is, I think, a body of implicit assumptions about the process of responsibility under a democratic system that makes up a theory something like this: [6] Up to some variable and ill-defined point, the politician has an eminently natural desire for re-election. Because of a basic democratic rule, to be re-elected he must receive a larger number of votes than any opponent. His desire for re-election, operating in conjunction with this rule, induces him to search out the views of his constituents and to act upon those of the largest number. Should he fail to do so, an opponent who will do so is sooner or later likely to arise and emerge the victor from the electoral contest.

Under the neoclassical explanation of economic life, competition ensured the sovereignty of the consumer. In a remarkably similar way in political life, competition among politicians interested in power guarantees that leaders will never stray too far from the wants of their constituents. Here, too, self-interest and morality conveniently coincide; competition for power under certain limiting rules is the central technique of responsible government.

Now I do not deny that the theory is—or at least has been—in pretty close correspondence with political reality in the field of domestic policy. Yet even there, reality, as I understand it, would require some significant adjustments of the theory. And what is true of domestic policy is even more true of foreign policy.

1. Active Constituents

To bring the hypothesis into line with reality, "constituents" probably have to be defined as politically active constituents. I think one may lay it down as a general rule that politics tends to maximize the values of the active and to minimize the values of the passive. Even in a democracy the passive, inactive, non-participating citizen is more likely than not a cipher when it comes to casting up an account of the forces that make for political decisions. The theory itself, indeed, implies as much. For it rests on the assumption that what the politician values primarily is his re-election, not citizen participation.

A comparison of voting in Congress with "public opinion" as reflected in polling samples appears to substantiate this qualification. (See Table XII, Appendix A.) Voting in Congress corresponds much more closely with the distribution of attitudes among "those with opinions" than with the sample as a whole, which usually includes a large number of people with no opinions. That is to say, the people without opinions—those who reply to a pollster with a "don't know"—often seem to be a politically neutral force so far as Congressional voting is concerned.

For two reasons, this is about what one would expect. First, whatever may be the way by which he arrives at his picture of public opinion, the Congressman has some reason to disregard people without opinions, on the assumption that they are among the passive elements; their voting behavior will be less influenced by his vote in Congress than will that of people who do have definite opinions. Second, the nature of the legislative process is such that the Congressman must generally be either for or against a measure. Unlike the citizen, as a general rule the Congressman cannot simply ignore an issue by registering a "don't know." He may sense that there are many among his constituents, perhaps a majority, who would be unable to articulate their stand on a proposed policy. Under such circumstances he may not vote on the issue. But if he does, he will have to vote yes or no, and not "maybe, maybe not." And in any case, most of the "don't know" group would not want the Congressman to register a "maybe." They would want him to make up his mind with the facts available to *him*—better facts presumably than those available to the constituent.

2. Passive Constituents

There are situations, too, in which so many constituents hold no definite views, or hold their views with such slight intensity, that their views provide the Congressman with no persuasive guide to action. In such a case, he must perforce act on his own best hunch or respond to influences other than his constituency —the executive, for example. How many citizens in Senator Vandenberg's state of Michigan had any views at all on the Mexican Water Treaty? Indeed, in a busy world of competing claims, how could they reasonably be expected to have any interest in such a treaty?

3. Self-contradictory Constituents

Even where his constituents do have views, they may reflect preferences within the individual so contradictory that the Congressman himself must choose which set of preferences he proposes to be guided by. Individuals may want A and B at the same time, although a more rational appreciation of reality would show that these exclude one another.

During the eighteen months prior to Pearl Harbor, Americans became notably self-contradictory in their attitudes toward intervention. (See Table I.) In July 1940, attitudes of an opinion sample were more or less self-consistent: 61 per cent

TABLE I

AMERICAN ATTITUDES ON INTERVENTION

	Sept. 1939	Oct. 1939	May 1940	June 1940	July 1940	Oct. 1940	Jan. 1941	Apr. 1941	May 1941
Per cent opposed to U.S. entrance in war...............	84	95	93	84	86	83	88	81	79
Per cent favoring aid to England at risk of war...........	44	29	36	36	39	50	68	67	61

Data from American Institute of Public Opinion polls.

of those with opinions favored "staying out" rather than "help-ing England win at the risk of war." At the same time, 85 per cent of the same group would have voted against entering the war. By January 1941, however, overwhelming majorities of the sample wanted *both* to help England at the risk of war and to stay out of war. From the point of view of a Congress-man making policy decisions, which emphasis should he have respected? It was impossible to respect both.

Or to take a more recent example: In July 1947, not long after Secretary Marshall made his speech at Cambridge sug-gesting aid to Europe, the American Institute of Public Opin-ion asked a number of citizens whether they would favor or oppose "giving European countries credit of about five billion dollars annually for three or four years so that they could buy the things they need in this country." Half the sample favored such action, and only one-third opposed it. But when the same people were asked, "Would you be willing to pay more taxes, if necessary, to raise this money?" the figures were reversed. Now only one-third of the sample supported the proposal and one-half opposed it. Because European aid was not specifically attached to a tax increase, a Congressman aware of these attitudes obviously could vote either way and believe he was doing what his constituents really wanted.

4. Difficulty of Communication

Because constituents are numerous, communication must be indirect. Thus the problem of the "pictures in the head" of the Congressman arises again, this time with respect to his constituents and their wants. Like "foreigners," "Germans," and "the Vatican," his constituents, too, are pictures in his head—although in this case there is a much better chance of comparing the pictures with reality. Even so, it is no easy matter today for a Congressman to arrive at any accurate picture of the particular reality that might be classified, "what my constituents want me to do."

Traditionally the Congressman unveiled the preferences and attitudes of his constituents by talking with them. But today the size of constituencies makes this scarcely feasible and often impossible. For the average constituency of a member in the lower house today contains about 340,000 individuals—a long way toward gigantism and away from village democracy! Then, too, because crisis is such a continuous feature of contemporary society, Congressmen have less and less time to spend in their constituencies. Senator Bridges testified in 1945: "The first year I came to the Senate we adjourned sometime in June and we did not convene until the first of the next January and I was able to close my office. . . . [Now] a Senator or Congressman is forced to be here, generally speaking, most of the time." [7]

Communication by mail has therefore replaced face-to-face contacts. But, as many Congressmen realize, mail may often be thoroughly unrepresentative.

In 1939, by his proposal to repeal the arms embargo, the

President created the same effect as did the sorcerer's apprentice when he split the broomstick. During the special session called in the fall of that year to repeal the embargo, Washington was inundated with a flood of mail unprecedented even in a city grown hardened to cloudbursts of public opinion. (On one day, Congressmen received 487,000 pieces of mail—an all-time high. An observer calculated that House members alone received over a million and a quarter pieces of mail on the arms embargo issue.) The mail of House members, it has been estimated on the basis of samples, ran about five to one *against* repeal; that of Senators, even higher.[8] Yet in a public opinion poll taken at that time 56 per cent of the sample *favored* repeal and only 44 per cent opposed it.[9] It is quite clear from the votes in House and Senate that Congressmen largely discounted—with whatever trepidations—the opinion reflected by the mail. For the embargo was repealed by a majority of 68 per cent in the Senate and 59 per cent in the House.

TABLE II

PERCENTAGES IN FAVOR OF TWO SELECTED MEASURES

	Mail	Polls	CONGR. VOTES	
			Sen.	House
1939: Repeal of arms embargo.......	20 *	56-60	68	59
1940: Selective service.............	10	70	68	64

* House only. Senate mail estimated at only 6% in favor.

A year after the arms embargo was repealed, the situation repeated itself with selective service. Once again, the "isolationists" dominated the mails. In a sample of 35,000 letters to fourteen Senators of differing views, 90 per cent of the writers opposed the measure.[10] Nevertheless, 70 per cent of a public opinion sample favored the proposed bill. When the bill was finally voted on, it was passed by a majority of 68 per cent in the Senate and 64 per cent in the House.

Recent sample polls indicate that one out of every five voters has at some time written or wired his Congressman or Senator. But as might be expected, mail reflects the educated and articulate classes. Thus in a 1949 poll, one out of every three members of the "professional and business" occupational group had written to Congressmen, whereas only one out of every eight manual workers had done so. Almost forty per cent of all college graduates had written at one time or another—as compared with only 11 per cent of those with merely grammar school education.[11]

In other words, mail may not be representative, and the Congressman may not be guided by it. He may look upon it as largely the work of chronic letter-writers and cranks. Or he may suspect that the avalanche has been carefully engineered.[12] To say all this is not to imply that mail is never influential. In at least one sample study of fifty-two Congressmen, mail was ranked as the most useful means of discovering public opinion on an issue. (See Table III.) The point is, however, that in the presence of contrary pressures and other indices of public opinion, mail is often disregarded, as the experience with the arms embargo and selective service clearly demonstrates.

The most recent technique for uncovering public opinion is the sample poll. As Table III indicates, even in 1945 many Congressmen looked with such suspicion on polls as to count them the least useful among the principal ways of determining public opinion. It is significant, however, that when asked, "Do you think public opinion polls help your fellow public officials decide what the public opinion is on public issues?" 87 per cent of the legislators said "yes"—although two-thirds of this group added "to a limited extent." [13] Although it is somewhat difficult

TABLE III

[USEFULNESS OF VARIOUS WAYS OF FINDING OUT
PUBLIC OPINION

	RANK ORDER	
	Legislators	*Administrators*
Personal mail..............	1	4
Visits to the public.........	2	2
Newspapers...............	3	3
Visits from the public......	4	5
Polls.....................	5	1

Table from Martin Kriesberg, "What Congressmen and Administrators Think of the Polls," *Public Opinion Quarterly*, Fall 1945, p. 334.

to interpret responses of this kind, one persuasive hypothesis is that Congressmen are more influenced by polls than they realize or care to admit, even to themselves: hence, they are willing to ascribe to other Congressmen a susceptibility to polling information that they deny in themselves.

There are, nevertheless, grave deficiencies in the polling process as an answer to the Congressman's desire for an understanding of his constituents' wishes. He is deeply suspicious of the accuracy of the polls, and rightly so.[14] By appearing to confirm the Congressman's convictions that polling techniques are basically at fault, the miscalculations of the pollsters in the 1948 election will surely reduce the influence of polls for some time to come.

But even putting the question of accuracy to one side, the utility of polls to the Congressman is seriously limited by their *generality*. Most polls fail to reveal the particular set of attitudes in the member's own constituency. Under the American party system, Congressman Jones has slight reason to vote in favor of a measure having support of, say, sixty per cent of the people in the country, or even in his region, if he has good reason to believe that a majority of active voters in his district or in his state oppose the measure. Some Congressmen have overcome this limitation by employing commercial polling agencies to sound out their own constituents. Representative Jacob Javits employed the Roper agency to poll opinion in the Twenty-first Congressional District of New York prior to the 1948 elections. But this is not a readily available technique; the expense rules it out as more than a rare device. One polling agency estimates that it would cost $2,000 to $2,500 to poll a "typical" Congressional district—pretty clearly an expense not many Congressmen or local party organizations can often afford.

A further weakness of polls—and one of profound importance to the politician—is the fact that however accurately they may measure articulated and "verbalized" attitudes, one's present avowed attitudes do not necessarily predict future behavior.[15] One may say, and one may genuinely believe, that he favors a proposed policy. But he may also possess certain preferences that run counter to that policy, preferences not necessarily probed by the polling question or adequately articulated in the response. Yet these preferences may dominate his motives when the moment comes for action.

In January 1944, 73 per cent of a national sample believed that the United States should govern Germany with an occupation force for several years; yet within little more than eighteen months, the clamor of citizens to bring the servicemen home virtually wrecked the occupation force in Europe. Within this period, moreover, the percentage of the sample favoring an occupation actually increased to 80 per cent.[16]

Many Congressmen shrewdly realize that a verbal response to a simple question is no real guide to behavior in actual situations. They may feel greater confidence in their own shrewd hunches about behavior. And they may be right.

What is more, polls almost never measure relative *intensities* of opinion. They fail to reveal whether the attitude is accompanied by sufficient emotional involvement to influence conduct in a significant way. The Congressman has much more reason to worry about the activities of a minority holding its views with intensity than about the attitudes of an indifferent majority. Eighty per cent of one's constituents may oppose, and only twenty per cent may favor, economic aid to Franco Spain. But if the issue is of marginal significance to the eighty per cent and of central importance to the twenty per cent, the Congressman had better listen to the minority if he wishes to be re-elected. For it is unlikely that his vote against the weakly held preferences of the majority will lose him much support in that group; the majority will be much more interested in his votes on the measures for which *they* have strong preferences. Yet by voting "with" the majority on the issue of aid to Spain, the Congressman feels he is almost certain to lose a very sizable number of voters among the minority bloc. He has, in other words, much to gain and little to lose by supporting the minority—yet the poll will fail to tell him so. As a result, he discounts the polls and seeks to discover as best he can not merely how extensive but also how intensive public opinion may be on a particular issue.

To be sure, some of these weaknesses characterize the commercial polls rather than the kind of opinion poll technically possible with adequate resources and a highly trained staff of social scientists and interviewers. Conceivably, Congressmen might place more reliance on this latter kind of poll. But at present there is virtually no communication between Congressmen and the social scientists conducting the more intensive and more carefully interpreted polls.

5. *Evaluation of Constituents' Views*

Finally, even when the Congressman has sounded out the attitudes of his constituents to his own satisfaction—whether by mail, interviews, polls or intuition—there is another consideration that may limit the influence of his discovery. This factor is his judgment of the competence and understanding of his constituents on this particular issue.

If in his view there is a great gap between his knowledge and understanding of what is at stake and that of his constituents—if, that is to say, he is pretty certain that the pictures of reality he has in his head are correct and the pictures in the heads of his constituents are false—he may choose to ignore the views of his constituents. He may act on the assumption, perhaps, that his subsequent explanations, or later events, will convince his constituents that his pictures and his policies were correct ones.

Views about the desirability and the morality of the representative acting on his own best judgment rather than that of his constituents have long been at variance, as a reading of Burke's reply to the electors of Bristol will show. It is probably correct to say that in the ethos of American democratic politics, the contention of the Bristol electors that Burke should adapt his policies to their wishes has probably somewhat wider influence than Burke's own view that he should exercise his judgment upon the basis of his own understanding.[17]

Yet it would be wrong to conclude that some such view as Burke's does not persist, particularly as part of the legislator's own idealized conception of himself. The Protestant-derived idea of the importance of the individual conscience, which, I suggested earlier, may be an important stimulus to the "independence" of the legislator, may also reveal itself in the legislator's conception of his relation to his constituents. Legislators probably like to think of themselves as capable of a certain measure of independence even of their own constituents. The more secure one is politically, the greater his opportunity to adopt a view somewhat like that of Burke's toward his function as representative. It seems probable, therefore, that Senators would feel freer than Representatives to ignore the momentary views of their constituents; and men from safe constituencies, freer than men from highly contested ones.[18]

To sum up, the influence of constituents on a Congressman's foreign policy decisions is limited by these considerations:

1. Only those who are politically "active" (to the extent of voting, at the very least) count for much.

2. Constituents may have no definite or deeply held views.

3. What views they have may be ambiguous or mutually exclusive.

4. Because of the problem of communication, it is extraordinarily difficult for the Congressman to find out what views his constituents do have.

5. In any case, the relatively greater ignorance among constituents of the facts or the stakes involved may cause the Congressman to ignore their views.

Constituents: Positive Influence

1. Local Mandate

Most Congressmen are probably influenced to a very considerable degree by their interpretaion of the individual "mandate" they received from their own constituents at the previous election. In the American party system, the Senator and Representative have great freedom in both creating and interpreting this "mandate." The Congressman, that is to say, goes before his constituents with his own program, which may deviate from that developed by the party at the last Presidential conventions. He enters into a kind of individual contract with his constituents, a vague, indefinite, imprecise contract, the terms of which only he and his constituents are free to interpret and enforce. Because of this, the candidates of a party may enter into so many individual contracts that when the Congress assembles, the party leaders discover that most of the *party* program has been contracted away. Execution of the *party* "mandate" is, therefore, frequently difficult and often impossible. But to say that the Congressman may place a relatively low value on the party "mandate" whenever it is different from his own, is only to say that he may place a relatively high value on his own individual contract with his constituency. And doubtless much of his action in Congress is determined by that contract and by the expectation that he must defend his execution of that contract at the next election.

2. *Group Action*

Constituents' views are less influential than constituents' *activity*. When constituents hold views about foreign policy with such intensity as to act "relevantly" upon them—by personal letters, visits to the Congressman's office, political rallies, advertising, threats of rivalry in the primaries, etc.—such constituents *can* have an important influence on their Congressman's voting behavior. Action is relevant if it influences (a) the Congressman's view of reality, including both international reality and the realities of power in his own constituency and the country at large, or (b) his preferences, including the value he places on re-election.

Typical issues that generate influential activity by constituents are those involving ethnic loyalties. In the 1948 campaign, for example, Congressmen from districts with Italian voters had to deal delicately with the disposition of

Italy's colonies. Perhaps the most notable issue of this sort in recent years has been the problem of American policy vis-à-vis Palestine, which evoked such intensity of feeling among Jewish voters that no Congressman with a significant Jewish minority could afford to ignore it. During the Spanish Civil War, the presence of a significant number of Catholics in a constituency unquestionably had an influence on Congressional support for neutrality vis-à-vis Spain.

Intensity tends to outweigh numbers. Thus the activities of ethnic and religious minorities will often be more influential than the passive views of a diffident majority. Marginal groups of about equal intensity and numbers will tend to cancel one another's influence. In conversation with the writer, a New England Congressman highly influential in foreign policy questions remarked of his district, which contains a number of articulate and often hostile minorities, "No matter how I vote, I am certain to lose *some* support." In such a case, influences other than constituents—party, President, newspapers, personal preferences—are likely to play the greater role.

3. Over-all Directives

Constituent opinion may set broad limits within which the Congressman must operate, even when this opinion does not define specific conduct within these limits. This is another way of saying that although electoral opinion may remain passive as long as the Congressman chooses among certain broad alternatives, his selection of an alternative outside this accepted range would activate constituent opposition. Thus it seems likely that in 1948, except in a very small number of special cases, few Congressmen could safely have adopted a position sympathetic to the foreign policies of the U.S.S.R. But *within* the broad range of anti-Soviet policies, many Congressmen probably had considerable choice among alternative ways of dealing with Soviet expansion. Their "mandate" defined certain broad objectives but not the specific means to those objectives.

4. Definite Majorities

In certain circumstances, what is majority opinion in the nation will be converted into something approaching unanimity in Congressional voting. Thus in 1937, when two-thirds of the electorate (at least as measured by a public opinion poll) seemed to prefer that a policy of neutrality be secured by strict legislative definition rather than "leaving the job to the President," the House voted almost unanimously for the popular course. (See Table XII, Appendix A.)

This experience suggests the following hypothesis: Congressional votes for (or against) a measure will significantly exceed the public support for (or against) that measure in cases where (1) a high percentage of the electorate holds its attitudes with intensity; (2) the distribution of attitudes is more or less the same in every constituency; and (3) public support for (or against) a policy is considerably larger than a bare majority, i.e., the majority is relatively clear and definite.

One would suppose that in a regime of rather weak political parties, where every Congressman is to some extent "on his own," if a majority of voters in every constituency clearly favored a given policy, the voting in Congress would tend to approach unanimity for the policy. In practice, obviously, this tendency is checked by other forces, including the party, executive and Congressional leadership, geographical differences in opinion, differences in intensity and activity of opinion groups, the Congressman's own convictions, and the Congressman's own intuitions about the "real" state of public opinion in his constituency.

On balance, so far as their constituents are concerned, most Congressmen probably have much more discretion on foreign policy (at least within a very wide range of alternatives) than is often supposed. This is not to say that constituents *can not* be influential. It is merely to register the fact that in many situations, particularly in the short run, they *are not*.

If this is a close approximation of what is in reality the relationship between constituents and Congressmen on questions of foreign policy, it must raise some serious issues in the mind of anyone concerned with the values of a democratic order. For, to stress again several of the criteria set forth earlier, can it be said with accuracy that the political leadership is fully responsible under such a system? Under this system is there any trustworthy guarantee that foreign policy as it is decided on in Congress will somehow be made to reflect the preferences of the citizens, or the greater portion of the citizens? Or does there exist the kind of two-way communication between Congressmen and citizens that will help the citizens to arrive at a more rational understanding of how to realize their preferences in the real world of international politics?

III. Parties and Pressures

THE political party, many American political scientists argue, is potentially the single most important guarantee that the preferences of at least a "majority" of the electorate will be translated into public policy. In the United States, however, the party is the stepchild of the political system. It is bullied at every turn by pressure groups. And the Congressman is not slow to learn who is boss.[1]

The Party

One of the significant aspects of American parties is their lack of discipline and cohesiveness—or, to put it another way, the significant amount of cross-party voting. Thus, if we take all the recorded votes on questions of foreign policy in the period 1933-48, we find that, with the exception of the Democrats in the House, on only about one-third of the issues were the parties able to muster as many as 90 per cent of their voting members on one side of the issue.

That House Democrats achieved such a large measure of agreement is to be explained partly by the influence of the President on members of his party in the lower house. Even in the Senate, however, on about two-thirds of the issues of foreign policy, more than eighty per cent of the Democrats voted together, whereas eighty per cent of the Senate Republicans voted together on less than half the issues.

The role of the party in Congressional voting on *foreign*

TABLE IV

PARTY VOTING ON FOREIGN POLICY, 1933-48 *

| | PERCENTAGE OF ISSUES ON WHICH AGREEMENT WITHIN THE PARTY WAS | | | |
	90-100%	80-89%	70-79%	Less than 70%
House				
Democrats.........	68	15	7	10
Republicans........	36	28	19	17
Senate				
Democrats.........	36	26	21	17
Republicans........	33	12	19	36

House percentages are based on 133 roll calls on 103 issues.
Senate percentages are based on 236 roll calls on 147 issues.

* For a more detailed table, see Appendix A, Table XIII.

policy nevertheless ought not to be underestimated. If it is not the "responsible party" of the political scientists' Utopia, neither is it the negligible factor it is sometimes thought to be.

Thus if we examine twenty-six important issues of foreign policy on which record votes were taken in Congress during the years 1933-48, we find that for a nation supposedly lacking in "responsible parties," a significant degree of party unity exists on important issues of foreign policy. If we define the party stand as that taken by the majority of party members in their voting,[2] we find that, on the average, between eighty and ninety per cent of the members of each of the two major parties supported the party stand. Where the parties took stands in opposition to one another, slightly more members voted against the party position than on those issues for which national consensus was so great that both parties took the same stand.

In attempting to account for even this degree of party unity,

TABLE V

PARTY VOTING ON 26 ISSUES OF FOREIGN POLICY, 1933-48

| | PERCENTAGE OF PARTY MEMBERS WHO VOTED TOGETHER | | | |
| | House | | Senate | |
	Dem.	Rep.	Dem.	Rep.
On issues where a majority of Republicans voted differently from a majority of Democrats..............	86	86	80	83
On issues where a majority of Republicans voted the same as a majority of Democrats...................	97	86	91	81
On issues since 1943 where foreign policy was made through bipartisan consultation with Senate Foreign Relations Committee *...........	95	79	95	82
Average percentage of party members who voted together for 26 issues...	91	84	88	79

* Slight discrepancies in percentages on "bipartisan" issues between this table and those of Table XI, p. 229, result from the inclusion of a larger number of bipartisan votes in the latter.

one can find only partial explanation in the formal party machinery in Congress. For the parties rely heavily, particularly in the Senate, on persuasion by discussion and negotiation. Caucuses on foreign policy are infrequent. On the Democratic side, indeed, there have been almost no caucuses at all on foreign policy for several decades. When a caucus is held, an attempt is rarely if ever made these days to take a vote binding on its members; few people now in Congress can recall when a party caucus in either house last took a binding vote. In the Senate Republican conference (as the caucus is called on that side of the Congress) even a *vote* is rare; no conference vote on foreign policy has been taken within recent memory.

The party policy and steering committees likewise depend upon discussion rather than the application of discipline. One important member of the Democratic steering committee in the House has gone so far as to characterize it as "a debating society, in which the members decide how they themselves are going to vote but do nothing to carry out the decision for the whole party." [3] In the House, to be sure, the Speaker and the Rules Committee exercise some degree of party control, but their powers today are a pale shadow of those held in the days of Reed and Cannon.

What are potentially perhaps the most effective devices for securing party regularity on an issue are scarcely employed: committee assignments and campaign funds. It is true that committee appointments are usually held up by the leadership until the Speaker is chosen, the rules adopted, the party posts (floor leaders and whips) filled—a ruse that insures party unanimity on the important issues of legislative organization and control. But once these decisions are made, membership itself is a presumptive claim to reappointment. This is not to say that the leadership will refuse to punish a member who consistently flouts the party program; from time to time a member is denied a coveted committee assignment because of his voting record. But such action is highly unlikely once a member has built up a little seniority on the committee; for on the whole, the leadership is timid with its sanctions. As for campaign funds, although each party appears to believe that the other party allots campaign funds in accordance with party regularity, the evidence indicates that such sanctions are used rarely, if at all.

How then can one account for the degree of party regularity that does exist? One obvious reason lies in the consequences of self-selection. Many members are Democrats, or they are Republicans, presumably because they started out with a general mind-set roughly like that of their fellow Democrats or Republicans. Except for the mavericks in one-party states—both North and South—who join the dominant party only because it is the sole one realistically available to ambitious men, most aspiring legislators no doubt select the one party or the other because its general orientation happens to correspond roughly with their own.

Other legislators select the party first, and only later become aware of the party's orientation. Representative Sol Bloom, the late chairman of the House Foreign Affairs Committee, described his own evolution as a Democrat:

> Shortly after the turn of the century, when I moved my principal office to New York, I again found it helpful to establish friendly relations with men who were active in politics. The fact that they were Democrats, so far as I was concerned nearly fifty years ago, was mostly a coincidence.
>
> In simplest terms, I became a Democrat in my youth because it was helpful to me to be one. As I matured I continued to be one largely for the same reason. I was approaching middle age before I sought, through reading and study, a philosophical justification for the side on which I found myself.[4]

Later, identification helps to strengthen party loyalty. "The party" becomes a symbol of the group to which one belongs; its battles are one's own battles, its victories and defeats a shared experience of the individual Congressman. A small quantity of group loyalty is perhaps the cheapest of all commodities; few men can get along without some sense of being a fraction of a larger sum. "Most members just don't like to go against the party," a leader in the lower house has remarked. Thus, Democratic leadership found it unnecessary to caucus on renewal of the Trade Agreements Act in 1948. "We just knew Democrats would support it," a top-ranking House Democrat explained.

There are also subtle social sanctions not so evident to the outsider but effective for the average member. The desire to "belong" is not merely a passive but also an active instrument in the hands of the leadership. One who consistently votes against the party may not suffer expulsion from the party as in England, but he may find himself regarded with hostility by people whose respect and approval he would prefer to have. "Independence" can be lonely and uncomfortable if one feels that one's colleagues and "natural" allies are increasingly cold. Disapproval may even be accompanied by the minor political sanctions available to the leaderships; one may be denied a seat on a committee he wants, or, more likely, he will find it difficult to get much accomplished. Both private bills and individually sponsored public bills depend even for consideration, in the lower house at any rate, on a high degree of reciprocity from the leadership.

Members of the President's party may be further motivated by a sense of loyalty to "the Chief," or by a respect for his power, particularly over patronage. Moreover, to break ranks on an administration measure, and thus to endanger the administration, may also threaten one's own seat. On the other side, the minority party has a stimulus to cohere, simply because it is in opposition; victory may cause a letting up of effort, while members of a minority party soberly prepare for the next election.

These are some of the forces that hold the parties together. The resulting organizations are characteristic products of American culture in their combination of undisciplined and erratic individualism with teamwork by discussion and negotiation. To say this is by no means to say that the parties adequately perform the task of providing responsible leadership for an informed citizenry. For as the parties are now organized it is difficult for citizens at election time ever to give their clear consent to a set of party proposals on foreign policy and to receive some substantial assurance that such policies will in fact be carried out when Congress assembles. First, because the parties at the Congressional level are, as we have just seen, loose alliances of individual Congressmen, it is difficult for them to work out a systematic program which they can present to the citizens for endorsement or rejection. And second, even should they leap this hurdle and obtain a more or less clear "national mandate" for their policies, it is by no means certain that the party program will, in practice, be translated into public policy. The serious difficulty in executing a national "mandate" is indicated by the fact that on a number of important foreign policy issues, 20 per cent of the Senate Democrats voted against a majority of their party and voted with a majority of Republicans. (See line 1, Table V, p. 47.)

If party machinery provides leadership that is, in this sense, irresponsible, by the same token it creates leaders who are not thrust by necessity into the task of discovering the broad areas of agreement implicit in the community. For it is one thing to arrive at policy by a process that searches out those common purposes on which various and often conflicting minorities may nevertheless agree. But it is quite another to make policy by patchwork-compromising that concedes everything to the special claims of an articulate minority, and nothing to the preferences of an unmobilized and inarticulate majority. Yet this is essentially what happens when American political parties encounter the battering ram of pressure groups.

Pressure Groups

It is a common observation among political scientists that effectiveness of pressure groups in influencing public policy seems to bear an inverse relation to the strength of parties. The stronger and more cohesive the political parties, the less opportunity for pressure groups to exert direct influence on the legislative process. In a regime of government by "responsible" parties, pressure groups are more likely to succeed in influencing legislation by action *within the parties* than by direct action upon members of the legislative body. Conversely, where parties are weak, the pressure groups can act *directly upon the individual legislators,* who have much more to fear from the sanctions of pressure groups than from those of their own parties.

However stylized this picture may be, it correctly expresses a fundamental phenomenon of American politics. As parties are relatively weak in controlling legislation, so pressure groups are relatively strong. This constitutes a major limitation on political responsibility in the American system.

The strength of pressure groups in the determination of legislative policy is no less evident in foreign than in domestic affairs. Given the conditions that (1) events frequently permit various interpretations, (2) it is difficult for the Congressman to be sure what his constituents will actively support, and (3) his party has few sanctions with which to punish him if he votes against the party program, the Congressman is a natural victim of organized pressures.

In pressure groups, at least, he finds specific and mobilized opinion. Unless there are equally specific and mobilized counterpressures, the legislator has, it would seem, everything to gain and little to risk by voting with the pressure group.

It may be that if he were to follow the preferences of a large majority of his constituents, he should vote otherwise. But their preferences are passive, unexpressed, inarticulate, unorganized, while those of the pressure group are active, specific, articulate, organized. The decision, to be sure, remains a gamble. And the Congressman may be wrong in his assessment of pressure group strength. There is some reason for supposing that his electoral survival is more closely associated with the fate of the party as a whole than with his vote favoring some pressure group on a particular issue. But to many Congressmen, it still seems the safer course to vote with the pressure group and trust that the preferences of the majority remain passive and unexpressed or happen to coincide with those of the pressure group.

In cases where the size of the pressure group clientele is known and where it is possible to guess at the degree to which the pressure group leadership actually expresses the active preferences of its clientele, the Congressman's choice is less of a gamble. Congressmen live in a milieu where this kind of market calculation must be constantly practiced, and no doubt the experienced Congressman learns to know within broad limits which pressure groups he can politely ignore— or openly oppose—and which he cannot. But playing the market is full of risks. And the odds are still with the pressure groups.

The arena in which foreign policy is fought out is noisy with the jangle of pressure groups. The historic role of pressures in shattering party lines on the tariff is too well known to need comment. Nor is it merely the old-fashioned and perennial pressures of economic interest groups that are important today. Issues of foreign policy activate men to organize for the pursuit of values more inclusive than the crasser ends characteristic of most pressure groups. Yet the organized pressures seeking to bend policy to their ends are, for all that, no less the instruments of minorities. International politics and the expectation of violence are so closely related, and in- securities and anxieties are so readily evoked by the threat of war, destruction, and death, that foreign policy must be con- ducted in an emotion-charged atmosphere where threats, fears, hates, and hopes are quickly mobilized into organized pres- sures. A large part of the history of American foreign policy since the First World War might be interpreted as a series of successful intimidations by pressure groups, of victories that occurred while the parties cautiously shadowboxed at a safe distance from the real conflict.

In the last days of 1934, to take an example, passage of a resolution of adherence to the World Court during the forth- coming session seemed almost certain. After polling their members, the majority and minority leaders of the Senate estimated that all but seven or eight Democrats and eight or ten Republicans would support the measure. Discussions began in the Senate on January 14, 1935. William Randolph Hearst and other "isolationists" immediately undertook a huge cam- paign in opposition to the Court proposal. With a staff in the Mayflower Hotel they telephoned influential people through- out the country, and soon telegrams in opposition began to pour into the Senate. On January 29, thirty-six Senators voted against the measure rather than the fifteen to eighteen originally anticipated.[5] This was more than enough to prevent the necessary two-thirds majority, and the measure went down to another of its long series of defeats.

Now there was nothing inherently "undemocratic" about this procedure or the result. The point is that the parties simply had to stand aside and let the dominant pressures de- termine the decision. There was slight possibility that one or the other party would stick by the proposal on the assumption that the views of the pressure group were those of a minority, and that the sensible course even from the narrow view of political advantage was to support the measure and look for party endorsement at the next election. There was equally slight possibility that one or the other party would, as a party, *oppose* the measure on the assumption that the pressures actually expressed a majority view. When the pressures run wild, it is every man for himself and the party take the hindmost.

Neutrality, the Spanish Civil War, repeal of cash and carry, lend-lease, United Nations, the British loan, Greek-Turkish aid, European recovery, Palestine—such basic issues of foreign policy as these were automatically at the center of a field of forces of which the private pressure groups were among the most important.

It would be wholly false to assume, however, that the mere strengthening of party responsibility would or should terminate the role of pressure groups in influencing policy. In a more or less free society composed of people with different and often conflicting interests, outlooks, aims, preferences, and ambitions, pressures will not vanish into thin air simply by the introduction of a more responsible party system. Minorities will organize to advance their preferences. If they do not, their preferences will be ignored or flouted; and in a pluralistic society a majority is, after all, largely composed of minorities. But responsible parties would force such pressures to work within the parties rather than in the legislature. Disputes now precipitated onto the floor of Congress would be resolved in advance by compromise and negotiation *within the parties*.

The Palestine issue typifies the kind of situation that remains inevitable in a society of complex attitudes. Some minority groups—historically the most important, perhaps, being the Irish, the Italians, the Poles, the Germans, and among the religious groups, the Catholics—influence American foreign policy out of all proportion to the size of the group because (a) many members of the minority hold their views with *intensity*, i.e., their views significantly determine their political conduct; and (b) the minorities are strategically located. The rising concern of the Jewish minority with the fate of the Jews in Palestine and in European displaced persons' camps is only the latest of a long series of similar actions by other ethnic or religious groups. In this case, probably most citizens had no very decided views about the extraordinarily complex problem of Palestine. Those citizens who felt intensely about the future of a Jewish state were distinctly a minority; but the intensity of their convictions, that is, their willingness to translate their beliefs into political action, far outweighed their numbers.

As has long been true with the "farm vote," the pro-Israel minority occupied a position of such strategic importance that both parties had to take pro-Israel stands if they did not wish to lose an important bloc of votes. Political candidates had almost nothing to gain by doing otherwise, and a good deal to lose. At their national conventions in 1948, both parties adopted pro-Israel planks. And the one foreign policy issue on which bipartisan exercise of self-restraint completely broke down in the last days of the campaign was American policy toward Israel. Both presidential candidates were unwilling to neglect the possibility of securing votes on that issue. Ultimately the American delegation at the United Nations, which was then concerned with the Palestine problem, found it necessary to postpone all discussion of the problem until the election was over.

The significant feature of these events is not only that a minority was able to influence foreign policy in a direction that might not have been taken if the majority had actively stated its preferences—or if, indeed, the majority *had* any preferences, given their understanding of the issues. For our purposes what is equally significant is the demonstrable inference that even if the parties *were* "responsible," "disciplined," "national" parties (which they are not now) they would have responded to the pressures of the minority.

It is true, nevertheless, that well-organized parties might be in a better position to lay down the terms of the compromise they make with organized minorities. It would be too much to expect that responsible parties could alter the tendency of politics to maximize the values of the active and to minimize the values of the passive. But the national political party is, potentially, the means by which the passive and the unorganized are activated and organized. And it is, potentially, the means by which purposes common to broad numbers of men may be brought to bear on public policy as a force offsetting the narrowly confined values exploited by pressure groups. As such, the development of responsible national parties is one of the prerequisites to both responsibility and wide agreement on matters of foreign policy.

IV. Leaders: Congressional and Executive

IN the past, periodic fluctuations in the status and power of one branch or the other—now the President in the saddle, now Congress—have depended in great measure upon the personalities and leadership qualities of the man in the White House or the men in Congress.[1] But in recent decades, the vast administrative resources and powers in the executive-administrative branch and the complex nature of public policies provide that branch with tremendous power over the formulation and proposal of policy and vast discretion over its execution, whatever the leadership qualities of the Chief Executive might be.[2]

What is characteristic of public policy in general is even more characteristic of foreign policy—particularly because the President has long enjoyed considerable discretion in this field. Perhaps the single most important fact about Congress and its role in foreign policy, therefore, is that it rarely provides the initiative. Most often initiative springs from the executive-administrative branch. It is an exaggeration perhaps, but one not too wide of the mark, to say that in foreign policy the President proposes, the Congress disposes—and in a very large number of highly important decisions about foreign policy, the Congress does not even have the opportunity to dispose.[3] This relationship gives rise to one of the central problems of this book: how the executive-administrative may be held responsible to Congress for the conduct of foreign policy.

Congressional Leadership and Expertise

One of the reasons for the influence over Congress of the President and those who work in the executive-administrative branch is the weakness of the leadership in Congress itself. We have already seen how uneasily the party leaders in Congress rest in their seats of supposed power, how slight are the sanctions they employ against party members who fail to carry out the party program, and how fully they depend upon persuasion by discussion and concession.

There are, to be sure, other sources of leadership in Congress than the party: individual members who exert influence, not primarily because of any formal position of party leadership, but because of power or status they acquire in other ways. Thus the committee chairman is in a position to influence members both of his own and the opposite party because he has some power over legislation and over committee reports—and therefore over the preferences embodied in legislative proposals and over the pictures in the heads of Congressmen who read the reports. He *may* exercise his influence as an agent of the party; but in the American Congress he may very well *not*. Because, indeed, his colleagues accept the principle that he is entitled to his chairmanship solely because of his seniority, he may well use his influence against his own party and suffer little or nothing at the party's hands. Nor is it only because he can shape the committee report, at least when he has a majority of the committee with him, that he can influence his colleagues. For it is he, customarily, who in debate is in charge of defending the committee position.

Yet it would be a gross oversimplification to assert that simply and solely because an individual is chairman of a committee, he thereby exerts more than ordinary influence on the voting behavior of his colleagues. As is generally the case, there are questions of one's personality, force, drive, capacity, and general prestige. Thus the chairman of the House Foreign Affairs Committee in the past has exerted considerably less influence on his colleagues than has his opposite number in the Senate.

The importance of the committee report now puts the experts on the committee staff in a position to influence Congressional voting. The committee staff exerts influence not merely by communicating and therefore interpreting events, but by suggesting, interpreting, and emphasizing the alternative policies available to meet the challenge of events. The Congressional expert is a relatively new influence in Congress, but his long-run significance may prove to be exceptional.

A third influential group consists of what one observer has called the "bellwethers." These are individuals, not necessarily official party leaders or committee chairmen, of whom it may be properly said, "They are influential because they are influential." Their influence may come from long experience in Congress and the prestige that sometimes accrues to those who know the ropes. Or, more typically in foreign affairs, the bellwether is one who has somehow earned a reputation for knowledge and understanding of some international problem or area; he is, in a word, one whom his colleagues regard as relatively more "expert" than they, and yet sufficiently akin to them to be trustworthy. In the Eighty-first Congress, one could point to Representative Walter Judd, of Minnesota, who had been medical missionary and hospital superintendent in China for ten years; or Mike Mansfield, of Montana, who had been stationed in the Orient with the Marines and later taught Latin American and Far Eastern history at Montana State University; or Christian Herter, of Massachusetts, whose work with the Select Committee on Foreign Aid gave him special status. Some bellwethers have influence because of their conscientiousness, integrity, or general knowledge. Until his retirement in 1948, Representative Dirksen was widely influential in the lower house because of his relentless accumulation of "facts" about any issue with which he was concerned.

The bellwether is less important in the highly individualistic Senate. But in the House, many members hopelessly outdistanced by the complexity of an issue pay special attention to the attitudes of certain members to whose judgment, for whatever reason, they defer. It would be difficult to underestimate the influence on voting conduct in the lower house when Mr. Dirksen shifted from a "militant-isolationist" to a "militant-internationalist" position.

When so much has been said, however, it remains true, on the whole, that the leadership within Congress is weak and dispersed. By contrast, the executive-administrative branch today is, in foreign policy at least, a citadel of power.

Leadership by the Executive-Administrative

The great influence of the executive-administrative stems from its occasional capacity for unity, from its superior organization for determining what realities exist at any given moment in international politics, and from the position of the President in his party.

The executive branch provides most of what leadership there is under the separation of powers. If anyone may properly be called the party leader, it is the President. After one term he may quite literally "write the program," as President Roosevelt did in 1936. He has a large measure of control over the dispensation of patronage.[4] His party leaders in Congress look to him for programs. Loyalty to the President is regarded as their chief virtue, and it is a major breach when a party leader is unable to "go along with the Chief."

More than that: however decentralized and uncontrolled the total executive structure appears from the White House, *as compared with Congress* it is unified, it is decisive, it is expert. And even when conflicts within the executive-administrative break out in public, as in the battle over unification of the armed services, the gain in Congress' capacity to assess the merits of the dispute may be slight. For Congressmen are then faced with a battle between two or more great bodies of technicians—and on the whole, as we shall see later, Congress lacks the mechanisms for judging a debate among technicians.

Added to this is the quasi-monopoly over important information held by the executive-administrative. Partly this is pure façade; but it is a façade of incalculable importance to Congressmen confused by contradictory public sources, bedeviled by pressures, and unfamiliar with foreign affairs. For those Congressmen who take their responsibility seriously— and the proportion is probably rather high—it is an inviting escape to say, "Well, *they* have the facts, and they must know what the situation requires better than I."

What is more, the impression that the executive-administrative has better information is not wholly façade. For it alone of all the branches of government has the world-wide reporting services necessary to intelligent judgment. It alone has steady access to the hourly and daily reports of consulates and embassies and military attachés throughout the world. And the reports, analyses, and forecasts of the Central Intelligence Agency are constantly available to it.

Congress has no such organizations. It has the newspapers and radio. It has the infrequent reports of Congressional junkets abroad, not uncommonly under the guidance of executive-administrative personnel. Whenever, therefore, these sources are inadequate, Congressional leaders, and the handful of foreign policy experts employed by Congress, must rely on reports prepared and submitted by the executive-administrative branch.

Because the executive-administrative has the information and provides the leadership, it most often formulates the alternatives. Of all the alternative methods of dealing with a given crisis in foreign relations, the executive-administrative selects that one which appears soundest to it, and henceforth its pressures are mobilized behind *that* alternative. What this really means is that the executive, by and large, determines the scope and nature of the debate. Congressmen may support, or they may oppose the executive proposals. But they are rarely in a position to examine the full range of alternatives that might be open to them.

These, then, are some of the people at work in molding Congressional opinion and decisions on foreign policy: the Congressmen themselves, with their own private preferences and reality views, newspaper editors and other "private" opinion leaders, constituents, party leaders, members of pressure groups, unofficial Congressional leaders who exert special influence, and people in the executive-administrative branch. It is not unfair to say that the total operation of these influences presents a far from happy picture to anyone concerned with the values of a democratic society.

First, it is difficult for citizens to enforce on Congress responsibility for decisions about foreign policy. And it is equally difficult for Congress to enforce on the President responsibility for his conduct of foreign affairs.

Second, because of the way in which the influences play upon Congress, there is no guarantee that the nation's political leadership will search out the areas of common agreement and base American foreign policy upon such consensus as may exist.

Third, the influences operating upon Congress by no means insure that decisions on foreign policy will be arrived at with even the rather limited rationality (given human beings as they are and the limits of man's knowledge) that is potentially available.

What ought we to do? There are three lines of approach. The last two of these are mutually exclusive; the first and the last are not.

1. We might try to raise the level of the citizen's competence in foreign affairs and intensify his interest in international politics so that he will use Congress more intelligently in translating his preferences into foreign policy. In the next two chapters we shall examine the problems in the way of this solution. We shall see there that, however desirable a solution this might be from the standpoint of our values, it is not one that is likely to develop soon enough to carry us through the present era of international crises. And in any case, it does presuppose some effective process through which foreign policy can be made to reflect citizens' preferences.

2. Congress might be deprived of its functions in the process of making foreign policy and turn full power over to the President—or more broadly, to the executive-administrative branch. In a later chapter we shall examine this possibility. And we shall there find that although this evolution is not wholly unlikely, given the present arrangements for making foreign policy, from the standpoint of our values it will prove to be a highly undesirable one. For it means, in effect, the creation of a kind of plebiscitary dictatorship through the Presidency. The more likely of these two "solutions," then, seems to be an undesirable one; and the more desirable solution seems

to be an unlikely one although wholly compatible with the third.

3. We might, therefore, try to force the evolution of a new pattern of decision-making in foreign policy—a pattern in which preferences and reality views of citizens, Congress, and executive-administrative can mesh in such a way as to increase the probabilities of responsible leadership, agreement, and competence in the making of foreign policy. To an examination of this pattern and its prospects—and particularly to the vital role of Congress in such a process—the major portion of this volume is devoted. There are many formidable obstacles in the way of achieving such a policy-making process. Yet the only other realistic alternative available to a nation bent on survival in this new epoch of international violence may well be some form of plebiscitary dictatorship.

PART TWO

THE DILEMMA OF COMPETENCE AND DEMOCRATIC CONTROL

V. Electoral Competence in
Foreign Affairs

WHAT are the prospects that the citizen's level of competence in foreign affairs can be raised to the point where great discretion by Congress and President in deciding foreign policy will be unnecessary? In this chapter we shall examine some of the difficulties that confront the citizen in making rational decisions on foreign policy. In the next chapter, we shall take a brief look at some possible ways of improving the rationality of the citizen in this area of policy.

Rationality—to put it with deceptive oversimplicity for a moment—is a matter of adjusting means to ends. I may be said to act with "optimum" rationality whenever I choose the best means available for achieving the desired ends. In making choices about things within our immediate experience, most of us stand a much better chance of acting rationally than in cases where the choices concern things remote from our experience. The experienced garage mechanic is likely to be pretty rational in deciding on the best way of repairing his automobile. But he is likely to be much less rational when he tries to make up his mind as to how the ravages of soil erosion should be repaired. And he may be still less competent to decide what his government should do, if anything, to repair the ravages of war in Europe and Asia.

Rationality and Foreign Policy

It is clear enough that one of the central problems of a democratic political system in a modern, highly complicated society turns upon the question of how—and indeed whether—the citizen can bring to bear on broad questions of public policy sufficient rationality to achieve his basic purposes. And in some respects there is no field of policy in which this problem is greater than in the conduct of foreign affairs.

Not everyone is a garage mechanic. Nevertheless, when my car breaks down, even though I do not know how to repair it, I can act with a high degree of rationality. For I take my car to a garage mechanic who has fixed it successfully in the past— to an *expert*, in other words, *in whose skills I have confidence*. I define the "end"—the repair of my car—to the mechanic, the expert. And the mechanic, an expert in means-selection in the special field of automobile repairing, exercises his discretion in selecting the means.

In one sense, this is also the way citizens * act in selecting public policy. The process of discussion, debate, and elections produces a decision as to some general purposes to be achieved. After these purposes are defined by the legislature in various degrees of detail, we often leave considerable discretion to "experts" in the executive-administrative to decide on the means.

But there is another sense in which we do not behave this way at all as citizens in a democracy. For there is a sense in which the citizens must choose the means, must tell the garage mechanic not merely to fix the car, but *how* to fix the car. For

* The word "citizen" in this discussion refers to those members of society who have the right to vote, but who are not holding office in government or in the political parties. The word "electorate" refers to these citizens as a body.

in practice—and this is the important point—in a democracy the citizen must always decide, not on abstract "ends," but on some more or less concrete "means." The great persistent issues of nineteenth-century American politics—for example, banking, currency, tariff, western lands—were quarrels over rather technical means. Yet behind the means lay differences over ends—over the kind of society that was to be developed in America, the location and use of political and economic power, the distribution of resources, the relative effects on one's opportunities, prestige, income, and status. The fact is, there has never been in American politics, nor probably in the politics of any nation, a sharp separation of ends and means. "Ends," John Dewey has said, "are ends-in-view or aims." In politics, as in most things, ends and means are a continuum, not separate elements that can be as easily detached as the parts of a child's Erector set.

The mechanisms of democracy can hardly be expected, therefore, to yield a "rational" decision unless at least one of the following conditions is met: (1) Knowledge about the means debated must be rather widely diffused—or, to continue with the analogy, all of us must be good amateur automobile mechanics. (2) Where wrong means to the objective have been chosen, there must be opportunity for experiment in selecting other means (trial and error)—that is, without too great disaster to ourselves, we must be able to take our automobile to another garage when the first one does a bad job. (3) The area of activity affected by public policy must be of only slight importance to us. In the last case we might, quite rationally, still prefer the democratic method for a wide variety of reasons, even though the specific public policies produced were, taken singly, rather irrational means to specified ends.

Now let us imagine the consequences involved in the selection of policy by citizens if none of these conditions is met: if, in other words, the means submitted by the leadership to the electorate are so complex relative to the intelligence and understanding of the voter that he cannot adequately foresee the consequences of his decision; if the situation does not give him opportunity to learn by failure—if, that is to say, his action is irreversible; and if, finally, the choice under debate is critical to the survival of the society. In such circumstances selection of means by citizens may lead to disaster.*

A moment's thought will reveal that for some time foreign policy has been more nearly characterized by the second rather than the first group of conditions. When we recall some of the recent issues (neutrality legislation, the Bretton Woods agreement, atomic energy control, the British loan, aid to Greece and Turkey, appropriations for western Europe, the veto in the Security Council, the organization of international trade, military alliance with western Europe) it is evident that if the citizen is asked to judge the adequacy of these means, even the most intelligent is given a task of virtually impossible proportions.

This is so, in the first place, because of difficulties inherent in the individual himself. To begin with, there is the staggering problem, not merely of having a sufficient quantity of pictures —correct pictures—in one's mind, but of arranging those pictures into a pattern that reveals the tendencies and potentialities of international reality, and then, what is perhaps most difficult of all, deciding on a policy that will mediate between the real world and one's preferences. For most of us, this is a formidable task.

Decisions on foreign policy involve matters that are not of

* It is important to remember that in extremely complicated situations selection of means by anyone else—"experts," dictators, or philosophers— may also be disastrous. But in this book, I am not concerned with the difficulties besetting nondemocratic systems.

immediate and direct experience to many of us, and, as has already been suggested, the more remote a decision from Everyman's experience, the less rational is he likely to be in making that decision. About automobiles, on which he has worked since boyhood, the garage mechanic has developed a pretty accurate set of pictures in his mind. About international politics, he has no such accuracy, for the process of acquiring correct pictures is infinitely more difficult.

Nor can the citizen fall back on "decentralization" to simplify the decision-making process. Historically, free societies have managed to solve an important part of the problem of rationality by devolving a large measure of decision-making on autonomous or semiautonomous individuals and organizations. The assumptions underlying this devolution are not merely that decision-making is thus more easily controlled by ordinary citizens, but also the corollary: the more intimately the citizen is involved in the decision-making process the more likely he is to temper it with experience, wisdom, and comprehension of reality—in a word, rationality. Yet, in making foreign policy, we cannot allow much autonomy to the citizens of Seattle, Miami, and Minneapolis, or to the members of the United Electrical and Radio Workers, the United Auto Workers, the Amalgamated Clothing Workers, or to the Catholics, Jews, and Protestants, or to the Chamber of Commerce and the National Association of Manufacturers. We do, to be sure, leave an area within which each of these groups may operate in international politics. But it is a circumscribed one, and perhaps increasingly so. By and large, foreign policy must be made through the instrument of national government and cannot be devolved on smaller units within which rational decisions on some kinds of policy are more within the reach of the ordinary man.

Not only are matters involved in foreign policy decisions

often remote to many of us. They are also extraordinarily *complex*—usually even to the "expert" of great learning and experience. What is complex to the expert is overwhelming to the non-expert. How can the ordinary citizen—or even the highly educated citizen who is not a specialist—hope to possess an intelligent judgment on techniques for atomic energy control? Who but an expert can guess intelligently whether the American proposals for atomic energy would, if adopted, accomplish their avowed purposes? The gap between expert and amateur thinking in this complex and esoteric field is necessarily enormous.

In 1946, a few months after the Acheson-Lilienthal report appeared, three-quarters of a sample of American adult population opposed putting the "secret" of the atomic bomb under the control of the United Nations.[1] And though the experts had recommended a system of international supervision and control on which they were prepared to stake the future of the nation, only thirty-seven per cent of the sample believed a system of international supervision and control could prevent use of atomic bombs; precisely half the people believed it would *not* work. Nevertheless, three-quarters of the people interviewed favored an international inspectorate in the abstract. But when asked, "Would you be willing for these inspectors to search American property if it meant that they would find out how we make atomic bombs?" only thirty-nine per cent favored the idea; and yet the fact is, such an inspectorate could not intelligently "search" American property unless its members *already* knew how the bombs were made.

It is not mere hyperbole to suggest, as many people have, that the future existence of the United States is more dependent on the outcome of atomic energy control than on any other single factor. But it is infinitely too much to expect intelligent judgment by the electorate as to the soundness of any given plan. The political process, nevertheless, pushes this complicated question into the political arena. In 1946, Secretary of Commerce Wallace broke with the Truman administration and began his appeal for electoral support on the issue, among others, of atomic energy control. In the 1948 campaign the Progressive Party was supporting the Russian proposals for the control of atomic energy, while the two major parties were substantially backing the American plan. Presumably, the voter was to pass judgment on the alternative proposals.

Atomic energy control perhaps seems unnecessarily complex and difficult. But is it any more abstract than international loans, on which so much of our foreign policy has come to depend? In 1946, while Congress was debating the loan to Britain, very few people in a nation-wide polling sample understood that the loan was anything more than a generous gift. Its relation to our own trade and security was not commonly grasped. The gap between the economist's argument for the loan and the ordinary citizen's understanding of it was fully as great as the differences between expert and amateur evaluation of means in the case of atomic energy.

Studies of opinion indicate that the tremendous increase in American concern with international affairs should not be taken to mean the existence of a well-informed public. Two students of public opinion have even gone so far as to say: "It would appear that a third of the people live in a world that psychologically does not include foreign affairs. As for the other two-thirds, it must be said that at best . . . only a minority of the people can be considered actively conversant with contemporary world problems." [2]

As is so often the case, moreover, a little learning is a dangerous thing. Those who know something about international relations are often more optimistic about the potentialities of international machinery than the ill-educated and ignorant.

Yet it is sometimes difficult to decide whether the one judgment has any more basis in fact than the other. "Internationalism" is often an undiscriminating mood, a mind-set, an attitude—which may or may not bear any appropriate relation to
current reality. Thus in 1946 the better informed of a polling
sample believed, by a considerably larger percentage than the
poorly informed, that we could count on the friendship of the
Russian Government. Yet those who so believed came almost
entirely from the group who also had optimistic expectations
concerning England, indicating a mood of pervasive and irrational optimism about international affairs rather than a specific
understanding of the different power positions of England and
the U.S.S.R.

The citizen is also limited in arriving at a rational decision
on foreign policy by irrational forces at work within himself.
Reality may be unconsciously distorted and falsified by certain
inner claims within the citizen generated by thwarted impulses.
So the citizen may unconsciously project—to use the language
of the psychoanalyst—a wholly false picture upon reality, a
picture created rather to satisfy the needs within himself than
to mirror the realities of international events. Complex means
and instruments of policy take on a symbolic significance that
evokes irrational responses. The individual interprets international activity through the screen of his own fantasies, wishes,
fears, anxieties. Although this is also true of domestic politics,
in international politics the perpetual possibility of violence,
destruction, and death evokes profound emotional reactions
which may distort one's capacity for evaluating events and
policy proposals.[3]

Added to the difficulties inherent in the individual are those
inherent in the political machinery for registering choices. Politics rarely presents the citizen with clearly formulated alternatives from which he can make a rational choice. In the United

States particularly, the absence of coherent parties, the lack of decisive influence by the party leadership over party voting in Congress, the perennial and deliberate ambiguity of the party platform and its inadequacy as a definite legislative program,[4] the rivalry of President and Congress exacerbated by the separation of powers system—all these serve to confuse the citizen as to the alternatives that might be available and inhibit him from making an effective choice.

It is not uncommon for the voter to find himself in a situation where—if it is a particular *policy* he favors—he would have to split his votes for a President, Congressman, and Senator. Let us suppose he decides to vote for each candidate regardless of party: note what this hallowed, if not often very effective, process of "voting for the man and not the party" requires in the way of sophisticated knowledge, understanding, interest, and rationality. In 1948, a few months before the election, Representative Jacob Javits of New York discovered as a result of an opinion survey of one thousand constituents by Elmo Roper that only 33 per cent of those questioned knew that he was their Representative. However, compared with the 8 per cent who knew the name of their Congressman in 1946, this was a rather high percentage.[5] The bulk of Mr. Javits' constituents, nevertheless, must have voted a few months later for a party label rather than for a particular man and his policies. It is doubtful if many even of those who knew his name were in a position to follow his voting record in Congress.

A recent study of voting in Connecticut from 1933 to 1946 offers persuasive evidence that citizens of that state vote for party labels and make little effort to distinguish individual Congressmen. The votes cast for an incumbent Congressman —presumably running on his record—were compared with the votes cast in his constituency for two other candidates of his party: the lieutenant governor (a relatively obscure state official whose policy views are of little importance) and the representative at large. The difference in the percentage of votes cast for these three candidates of the same party averaged less than one per cent over the thirteen-year period—to be precise, .99 per cent for Democratic candidates and .83 per cent for Republicans. In the sixty cases studied, the difference was never more than 2.6 per cent.[6]

In sum, the decision of means to be employed in foreign policy is a terrifying demand to place on the citizen. One should be little astonished, therefore, if the citizen rejects the burden. The real danger, however, is not his refusal to accept the load; it is the possibility that one day he will fly to leaders who would relieve him not simply of this crushing weight but of the whole burden of rationality and freedom. The problem of democrats, therefore, is to find an alternative that would enable the citizen to discard some of his burden and yet render meaningful his power to determine the basic preferences pursued by the nation in its foreign policies.

Means-Selection in American Politics

Why do citizens in a democracy—particularly in the American democracy—select means? * To begin with, it is difficult to cast a political problem into any clear-cut and sense-making framework of "means" and "ends." What are the "ends" of foreign policy? What is it that the citizen wants from the conduct of foreign policy? "National independence?" "Peace?" "Security?" "Justice?" "Freedom?" Under what conditions?

---

* To sharpen the problem, let us ignore in this chapter two complicating factors: (1) questions of means are sometimes deliberately withheld from political campaigns; (2) discretion over lesser means normally *does* lie with the Congress and with the executive-administrative.

And at how great a price? Does the citizen want "peace" more than "independence," or "security" more than "justice"?

It would be possible to construct formulae for the relationships among alternative ends, but such formulae would be of little practical utility. Suppose we assume the "ends" of foreign policy to be the five just listed. Conceivably one might ask the electorate to ballot on a series of alternative rankings of his preferences. Then we might apply the principles of proportional representation to the choice of "ends."

But not only is each of these "ends" without agreed meaning; what is more, most of us understand the relative values of each only in concrete situations. Few of us can make up our minds effectively about abstract preferences. We need concrete situations to give our preferences shape and meaning. We want to know the relative advantages and sacrifices, the alternatives to be foregone—the "opportunity costs," as the economist says.[7] To quote John Dewey:

> The "end" is the figured pattern at the center of the field through which runs the axis of conduct. About this central figuration extends infinitely a supporting background in a vague whole, undefined and undiscriminated. At most, intelligence but throws a spotlight on that little part of the whole which marks out the axis of movement.[8]

And not only are means and ends conceptually difficult to distinguish. In practice, "means influence ends." The ends one pursues may shift as a result of changes in preferences resulting from one's employment of means. In a broad sense, a society may intend to select a policy that will give it result X; but the policy chosen may bring about new behavior and new attitudes that give rise to a shift in the preferences of that society—or of those who make the decisions in that society—so that a new end, Y, emerges as more desirable. Means and ends are thus in a state of flux that requires constant reassessment. To give leadership a blank check on the choice of means is, in fact, to let it dictate the ends of society.

Nevertheless, in our fantasy about applying proportional representation to a set of abstract ends, there is a guide to the direction in which a partial answer might lie. If it is fruitless to pose to the electorate abstract ends, and if it is sometimes dangerous to ask them to choose among specific and complex means, there may be a middle ground. The citizen may not be able to decide intelligently whether a loan to Britain is necessary to solve the British balance-of-payments problem; but he can choose with a degree of insight whether or not he would make some sacrifices in order to strengthen Britain's economic and military position. He may not have sufficient grounds for deciding whether appropriations for western Europe will help restore the European economy and diminish the influence of the U.S.S.R.; but he can say with some perceptiveness whether or not he is willing to make sacrifices if these will help to restore the European economy or control the expansion of the U.S.S.R. He may not be competent to judge whether a military alliance with western Europe could increase our chances of preventing (or winning) a war; but he can say with some assurance whether or not he would support a military alliance *if* it would help to prevent or win a war. In a word, the citizen is not in a position to decide what means will *produce* a given set of consequences. But he is in a position to decide *what set of consequences he prefers*.

Why then do we insist on putting the first kind of question to him rather than the latter? There are two basic reasons.

First, the nature of the political process itself tends to require discussion, debate, and controversy over "means" rather than over the general preferences and purposes on which there may be considerable agreement in American society.

The political arena is a standing invitation to conflicts over means. Individual and party competition for power thrusts the debate over technical means out into the forum of public opinion. In foreign policy, as in many areas of public policy, means cannot be easily neutralized or "de-politicized." It is as if the garage mechanics were required to organize themselves into two or more great guilds, each contending before the public in behalf of a particular set of techniques for repairing automobiles. The citizen must decide between candidates espousing rival means, often ostensibly to the same end. Rivalry between President and Congress growing out of the separation of powers adds to the confusion. For the President may differ over means even with members of his own party in Congress, as did President Roosevelt in his demand for lifting the arms embargo in the spring of 1939. So long as political questions are posed to the citizen as choices among alternative sets of leaders espousing different sets of complex means, the citizen must register his choice if he is to exercise any control over his leadership at all.

In a pragmatic nation like the United States, furthermore, the mythos of practicality makes it unlikely that power will accrue to those who discuss "ends." One of the aims of the political leadership is to stay in office. The struggle for political control turns on the immediate, the practical. And the effective symbol of good or evil employed by the political leader more often than not is something concrete and close to human experience. In opposing the European Recovery appropriations, Senator Langer was not likely to overlook the symbolic value inherent in an appropriation of $299,000,000 for western Europe to spend on tobacco, when Congress had provided only $20,000,000 "to feed all the hungry children in this world." [9]

But there is a deeper reason even than the political process. And this is the difficulty—often, indeed, the impossibility—of arriving at any widespread agreement, in the present stage of understanding society, as to what the consequences of a public policy measure may be. The great debate over neutrality legislation in 1939 was not conducted primarily (at the verbal level) as a debate over "ends." Participants on both sides were virtually unanimous in their alleged aim: to keep the United States out of war. Disagreement was consistently cast in terms of different predictions as to the outcome of the proposed means. Those who espoused strict and undiscriminating neutrality, including a complete arms embargo, argued that this was the only means by which the nation could stay out of war, while those who proposed a repeal of neutrality legislation in order to provide aid to the western democracies argued with equal vehemence that *their* policy was the only means by which we could be kept out of war.[10]

Representative Taber, in opposing the 1948 appropriation totals for western Europe urged by the executive and passed by the Senate, did not contend that he wished for a different set of consequences; he argued that reduced appropriations would achieve the *same* consequences at less cost.[11] Conversely, Senator Kem, like a number of others in the Senate, opposed the appropriations for European aid although ostensibly he favored the major consequences alleged for the expenditures; but, he argued, the appropriation would in fact have quite different consequences from those intended; it might "undermine the American economy and . . . make our Nation as vulnerable to communism as are those we are seeking to aid." [12]

If it were possible for experts to predict with reasonable certainty the outcome of a policy measure, and if the experts agreed, the citizen might substitute for the conflicting assertions of politicians the predictions of the expert. Thus although reclamation policy is subject to intense controversy, we do not require public debate over the amount of concrete needed for a Reclamation Bureau dam.[13]

But in the case of foreign policy, even experts may have to grapple in the dark. Senator Bridges, in reporting the larger figure for European aid to the Senate, confessed that "in the committee hearings testimony was offered by many witnesses of the Government, by the individuals who will administer the funds appropriated, and by private citizens who the committee felt had pertinent experience and knowledge." But he added later, "In all the great detail of testimony submitted to the committee there was little information on which the committee could base a firm, precise, stable, and undisputed appropriation figure." [14] So incomplete were the raw data with which the experts might work, so many were the variables, and so uncertain were the influences on these variables that in May and June of 1948 no group of experts could predict with confidence the consequences of a particular appropriation figure for European recovery submitted to them for analysis. Yet the very essence of the policy was speed, and if the policy were to be adopted at all, it would have to be adopted as a calculated risk.

Among those who make predictions about the dynamic and multicausal succession of events known as international politics, furthermore, how is the Congressman or the citizen to determine who is "expert"? It requires expertness to evaluate the experts. In 1939 who was to be regarded as an "expert" on the consequences of neutrality legislation—Charles Beard, who favored it, or Henry Stimson, who opposed it? Indeed, how does one qualify as an "expert" in this tangled field? Was Beard, the historian, who surveyed politics from the quiet of his dairy farm in New Milford, Connecticut, *more* or *less* expert than Henry Stimson, the lawyer, who had acquired his expertness as Secretary of State?

Like any human being, the "expert" in the social sciences encounters peculiar difficulty in rising above his own predilections; he, too, tends to project his preferences upon reality. And sometimes the strength of his preferences may render his predictions no better—and perhaps even worse—than those of the average citizen. In a poll taken before war broke out in Europe in 1939, the Society for the Psychological Study of Social Issues found that only half the social scientists in the United States thought an increase in the size of the armed forces was desirable—whereas 75 per cent of the public gave its approval. In retrospect it seems clear that the social scientists were making a policy choice less rationally adapted to achieving their preferences than was the general public. Accelerated rearmament was, as it turned out, a necessary means to securing preferences that were probably shared widely by social scientists and the public at large. But it seems evident that social scientists permitted their interpretations and forecasts of international politics, their pictures of reality, to be seriously influenced by their inner wishes for peace.[15]

What then are the prospects, if any, for developing a higher degree of competence on foreign policy among ordinary citizens? And even if this were possible, is it enough?

VI. What Hope for Greater Competence?

IN the last chapter we examined some of the major barriers to citizen competence in foreign affairs. Are there reasons for hoping that these barriers might be minimized? It is the argument of this chapter that:

1. The experience arising from greater American participation in world politics, although an important educating influence, does not promise a solution adequate to the need. Trial and error is not enough.

2. A significant increase in the competence of ordinary citizens in foreign affairs requires a cure for two fundamental defects in our present social arrangements for communication: the lack of well-oriented discussion and inquiry among citizens, and the failure of communication between certain parts of the intelligentsia (particularly social scientists) and ordinary citizens.

3. But even if these defects could be cured, in order to maximize the values of rationality, responsibility, and agreement in the foreign policy sector, there needs to be a better system for the communication of preferences from citizens to policymakers.

Trial and Error

The child touches the stove, feels pain, withdraws his finger, cries—and perhaps keeps his finger off the stove in the future.

Later he learns to respond, more or less, to certain cues furnished by his parents, siblings, and teachers: "Don't touch!" "Hot!" "You'll fall!" "This way!"

People in groups learn by experience. They discover how they may satisfy preferences by following some lines of collective action and avoiding others. They learn to respond to certain cues furnished directly by their environment, by leadership, by specialized agents of the group. These cues and the "appropriate" responses are transmitted from one generation to another until new group experiences lead to new cues and new responses.

No doubt there is a sense in which a national group—or its dominant elements—also learns to adapt its behavior to changes in its environment. Certain techniques seem to fail—disarmament, unilateral action, neutrality. New techniques are experimented with—large armaments, alliances, intervention. Can we count on this kind of process to bring us through the new period of international violence?

Undoubtedly the decade from 1937-47 witnessed a revolution in American public opinion on foreign affairs. The profound growth in public awareness of international problems and the increased willingness to accept the "obligations" of a world power might give one ground for hope that the electorate can continue to grow in awareness, in comprehension, and in judgment. Three unhappy considerations must, however, be borne in mind.

For one thing, the growth in awareness of international problems does not necessarily indicate increased understanding of technical means. Rather it indicates a fundamental change in mood, in the acceptance of sacrifices necessitated by active foreign policies. Such problems as the veto in the United Nations Security Council, or atomic energy control, or the International Trade Charter, are little more susceptible today of rational evaluation by the electorate than they would have been ten years ago. The complexity of techniques increases apace. The rapid specialization within skill groups characteristic of modern society shows few signs of declining, precisely because the complexity of techniques increases faster than either human intelligence or techniques for accurate simplification and generalization.

Secondly, the dynamics of the international situation may forbid experimentation. To the extent that each situation is unique, the experience gained from one may be inapplicable to the next. To the extent that each situation is *complex*, only the expert—and often enough not even he—will recognize whether the situation is unique or a substantial repetition of an earlier event. The widespread and fatal tendency of professional military men to act on present events as if they were replicas of earlier experiences indicates the degree to which experts, too, may be misled.[1]

Finally, insofar as a wrong policy choice may mean decisive defeat or annihilation—which is precisely what a wrong policy choice on atomic energy control may well involve—the opportunity to learn by experience does not exist in any meaningful sense. The enormously enhanced effectiveness of modern techniques for exploiting power represents an epochal change in the climate of politics in the twentieth century as compared with that of the nineteenth.[2] This is an alteration no less characteristic of international than of domestic politics. The concentration camp and the atomic bomb are not merely quantitatively but qualitatively different from the political repressions and the military techniques of the nineteenth century.[3]

Friedrich Engels, who was not only a political strategist but a journalistic military strategist of some competence, reflected the turning point in power relationships when at the end of the nineteenth century he remarked, "Rebellion in the old style, the street fight with barricades, which up to 1848 gave everywhere the final decision, was to a considerable extent obsolete. . . . Since then [1848] there have been many more changes and all in favor of the military."

If the nineteenth century, politically speaking, was the era of multiple opportunities, the twentieth century by stark contrast is the day of the single chance. This is not to say that the experiences of the United States in international politics are unimportant in providing some important prerequisites to learning: motivation, interest, attention, concern. It is simply to say that concern is not enough.

Citizen Organization for Discussion and Inquiry

What then can be done to raise the probabilities that citizens will obtain a sufficiently accurate picture of international reality to enable them to make competent choices among the alternative foreign policies thrust at them by competing political leaderships?

First of all, competent choice on questions of this kind requires a preliminary process of discussion and inquiry, not only to clarify reality, but to discover what one's preferences are in that context of reality and what, if anything, may be done to realize those preferences in the real world.

The current state of discussion and inquiry in American life is inadequate to the task. If the public opinion polls cited in the previous chapter frequently reveal a confused and at times ignorant electorate, it must never be forgotten that democratic theory has always presupposed—as the polls do not—a discussion process prior to a politically effective expression of opinion. To be sure, discussion is a commonplace of life, but well-oriented discussion is not. Most Americans belong to several informal or unrecognized discussion groups—the family, the circle of friends, the shop, the union hall, the office, the small town barbershop, the ubiquitous club, the taverns—and a few belong to specialized organizations like the Foreign Policy Association or the Council on Foreign Relations. But most of the discussion that takes place in most of these groups is casual, unoriented, fragmentary. Undoubtedly it changes the views of some participants.[4] But it does not necessarily lead to more *rational* views.

The likelihood of a widespread generation of small, local discussion groups systematically devoted to the critical examination of public policy seems slight. A growth of this kind would have to take place as a broad movement, not as a specialized attack on the single problem of foreign policy. The assorted foreign policy organizations reach too restricted a clientele to be more than pitifully inadequate. The problem requires nothing less than a revolutionary development in the technique and practice of public discussion and inquiry.

There are many obstacles to such a development. For one thing, there is a vicious circle that cannot easily be broken. Discussion and inquiry do not flourish spontaneously unless the problems discussed involve, in a broad sense, the "interests" of the participants. Yet, because inquiry and discussion are inadequate, the citizen often does not understand how his "interests" are involved. A multiplicity of satisfying (or at any rate, anxiety-relieving) activities makes a greater claim on his attention, and until this bulwark of competing interests is broken through by decisive attack, it is hopeless to expect that citizens will spontaneously form into discussion and inquiry groups. That the monopoly of these competing activities *can* in some circumstances be broken and that under some conditions interests *can* be engaged in organized political discussion at the group level is suggested by the relative success of the British Army discussion program in World War II.[5]

Our highly urbanized society likewise presents difficulties. Modern urban life is not conducive to the kind of intermediate organizations implied by, say, the neighborhood discussion group. Individual hostility, anonymity, and moral isolation; the physical layout of the city; the bothersome aspects of transportation; the lack of facilities for group life; the intensified satisfactions of passive participation, exploited by highly organized and influential commercial and advertising groups; the centralization of control over techniques of influencing attitudes and the consequent standardization and banality of opinion—all militate against the spontaneous growth of local discussion and inquiry groups.

If the local group is to grow into an influential factor in national life, the ground will have to be deliberately prepared; the soil is now too barren for the local group to take root. And yet we do not have time to wait for a reorganization of urban life that would buttress the forces of rationality—a reorganization that in any case shows few signs of occurring.

One observer has argued that only the government has the power and resources with which to rekindle the spirit of democracy by discussion. And particularly is this so in the field of foreign policy, where "to an even greater extent [than in the case of domestic policy], action and information . . . lie in the government's hands." [6]

The basic difficulty of such an approach, however, lies in its very novelty. Here is an area in which we have no tested techniques for citizen control. Can "government-stimulated" discussion be controlled by the citizens? Can we prevent the development of the very situation we are trying to avoid? Will the power relationships developed in such a program inevitably turn the local discussion groups into devices by which the leadership may further manipulate public opinion to its own purposes? Or to put it differently, how can we arrange so that the local groups, on the one hand, are as autonomous as possible in their discussions, and, on the other, are assisted by government personnel, power, resources, and information? One cannot help feeling that there is a certain paradox in turning to the modern leviathan state for help in bringing that state under a fuller measure of citizen control.

But to pose the problem in this fashion is perhaps to prejudice the answer and the solution. If there are not now in American society potential leadership groups which place a high value on discussion and inquiry, and if there is not now a large part of the electorate potentially interested in such activity, then free discussion and inquiry of a highly autonomous and decentralized kind is almost certain to die out in American life. In this case, the future almost certainly lies with the authoritarians. But *if* there now exist leaders and citizens of this kind, the problem is to activate them, to mobilize their interests, and to enable them to secure whatever resources are necessary to their task.

In only a limited sense is this in its initial stages a problem of "the government." To a much greater degree it is a question of first securing recognition among citizens that the problem exists, and only then approaching a solution experimentally. We are still in the preliminary stage, not yet capable of an immediate solution. We need nation-wide debate on the question, in the process of which additional leadership and citizen interest might be activated. If there seems to be a certain circularity in this proposal for developing discussion by discussion, it can be replied that the process must indeed be a spiraling one, beginning with initial recognition of the problem by a small group of leaders who activate latent citizen interest, which in turn stimulates the emergence of additional leaders, and so on over a wider and wider radius. Thus when the time comes for more direct and vigorous governmental support for the organization of discussion about, let us say, foreign policy, a protective layer of social institutions will already partly exist to provide some insurance that the discussion process will not be exploited merely to secure the preferences of the national political leadership in power at the time.

The Citizen and the Social Scientist

Even a sudden burgeoning of organized citizen discussion about public policy could not significantly raise the level of citizen rationality in foreign affairs unless a second weakness in our social structure were repaired: the breakdown in communication between social scientists and citizens. For in the present complex world, the citizen desperately needs the assistance of trained observers, not only in interpreting reality, but also in deciding what may be done to satisfy his preferences in the real world.

Paradoxically, for the past half century social scientists have eagerly adventured into every hidden corner of the social system—without, however, devoting much systematic examination to the relationship between the social scientist and his society.[7] Yet it is no exaggeration to say that in a society where a considerable measure of agreement and rationality among ordinary citizens is a prerequisite to competent public policy, a breakdown of communication between intelligentsia and citizens may seriously reduce the chances of national survival, or at the very least, of following the kinds of foreign policies best calculated to satisfy the basic preferences of the most citizens.

There are great variations in the effectiveness with which the professional elites in our society communicate their views to laymen; but it is probable that in the matter of communication the social scientists are among the least effective. Thus, changing ideas on techniques of child rearing are quickly disseminated from "skill group" to laymen; but by contrast, the post-Keynesian analysis of the employment problem, known to every competent Ph.D. in economics, is probably grasped by less than half a dozen members of Congress. Or contrast the agricultural scientist with the social scientist: the ubiquitous agricultural college and extension service lead to a much more effective integration between agricultural scientist and farmer than exists between the urban citizen and the typical political scientist, sociologist, economist, or psychologist.

Any satisfactory solution to the problem of establishing better communication between social scientists and laymen also presupposes some kinds of protective devices for the citizen in order to prevent the growth of "expert authoritarianism." That is to say, it is wholly within the competence of the social scientist to help clarify not only the citizen's picture of reality but the citizen's understanding of efficient ways to mediate between reality and his own preferences. The danger lies in the fact that the social scientist also has preferences. Consciously or unconsciously he may pervert his interpretation of reality in order to persuade the citizen to support a policy adapted to the private preferences of the social scientist himself.

It follows, then, that here is another case where the citizen cannot rely on techniques of casual and haphazard communication. Communication needs to be organized. The whole problem of organizing the relationships between the social scientist and citizen needs to be intensively examined—a task outside the scope of this volume. But it is difficult to see how citizen discussion can produce fruitful results in complex sectors of public policy, such as foreign affairs, until this gap is closed.

Some Conclusions

What must we conclude about attempts to raise the citizen's competence in foreign affairs? First, the effort—assuming the values of responsibility, rationality, and agreement—is highly important but beset with difficulties. It would require a long-time readjustment in social processes. And even if this could occur, it would be utopian to expect more than a modest increase in the layman's competence in this one sector of public policy. Given the complexity of modern life, even a highly skilled person who devotes all of his energies and talent to the task cannot attain a uniformly high level of capacity in all fields of public policy. Which is to say, very considerable discretion would still have to remain in the hands of the political leadership.

Second, even if the desired readjustment in social processes took place, we should still face the problem of securing adequate techniques for translating the citizen's preferences into public policy. It is one thing to improve the communication of reality *to* the citizen. It is quite another to improve the communication of preferences *from* the citizen to policymakers. The first does not automatically result in the second, as so often seems to be assumed.

Without attempting, therefore, to make any precise forecast about the likelihood of raising the level of citizen competence in foreign affairs, one conclusion is evident. Even this, if it were possible, would not be enough. For the citizen also needs effective techniques for communicating to political leadership his own preferences.

The question remains, then, as to what these techniques should be. There is an important line of contemporary thought and action that would place main reliance on the determination of foreign policy by the President operating as a close ally of the administrative branch.

The central argument of this book, as indicated earlier, is that this kind of decision-making process will not maximize the values of rationality, competence, and agreement. In the two succeeding chapters, therefore, we shall examine the case for presidential supremacy so that we may see its deficiencies.

VII. Presidential Supremacy:
An Irreversible Trend?

IN 1917 a distinguished French student of democratic constitutions observed that "Mr. Wilson exercises a virtual dictatorship over foreign policy. There are few sovereigns of authoritarian countries who have as much power over the international destinies of their kingdom as that temporary monarch." [1] Yet within four years this "virtual dictatorship" was in ruins.

In 1917 President Wilson's legal and "constitutional" prerogatives on the one side and his political influence on the other were both nearing their peaks. But at the very time Wilson's legal prerogatives reached an apex, the elections of 1918 revealed a decline in political influence that ended in political rout a few years later.

As a political scientist, Wilson had understood that the President must maintain a close liaison with the Senate. But he had also arrived at a view of the Presidency as the predominant power in our political system. This dominance of the executive, he believed, was partly a result of the evolving importance of foreign affairs; for it was particularly in that field that the President's powers were greatest. "The initiative in foreign affairs, which the President possesses without any restriction whatever," he said in 1907, "is virtually the power to control them absolutely. . . . He need disclose no step of negotiation until it is complete, and when in any critical matter it is completed the government is virtually committed. Whatever its disinclination, the Senate may feel itself committed also." [2]

Surely there is a sense, as Wilson's experiences confirmed when he became President, in which the President's influence on foreign policy is "virtually the power to control them absolutely." But there is also a sense, as Wilson discovered, in which his formal "constitutional" and legal prerogatives may far exceed his influence with other participants in the policy-making process.

In such situations, the nation's foreign policy, as influenced by the President, may not be based upon a broad agreement reflected in Congress or even in the electorate. And when Congress or the electorate finally expresses itself effectivly by rejecting a treaty or voting out the President, the major foreign policies of the nation may abruptly give way to quite different ones, with disastrous consequences for the international structure of power erected with the assistance of the President.

The Case for Presidential Supremacy

Such violent and cataclysmic shifts in foreign policy are not implicit in democracy. Some people would argue that a high degree of continuity and wisdom in foreign policy, based upon agreement and responsible leadership, might best be achieved by granting the President "supremacy" in the field of foreign affairs. The case for presidential "supremacy," it might be reasoned, rests on the extraordinarily powerful constitutional, administrative, and political position of the Chief Executive. In practice, these assets of the Chief Executive have given him the dominant role in the formulation of foreign policy. And, it might be argued, this tendency of the policy-making process should be strengthened. Presidential discretion over foreign policy should be virtually complete.

The argument in favor of this position would run something like this: Because contemporary international politics is crisis politics, because we need speed and flexibility in creating and operating our foreign policies, because we need the kind of planning and expertness that are accessible only to an executive, we should delegate to the Chief Executive exclusive responsibility for foreign policy. Only in this way, can we hope for competent policies.

And not only is rationality at stake. Responsibility and nation-wide consensus can only be achieved through the Presidency. The President alone under our political system can secure a national mandate for his foreign policy. Admittedly there must be responsibility, but the President's responsibility is enforced directly by the people in periodic elections. He is "the steward of the people." Responsibility to the Congress is therefore unnecessary; indeed, because Congress is composed primarily of representatives of local interests, to enforce on the President a responsibility to Congress for the conduct of foreign policy is to reject the possibility of basing foreign policy on a nation-wide consensus. Thus the refusal of Congress in June 1939 to grant the President's request for repeal of the arms embargo could only be interpreted as a product of the inherent inability of Congress to view a problem from a "national" point of view.

It follows that the President must be given virtually a free hand and Congress must withdraw its attempt at controls. In any case, Congressional controls are largely futile, for the President's inherent powers give him the trump card. Of what avail was it for Congress to secure the promise of the executive in the winter of 1941 that American naval vessels would not be used to convoy lend-lease shipments?

It might be argued, in sum, that the President is the only political leader who (1) is responsible to a nation-wide electorate, (2) is capable of basing policy upon the widest areas of agreement in the nation, and (3) has at his disposal the organization and information necessary for relatively rational action amidst the tremendous complexities in international politics. And because of this, one could argue, he should have complete—or very nearly complete—power to decide what the nation's foreign policy should be, without regard to Congressional claims.[3] Although there is much truth in the premises, does the conclusion follow?

Responsible to Whom?

The argument of this chapter is that the "solution" of presidential supremacy represents in fact a flight from the very values it purports to pursue.

To begin with, the kind of "responsibility" the proposal envisions is so vague as to be virtually no responsibility at all. If the President receives a national mandate, it is a very vague mandate indeed. A presidential election is normally a conflict fought over a variety of issues, and it is difficult to assay the relative importance of foreign policy as compared with domestic issues. One diplomatic historian has argued that only three elections in American history—1796, 1844, and 1920—have turned on issues of foreign policy.[4] One could, no doubt, debate his choice. But the important point is that there are very slight historical grounds for supporting the idea that the President derives a "national mandate" for his foreign policy.

To the extent, moreover, that bipartisanship suppresses debate between the candidates over foreign policy, there is small chance of enforcing responsibility at all by the electoral process.

In any case, the presidential election by itself can be interpreted only as a national vote of confidence and not as an approval of any one specific policy.

What, for example, was the meaning in 1920 of Harding's victory and the seven million vote defeat of Cox and Roosevelt who carried the torch for Wilson's League of Nations? That this was a rejection of Wilson's leadership and his party was clear enough. But what, if anything, was the electorate endorsing? Harding's ambiguous position on the League? The views of the Republican Senators who wholly opposed the League? The Republican Senators like Lodge, who (publicly at least) agreed to it with reservations? Those Republican members who supported it? [5] Even if Harding's position had been clear and precise, could he logically have contended that it was his specific position the voters were endorsing? Was it not more nearly that they were rejecting Wilson and the Democrats? It would be even more difficult to determine whether Harding's subsequent endorsement of the World Court stemmed from any "mandate."

And did the four million vote majority for Coolidge in 1924 indicate a mandate for his previously announced support for the World Court? It would require much logic-chopping to argue the case convincingly. Indeed, the closest thing to a "mandate" on the Court issue came not from the presidential election but from a 301 to 28 vote by the House of Representatives (in 1925) in favor of the Court.

The most profound student of semantics would be unable to discover what the foreign policy mandate was that emerged from the 1940 presidential elections. The presidential campaign was carried on in a surrealist atmosphere as baffling as that of a Kafka novel.

On the one side was Wendell Willkie: a long-time Democrat; a Wilson League of Nations supporter; a "Baker boy" at the 1932 Democratic National Convention, supporting the "internationalist" Newton D. Baker against Roosevelt and Garner; prior to his nomination in June 1940, unequivocal advocate of aid to the Allies; by September of 1940 a contender for the Presidency on a promise that he alone would keep "our boys" from being sent to war; and by the end of October, the author of the assertion that if President Roosevelt were re-elected "you may expect war in April 1941" (a charge that in February 1941 he referred to as a "bit of campaign oratory").

On the other side was Franklin Roosevelt: a long-time Democrat; a Wilson League of Nations supporter; a critic of the League immediately prior to his nomination in 1932; an advocate of neutrality legislation in the Spanish Civil War; an unequivocal advocate of aid to the Allies by 1939; and a contender for the Presidency on a promise (October 30, 1940) that "your boys are not going to be sent into any foreign wars."

What sort of "mandate" did the elections result in? On what logical grounds could either candidate have argued, purely on the basis of his own election, that he had been given a foreign policy mandate more lucid than that granted to Congress by the same elections? [6]

It would be equally absurd to contend that the elections of 1944 in any sense conferred a specific "mandate" on Roosevelt and Truman to engage in their respective agreements at Yalta and Potsdam. Had Congress disagreed with these commitments, it would be implausible to argue that the executive mandate was somehow more specific or binding than that of the legislative.

The argument on behalf of presidential supremacy, furthermore, proves too much. The ultimate impact of modern foreign policy is at least as great as, and perhaps a good deal greater than, that of domestic policy. Probably no powers granted to the President by Congress were quite as significant to the nation's future in the summer of 1948 as the President's inherent discretionary power over our conduct in the Berlin crisis. If the President can be said to secure adequate "consent" to his foreign policy by means of his election, then a fortiori he receives sufficient consent for his domestic policy. If both domestic and foreign policy are excluded from Congressional control, then we have eliminated the legislative process as a part of the democratic method. Is the Congress truly so anachronistic an institution that it can have no place in enforcing the responsibility of the executive to the public? Must we carry the plebiscitary doctrine of the Presidency to its final conclusion and extinguish the Congress?

So far we have accepted at face value the assumption that the *President* could, in fact, dominate foreign policy if he were relieved of Congressional controls. But can he? Can the lonely amateur in the White House ever have the time and ability to do much more than support or reject foreign policy proposals brought to him by his advisers? Out of his own experience, Cordell Hull concluded: "With the present immense network and mass of details involved in conducting our foreign relations, the President finds it impossible to keep familiar with more than the principal acts of the State Department. The Secretary of State must do the rest." [7] If one realistically examines the probable limits of any one human being in influencing the process of making policy where complicated questions of fact and forecast are involved, does not the proposal for presidential supremacy imply, in reality, the supremacy of the President's advisers? Thus in the last analysis, the mantle of responsibility comes to rest upon the shoulders of some shadowy figure responsible to—whom?

Competent for What?

But the most important assumption behind the argument for presidential supremacy is not that the President is more *responsible*, in the sense in which that term is employed here. It is that the Chief Executive is more competent, that he is more likely, therefore, to adopt "right" policies.

Now whatever may be the case in domestic affairs, it is undoubtedly true that in international politics the executive-administrative branch has much better facilities than does Congress for interpreting reality and formulating means for dealing "correctly" with that reality. As we shall see later, this gap in competence between executive-administrative and Congress represents a problem of crucial importance to the future of Congress. But conceding so much, we must remember two vital characteristics of "policy," as distinct from a mere "finding of fact." For it is policy with which we are concerned.

First, a "correct" or competent policy requires more than a knowledge of reality. A policy is "correct" only insofar as it maximizes the achievement of some results that are preferred over other results: security, power, prestige, wealth, freedom, or what not. But since people have differing preferences, a policy "correct" for Smith, because it helps to satisfy his preferences, may be quite "incorrect" for Jones, whose preferences suffer in the process. Thus a basic question in public policy inevitably is: *Whose* preferences are to be maximized? Unless it can be shown, therefore, that the executive-administrative is likely to maximize the preferences of the greater number, its superior capacities for interpreting reality may merely lead to the adoption of policies "correctly" designed for the achievement of the private preferences of the President or his more influential advisers.

Second, the selection of a policy must be a complicated interweaving of interpretations about reality, the preferences relevant to dealing with that reality, and the ways of mediating between those preferences and reality; hence, competent or "correct" judgment in the policy area requires a special kind of skill. This is the political skill.

The political skill is, of course, needed at all levels of policy-making. Where the need for the political skill is slight, as compared with the need for skill in interpreting some sector of reality, as a general practice we recruit an "expert." The more important the questions of preference become, the less competent becomes the expert. At the other end of the spectrum in the policy process is the ordinary Congressman. He may be reasonably competent at searching out preferences and securing their expression. But the more difficult it is to interpret reality, the less competent he becomes. As we move "up" the hierarchy of authority from expert to top administrator on the one side, and up the hierarchy of specialization from ordinary Congressman to specialized committee member on the other, the less different are the skills involved. And at the top of the pyramid, the skills of an Acheson and a Vandenberg may be of much the same kind.

The solution of presidential supremacy ignores this central fact. The superior facilities of the executive-administrative for interpreting reality are important assets. But the problem is not so much one of excluding the Congressional elements of the political skill group in favor of the executive-administrative elements; the problem is to bring the highest competence of the *entire* skill group to bear upon the making of policy. This problem we shall turn to in a later chapter.

Agreement for What?

If the case for presidential supremacy on grounds of superior responsibility or competence is a shaky one, what is the case for the President as an agent in discovering broad areas of agreement?

There is much to be said for the view that in the latter respect the President is vastly superior to Congress; that the President is the instrument of majorities, and Congress of minorities; that the President's political aims and opportunities require him to search out the widest possible national consensus. Here again the weaknesses of Congress are manifest. But here again, is presidential supremacy a solution or a mad flight away from the value itself?

The plain fact is that Congress now exists with certain constitutionally stipulated opportunities for influencing policy. And American foreign policy rests squarely on the kinds of "powers" which constitutional doctrine stipulates for Congress. American foreign policy rests on government loans and expenditures which require appropriations; on military aid, trade negotiations, resources control, which require enabling legislation; on the existence of military forces in readiness, which requires legislation and appropriations; and on the imminent possibility of war, which requires a Congress ready to accept the responsibility of war and beyond that a nation ready to accept wartime sacrifices.

Nineteenth-century American foreign policy might be carried on, like the Monroe Doctrine, without affirmative Congressional action. In the changed American international role after World War I, when treaty action was important, the executive might be brought up short by the Senate. But now the problem is far broader than it was either in the nineteenth century or even after World War I: not merely the treaty power and the Senate are called into play by our foreign policy, but the appropriations and law-making process itself. The whole Congress is as deeply involved in foreign policy as it is in domestic policy; for measured by the demand placed on Congressional power, there is far less basis today for distinguishing foreign from domestic policy than there was a century ago.

For the President to attempt to deprive Congress of the prerogatives stipulated for it by constitutional doctrine would be to involve foreign policy in a procedural controversy that would certainly shatter any consensus that might otherwise exist for the policy. The "solution" of presidential supremacy cannot promise to satisfy the test of consensus unless there is some relatively painless way of liquidating Congress as an effective participant in the making of foreign policy.

Yet, it may be asked, is this last step as improbable as it sounds? Before turning to a solution that seems more in accordance with our values, let us first examine the possibility that the President might conduct foreign policy with a free hand simply by manipulating Congress into accepting whatever policies he proposes.

VIII. A Constitutional Dictator?

A PRINCE who wishes to maintain the state, Machiavelli reminds us, is often forced to do evil. Is this the case with the American President?

In the last chapter we saw that Congressional prerogatives stipulated by constitutional theory and practice stand directly athwart presidential supremacy in foreign affairs. But one may easily fall into error by assuming that constitutional prerogative is the equivalent of power. Is it not possible that in foreign policy the executive can take the substance of power and leave Congress the shadow? If Congressional consent is required by certain widely accepted constitutional stipulations, cannot the President use the powers of the executive-administrative to feed foreign policy into one end of the Congressional hopper and run it through the formalities of the lawmaking process without significant change? Or to put it differently: Whoever can decisively affect the Congressman's preferences or his views of reality can substantially control his voting behavior. Does the executive-administrative have at its disposal adequate means for influencing the Congressman's preferences and reality views on questions of foreign policy?

The argument of this chapter is that the executive-administrative does indeed possess some important means of this kind. Any realistic examination of the power relationships existing between President and Congress must take these influences into account. It may well be that the dynamic of events will strengthen these influences to the point where the Chief Executive is a kind of constitutional dictator in foreign policy. But this is not to say that the constitutional dictator is the only alternative still open to us, nor that it is the most preferable, assuming the values of rationality, responsibility, and agreement. The remaining chapters will be devoted to an examination of an alternative that may yet be open. But first, let us take a brief look at the tool kit of the potential constitutional dictator.

Mobilizing Public Opinion

The President may—indeed often does—attempt to manipulate the Congressman's preferences and opportunities for re-election by mobilizing public opinion behind his own policies.

In domestic policy this practice dates at least from Jackson's administration, when the President sought to use public opinion as a weapon against Congress in the conflict over the Bank. It is perhaps worth recalling, however, that although Jackson was re-elected in 1832, even that popular President failed to gain a favorable Congress and therefore had to resort to his executive powers to achieve his ends.

In foreign policy, the use of public opinion as a force in the President's struggle with Congress is a weapon too ready at hand to be underestimated. It should not be overly difficult for the executive branch to create a "crisis" in foreign affairs by the release of appropriate information at its disposal. Lincoln Steffens tells us in his autobiography that as a police reporter in New York he created a local "crime wave" merely by a somewhat more intensive reporting of crimes than had theretofore been the practice. It is perhaps not too much to expect that the executive branch, by withholding or releasing information at its disposal and by its silence or its public statements, may significantly influence public impressions as to whether or not a serious crisis in foreign relations exists at any given moment or in any given area. There are, to be sure, limits within which the picture of reality can be manipulated, but within these limits executive decisions can sometimes play a decisive rôle.[1]

Thus in the postwar period the executive evidently began to play up an interpretation of events in Europe as a crisis which the United States had to meet with definite foreign policy measures; and at the same time, it played down—until much later—such an interpretation of events in China. Congressmen and others who sought release of the suppressed Wedemeyer report on China were probably right in their belief that the report would have an impact on public opinion about our China policy roughly comparable to the impact on public opinion of speeches and comments by members of the executive on the need for a new American policy for Europe. In retrospect it seems clear that had the executive chosen to do so, by co-operating with events it could have created a popular sense of crisis over happenings in the Far East more nearly like the one developing at that time over European events.

But in the strategy and generalship of foreign relations how useful is the technique of manipulating Congress through public opinion? As a method of overcoming deadlock, a presidential appeal to public opinion is not without practical difficulties. Short of waiting for another election, it is sometimes difficult to know how the various publics have made up their minds. Public opinion polls, letters, or newspaper editorials may not be influential in breaking the deadlock. And in various respects these may distort the way in which the various publics will act on election day or when concrete sacrifices are demanded in behalf of the policy. Yet to sit back and wait for the next election is to play into the hands of crisis. Even the election may not resolve the conflict; given the separation of powers and a weak party structure, the election may only return both contestants in the controversy. At least for domestic policy, this appears to have been the case in the elections of 1948.

Or the President's appeal may be rejected, as was President Wilson's demand for a Democratic Congress in 1918. If the President is engaged in negotiations, this defeat may place him in a most delicate situation, particularly today when the executive-Congressional relationship is much better understood in foreign chancelleries than it evidently was in 1918.

If the technique is to be successfully employed, therefore, the executive branch must be given such a superiority of means for manipulating public opinion that it would regularly emerge the winner in any executive-Congressional conflict. There are values according to which such a development might be justified. But they are not the values of a democratic society.

State Department as Ward Heeler

There are other methods of manipulating Congress short of a drastic control of public opinion, and these are a part of the traditional practice of executive relations with Congress. In various ways the executive branch may apply gentle pressures on Congressmen: the President may employ patronage; the Departments may provide certain helpful services to members of Congress; influential pressure groups under executive influence may be brought into action; the favorite projects of certain members of Congress may be looked on with more tolerance. These are all devices that have grown up as essentially irrational substitutes for the more rational executive-Congressional relationship that is inhibited by the separation of powers. From a democratic point of view, the techniques are decidedly unattractive, for they secure legislative action through influences that have no necessary relationship to the wants and desires of the electorate. But such influences undoubtedly help to grease the squeaking wheels of constitutional machinery designed rather for maintaining the power of minorities within a negative state than for meeting the needs of majorities in the modern, positive state.

Yet even as a *pis aller*, this technique for manipulating Congress has limited utility in the operation of foreign policy. For one thing, the techniques may bring about an empty victory unless Congress and the public *are* genuinely behind the policy. To develop an arrangement that will insure a positive relation between public policy and public support is the basic problem, not the mere winning of temporary executive victories over Congress.

Congress has a way of taking its revenge on the executive when it is manipulated into consenting legislatively to a policy that it does not really endorse. It may harass the executive by investigations, by using the appropriations process to weaken the organization or to secure policy changes, by legislating certain personnel out of office, and if need be by modifying the statute itself. The perennial phenomenon of Congress delegating power with one hand and retaking it with the other, which leads to so much instability in policy and administration, probably stems in part from the fact that the original delegation was secured less because of basic agreement on policy than because of the manipulative techniques customarily employed by the executive in getting policies approved.

An even more important limitation on these techniques is the weakness of the State Department as an instrument for this kind of manipulation. To begin with, the Department has very few personal services it can provide for individual Congressmen. To be sure, there are some. It can facilitate passports.[2] Foreign Service officers abroad can provide special assistance to Congressional delegations or individual Congressmen and their families.[3] The State Department may also write speeches for Congressmen, a service all government departments are happy to perform. It is well authenticated that more than one member of Congress has acquired a reputation for a profound understanding of foreign policy on the basis of speeches written for him by the State Department; occasionally a member is even "built up" into something of a figure by the solicitous coaching of State Department officials.

Services such as these may help; [4] but they cannot overcome the real weakness of the Department as a player in *this* kind of political game. The State Department has virtually no "constituency." It is not the kind of service agency whose benefits are immediately visible to important voting blocs; therefore it cannot easily mobilize citizen pressures on Congress. In this respect, it differs fundamentally from the Department of Agriculture, which as a service agency to farmers is a political power in its own right; or the Department of Labor with its services to trade-unions and workers; or the Department of Commerce with its services to businessmen; or the Department of Interior with its variegated services to electric power consumers, irrigated areas, reclamation districts, and the like. Citizen groups like the United Nations Association or the Foreign Policy Association can scarcely match in potency even one important local of the Farm Bureau Federation, the CIO, or the National Association of Manufacturers. The State Department, moreover, is a small department; its personnel is recruited almost wholly on a career basis; it has little patronage to dispense. Aside from an occasional ambassadorship, which is too important and too infrequent a plum to waste on Congressmen, there is little help the individual Congressman can get in strengthening his organization back home. Worse yet, for a variety of reasons, Foreign Service personnel until recently has been recruited in significant part from social, educational, and economic strata that many members of Congress distrust. A distinguished young Congressman of intelligence and balance remarks: "The State Department is an old class bureaucracy based on seniority, protocol, and everything else of that kind." [5] The myth may be false, but it persists (although, as we shall see in a moment, the Foreign Service is sometimes an asset.)

There are other, more irrational factors, on the debit side of the Department's balance sheet. The State Department is by the very nature of its function a "troublemaker" for Congress in the present state of the world. It can rarely bring a happy word—a budget surplus, a decrease in expenditures, a spectacular solution to a pressing problem. More often it must demand increased expenditures in election years; it proposes policies that require a large military establishment and a draft; it presents the Congress with issues from which a Congressman can gain few votes but which he cannot successfully dodge. It would be interesting to speculate on the hatreds that were projected by Congressmen on the State Department in 1948 as a result of having to appropriate six billion for foreign relief and pass a peacetime draft act, both in in an election year.

Moreover, desire to locate guilt for the state of the world leads directly to the door of the Department that is "responsible" for that condition. If foreign relief and a peacetime draft are necessary, it is easy to believe that the State Department has bungled. If the Department operated more effectively, one would like to believe, the country would not be faced with its great crisis in Soviet-American relations.

The State Department therefore meets a much more hostile and distrustful Congress than do most other departments. Congressional distrust is revealed by such items as its initial refusal to allow complete State Department operation of the Voice of America programs, and perhaps even more clearly, by the establishment of a separate agency for the administration of the European Recovery Program. One has only to spend a few days on Capitol Hill to realize how widespread is Congressional distrust and resentment of the Department of State.

Manipulating the Picture of Reality

The real power of the executive-administrative in playing the game of politics with Congress cannot rest on the old-fashioned techniques of the ward leader. Nor does it need to. For the trump card of the executive-administrative in foreign affairs is not its capacity for influencing the Congressman's preferences by ward-heeling methods. Rather, it is the capacity for influencing the Congressman's picture of international reality. This it does in two ways.

First, the Department of State has in the Foreign Service an elite corps whose assertions about international reality may sometimes be highly influential. For despite the hostility of some members toward the stereotype of the "striped pants cookie-pusher," the Foreign Service—perhaps the most group-conscious guild in the federal government—does have some influential allies in Congress. The authors of a recent detailed study of the Foreign Service Act of 1946 remark:

> During the course of the eight hearings in executive session before the Subcommittee [of the House Foreign Affairs Committee] . . . a spirit of camaraderie developed between the Foreign Service representatives and the Subcommittee members. There was some social intercourse between the Foreign

Service officers, especially Chapin [director of the Foreign Service] and Harrington [deputy director], and the congressmen. As the bill became more and more "their bill," the Subcommittee members seem to have adopted a rather paternal attitude toward the Foreign Service; the Service became for them somewhat like a constituent, whose rights and interests deserve Congressional protection.[6]

As an elite corps almost wholly insulated from the crasser political influences and completely untainted by charges or innuendo about "party politics," as a guild whose members are carefully recruited according to standards until quite recently severe for the federal government, the Foreign Service evidently appears to some Congressmen as a model of what the civil service ought to be. Testimony from a member of the Foreign Service at times may be extraordinarily influential; Congressmen may be inclined to take Foreign Service views on faith and not subject them to the critical scrutiny they need.[7]

Second, as pointed out in an earlier chapter, the fact that the executive-administrative as a whole appears to possess a superior claim to information about, and expert interpretation of, international politics does give the President and State Department a certain lever on Congress as on the electorate. For just as the executive-administrative can, within limits, deliberately and systematically shape public opinion by giving different emphasis and interpretation to events, so too can it influence Congressional opinion by the same techniques.[8] Moreover, the growth of the Central Intelligence Agency may over the long run give the executive-administrative enormously better information, and better evaluation of information, than it has ever had before.

It is difficult to evaluate the effectiveness and potentiality of these powers. But the theoretical possibilities contained in the development of a great disproportion between executive, Congress, and electorate in access to information may be imagined by the following mental experiment: Suppose the Chief Executive and his aides were to decide that a preventive war had become indispensable to national survival. Suppose the Congress and the electorate did not share this view. Suppose, finally, that the President and his aides appeared at a hastily summoned, closed meeting of Congress and informed it that Russian war planes were about to begin winging their way to the United States with quantities of atomic bombs. What would Congress do? Indeed, what *could* Congress do?

The Constitutional Dictator in a Mass Society

It is at least possible that these techniques for manipulating Congress and public opinion might, under the proper circumstances, transmute presidential supremacy into a peculiarly American form of modern dictatorship. Indeed, our analysis suggests that only some such development will provide the necessary guarantees that the President will be supreme in foreign affairs and untrammeled by "interference" from the national legislature.

Modern society in an age of acute crisis provides fertile soil for such a growth. The onerous burden of freedom, the imperious desires of leadership groups for domination, the crucial need for a "right" decision that will promote security and relieve anxiety—these are some of the preconditions for a flight into authoritarianism.

In the blatant form practiced in the Third Reich or the U.S.S.R., most of us easily recognize that the mass of the people is exploited to satisfy the preferences of the leadership. But the growing discrepancy between the capacities of the electorate and those of certain leadership groups may lead in democratic societies to pressures of a more subtle kind.[9] The universal impulse of the leaders to guide the mass to the "right" policy conclusions is easily converted into a desire to short-circuit the democratic process, particularly, as in foreign policy, when the "right" choice may seem to be a precondition of national survival. The leadership feels that it knows "what the realities of the situation demand." Yet it must submit its policies to the electorate for approval or rejection, even though the irrationalities of the political process may lead to a "wrong" choice—which is to say, to policies that do not secure the preferences of the leadership. The leaders, moreover, may be fortified by the easy conviction that their ends and purposes embody the real preferences of the electorate—preferences obscured by the operation of the political process.

Perhaps, despite these hesitancies, the democratic game must be played out according to the accepted ground rules. The wish to by-pass the rules runs afoul of a deeply rooted institutional framework, reinforced by a powerful body of habitual activities and beliefs. It also runs counter to the tremendous inheritance of democratic slogans, myths, and practices that have surrounded political and administrative leadership from infancy, and which inhibit a conscious declaration or even realization of one's anti-democratic purposes. These conflicting desires of the leadership might perhaps be reconciled if only the citizens could be guided to a "right" decision by surrounding them with the "correct" information, or by withholding intelligence reports adverse to the policy, or by repeating and dramatizing the appropriate symbols. Thus the illusion of freedom and democracy might be maintained; the electorate might continue to believe that it was enforcing its preferences on the leaders; while in reality the leadership would be enforcing its preferences on the electorate.

Unattractive as this picture may appear when drawn so starkly, its appeal must not be underrated.[10] For it would simultaneously satisfy the power needs of driving, aggressive, and perhaps charismatic leadership, the desire of followers to be relieved of the responsibility for making burdensome choices, and the verbal and institutional apparatus of democracy. Of all the alternatives, moreover, it may be the easiest to achieve in a crisis world.

Another Way Out

Presidential supremacy—even some form of constitutional dictatorship—*may* be the wave of the future. But if so, then the future lies with values other than rationality, responsibility, and agreement. The central argument of this book is that another way out is still open to us. What is this way?

We must begin with the assumption that discretion over foreign policy by political leadership—often very great discretion—is an ineluctable requirement of survival in modern international politics. As we saw in Chapter VI, foreign policy is too complicated an affair to be conducted by plebiscite. The basic question is not *whether* political leadership is to exercise discretion in foreign affairs, but *how*. Or put in another way, the question is: What can we do to make it reasonably probable that in exercising its discretion political leadership will maximize—so far as is possible in the kind of world we live in—the values of responsibility, rationality, and agreement?

The argument here is: First, that Congress can be converted into a basic institution for deciding what and whose preferences are to guide the conduct of foreign affairs. There are, however, many obstacles to such a conversion, and these must be removed.

Second, that the executive-administrative will probably

remain the basic institution for interpreting international reality and formulating proposals for dealing with that reality. But if Congress is to perform competently in mediating between preferences and reality, it must develop techniques for more rational evaluation of executive-administrative reports and policy proposals.

Third, that these developments in themselves will greatly facilitate the process of making foreign policy on the basis of the widest possible agreement. There are, to be sure, some potential conflicts between the goals of rationality and responsibility on the one side, and the goal of agreement on the other. To some extent, however, these conflicts can be resolved.

In the two succeeding chapters we shall examine the problem of Congressional competence in foreign affairs and some ways by which its competence may be raised. Thereafter we shall turn to the problem of whether and how Congress can be converted into a more satisfactory institution for formulating preferences about foreign policy. We shall then consider the problem of agreement. And finally we shall attempt to determine what might be the implications of the proposed structure for the making of foreign policy.

PART THREE

A NEW PATTERN OF POLICY-MAKING

IX. Obstacles on the Road to Reason

TO say that Congressional rationality in foreign affairs is limited is only to say in a somewhat complicated way what everyone already knows: that Congressmen are human beings. Therefore, in examining the obstacles to rational action by Congress on foreign policy, we should not lose sight of one important point. This basic limitation—the fallibility of man—is shared by all who may assert a superior claim to rationality; for were we to undertake an examination of such rival claimants as the "experts," the State Department, the President, the journalists and pundits, we should no doubt discover many frailties there, too.

Accepting this, what are some of the special difficulties stemming from Congressmen as people and Congress as an organization?

Decision-Making by Discussion

An action is rational, according to our assumptions, if it is designed to achieve the preferences of those for whose benefit the action is taken. From this point of view, an organization might be described as "democratic" to the extent that (1) it facilitates relatively "free" choice by the adult members of the organization of the policies to be followed, and (2) in cases of conflict, it carries out those policies having the support of the greater number of members.

Emphasis on the first of these criteria has led some writers like the late Henry Simons to describe "democracy" essentially as a process of arriving at decisions by discussion. If such an interpretation overlooks some of the implications of the second criterion, it nevertheless does focus attention on an element that has long been regarded as fundamental to the operation of a democracy—discussion.

Now the paradox presented by some kinds of policy situations, and not infrequently international situations, is that *the process of discussion itself may preclude choice of the very policies that members of the society would have chosen as a result of their discussions.* Let us examine the discussion process at the Congressional level for a moment and see why this is so.

If discussion is held to be a vital prerequisite to rational choice about complex questions of public policy, and if the opportunity to make rational choices is highly valued, then Congress should perform two functions in the discussion process.

In the first place, the decision *within* the legislature itself must be arrived at after discussion. And it is probably correct to say that the decision-making process in the legislature, more than in any other significant power institution, is in actual practice conducted by discussion. This is as true of the American Congress as of the British Parliament, although the one emphasizes discussion in committee, and the other full-dress debate. In the United States the need for protracted discussion has been intensified by the nature of the parties, which have been loose alliances of regional and functional interest groups with claims, often sharply conflicting, that must be accommodated. The importance of these discussions and negotiations can scarcely be exaggerated, particularly in the United States where the interest groups are manifold and internal conflicts are more often resolved within the legislative body than within the confines of the party.

But Congressional inquiry, discussion, and debate ought to serve a second function: facilitating a rational decision by the electorate *outside* the Congress. Congress is a forum from which the decisions made there and the issues outstanding between the parties are periodically appealed to the electorate. The second function of Congress, therefore, is to clarify these decisions and issues so that the citizens can make reasonably intelligent judgments from the standpoint of their own preferences.

These functions are of crucial importance to the operation of a democracy. But they do not necessarily adapt themselves to effective pursuit of foreign policy, if we employ "effective" here to mean success in achieving objectives on which there is explicit or implicit agreement within Congress or the electorate. For the very process of reaching *agreement* on objectives may militate against attaining those objectives.

This is so, in the first place, because international events move with speed; there is therefore a premium on the ability to decide and to act quickly. But the process of inquiry, discussion, and debate in the legislature is inherently ill-adapted to speed. The greater the speed, the less successful the process generally is in fulfilling its two major functions.

Second, unity of decision is a positive asset in international negotiation. When Secretary of Commerce Henry Wallace attacked the Truman foreign policy in his Madison Square Garden speech on September 12, 1946, the effectiveness of the American delegation at the Paris conference on peace treaties was temporarily reduced to nullity.[1] But an essential quality of the legislative function is the exposure of differences, of "disunity." So long as the nation is not basically in agreement on its foreign policy, this limitation on effectiveness is inevitable.

Even bipartisanship may only serve to create new, non-party alignments in Congress, and will not—certainly under our assumptions ought not—put the quietus on debate and discussion of issues where agreement is absent.

In some sense, neither speed nor unity can be completely won without wholly nullifying vital parts of the democratic process. But the significance of that process in limiting our effectiveness in international bargaining can perhaps be reduced without sacrificing to the impelling claims of foreign policy the fundamental values of a democratic order.

The Dead Hand

A gray head is a wise head, according to a folk belief that manages to live side by side with its contrary—no fool like an old fool.

It may be said that Congress does not always "act its age"; nevertheless one of the most important characteristics of our national legislature is its age as an institution.[2] Although the American Congress has not existed as long as the British Parliament, there is nevertheless a sense in which Parliament is the more youthful institution. For in a century and a half of existence, Congress has undergone no internal changes comparable to the extensive evolutionary alterations in the structure, operation, and techniques of Parliament during the same period. In a country with few visible signs of age, where antiquity has little value and antiquarianism is a synonym for eccentricity, the Congress is uniquely an institution of which it may be said that the old is more venerated than the new. It is a common observation that even the Congressmen most unorthodox in their views on social policy are likely to accept, and perhaps to approve, things-as-they-are in Congress.

Congress is a conservative institution. And perhaps this factor as much as any will stand in the way of a reorganization that will help to make the national legislature viable in the modern world. It is conservative primarily because it is old. The established Congressional relationships and techniques are products of, or have survived, a lengthy experience. As often as not they are customary rather than formal, but no less binding because of that. Thus the "seniority rule" for committee chairmen is entirely based on custom and yet is so firmly embedded that in 1946 the most systematic Congressional reorganization in history was unable to tamper with it.[3]

The Congress is an *institution;* it is a conglomerate of collective habits and sanctions that can only be fully known to the initiated. The initiated therefore have more prestige than the new members. It is common practice for a member of Congress to preface a remark by an affidavit of his Congressional age: "In my fifteen years in Congress . . ."; "Although I have been in Congress only three years . . ."; "My experience as Senator and Representative since 1925 is . . ."

A perceptive ex-Congressman with a reputation for heterodoxy has set down his reactions as a freshman in the House:

> Very early I discovered that, like New York, Keokuk, and Centerville, Congress has its "select circle." It consists of a number of highly prepossessed members, who have considerable influence in the Congress and who are well aware of that fact. Practically always they are members of long service. A few of them seem to make a point of failing to note the presence of newer members or those not belonging to the select influential group. . . . Most of these highly influential members are conservatives; almost without exception they are people of admirable character. I confess to having had a deep desire to have the friendship and understanding—if not the agreement—of certain of these men. I have experi-

enced the hollow, empty feeling of having others of them
turn away, almost deliberately, and begin a discussion with
another of their circle when I was attempting to speak to
them.[4]

The member who is conservative about the organization
of Congress uses the arguments of the conservative everywhere—arguments that many Congressmen find persuasive
with respect to Congress, but objectionable when applied to
different realms. We are all conservatives, we are all radicals—
to paraphrase Jefferson; it depends on the institution in view.

Conservatism vis-à-vis Congress has the old familiar ring:
We are an old institution. Out of our lengthy experience we
have evolved certain ways of doing things. These are, on the
whole, satisfactory ways. The ways are known to us, the
initiated, but they are not always known to the novice or the
outsider. Therefore any proposal from such sources is likely
to be "impractical," "unrealistic." We have dealt with these
problems in the concrete; they cannot be dealt with by theory.
To be sure, we see the need for some changes. But these
are minor. We shall have to move slowly and cautiously,
or we shall injure this complicated instrument, perfected out
of a century and a half of experience.

In addition to the relative age of both the institution and
the initiated elite, there are several additional forces for
organizational conservatism. For one thing, the concerns of
the Congressman militate against any preoccupation with
internal organizational problems. He is primarily concerned
with manipulating the relationship between himself and
his constituents, or with manipulating Congressional relationships for his particular political ends. He is less likely to be
interested in the over-all problem of organization unless he
is one of the leaders; and if he is a leader it is more than

probable, as Mr. Voorhis points out, that he has already grown gray in the institution and has become accustomed to—indeed fond of—the genial inefficiencies of Congressional operation.

Moreover, the training, education, and personality of the Congressman are not particularly conducive to the managerial, executive kind of outlook. Organizational problems are not so likely to lie within his focus of attention and interest. The politician, as Max Weber suggested, tends to be at the opposite end of the spectrum from the bureaucrat; the politician is less interested in creating order, rules, organizational "efficiency," and more interested in manipulating order, rules, organization to suit his purposes. The least bureau in the administrative branch may have a staff unit on "organization and management." But not the Congress of the United States.

Time

Such truth as there may be in the adage that wisdom arrives with years reflects the elemental limitation imposed by time on a man's knowledge. Wisdom, someone has said, is brains plus years.

One of the central problems of the modern Congress (one might almost say, of the modern democratic legislature) is the lack of time for the performance of its functions. Witness the following exchange between the Staff Director of the Republican Senate Policy Committee and a Senator:

> Mr. SMITH. Now, Senators, for your amusement as well as to bear out my point on the impossible work load put upon Members of Congress, I have gathered here a group of the books and reports, limited solely to an official character, you should be reading right now on the Marshall plan.

(Mr. Smith here presented a stack of material 18 inches high.)

You are going to take the most momentous step in the history of this country when you pass upon the Marshall plan. . . . That is what you ought to be studying. It contains the Krug report, the Harriman report, the State Department report, the reports of the Herter committee, the Foreign Relations Committee digest; it includes part of the hearings just completed of the Foreign Relations Committee. It does not include hearings yet to be held by the Appropriations Committees. This is one work load you have now on a single problem out of the many problems you have to decide.

Senator FERGUSON. How long would it take in your opinion . . . for a person to read it?

Mr. SMITH. Well, Senator, I have been reading for the last 35 years, nearly all my life, in the field of research; and if I could do an intelligent job on that in 2 months of solid reading, excluding myself from everything else . . . I would credit myself with great efficiency.

Senator FERGUSON. A normal person would probably take 4 to 5 months.[5]

Accentuating the shortage of time for major legislation is the extraordinarily high percentage of the Congressman's daily activity devoted to the needs and plaints of his constituents. The American Congressman is above all else an ambassador from his constituents; he is expected to serve as their liaison man for every problem that might conceivably be solved in Washington—and for a good many that cannot. He dare not take time from this function to perform his legislative duties, for his service activities, he believes, are more important in vote-getting than his action on general legislation. As the functions of government expand and the citizens' contacts with their government multiply, the service demands on the Congressman flourish.

Here is what the Congressmen themselves say:

> Mr. VOORHIS. The people of the districts of this Nation need somebody to act in the nature of an ambassador in their behalf in Washington. Some people call it an errand-boy.

> Mr. RAMSPECK. For the past 2½ years I have been the Democratic whip in the House. Perhaps I ought not to say this, but, without being critical of anybody, I know that the Members of the House are finding great difficulty in giving sufficient time to legislative matters because of the constant and pressing demand from their constituents to deal with matters in the executive branch of the Government. . . . It is my observation that most Members feel it is necessary, if they have to neglect either part of the job, to neglect the legislative end, because they get elected through votes, and most people are not interested in legislation . . . I feel very few read the bills, or, for that matter, know that they are coming up.

> Mr. DOYLE. I would say that most Members of the House are not present when many important bills are being read. . . . They cannot be present at all times on the floor of the House and also do the errand work which we have to do.

Nor does the Senate escape condemnation, as this colloquy reveals:

> The Chairman [Senator LaFollette]. We have had before the Foreign Relations Committee a Mexican water treaty, and as I recall, the hearings lasted 5 weeks. It was, in my opinion, one of the most complex situations that any committee ever had to deal with.

> Senator DOWNEY. Yes. Now the significant thing about that situation, Mr. Chairman, is that I do not believe any Senator

can fairly comprehend that particular treaty without at least 3 or 4 months' concentrated study of it.

The Foreign Relations Committee of the Senate has 23 members. They are all men of genuine ability. Yet I am duty bound to point out that never during those protracted hearings on the Mexican water treaty before the committee did we reach the point where we had more than 3 or 4 members present.[6]

The Reorganization Act of 1946 in no sense solved this problem, although it did decrease the number of committee assignments (assignments on subcommittees promptly increased) and restricted, but did not abolish, private bill legislation. The simple and obvious problem of time remains, and if Congress is to discharge its responsibilities in foreign affairs, as in other major fields, it will somehow have to overcome this elemental limitation.

The Powerful Novice

One special complicating factor arises from the fact that the House of Representatives is now called upon for extraordinarily grave decisions on foreign policy. Yet it is, comparatively, a mere stripling in the field.

Where for a century and a half the House had little or no responsibility for foreign affairs, today three significant tools of foreign policy require its consent. In the first place, parts of foreign policy have come to rest upon *legislation*. Equally important is the recent development of foreign loans and grants, which place upon the House the responsibility for *authorizations* and *appropriations*. Finally, the use of *executive agreements* as a substitute for the treaty process has also brought the House into the determination of foreign policy, for in a large number of cases the executive has considered it necessary or desirable to have Congressional support, in the form of a joint resolution, for an executive agreement.

The House of Representatives, then, has inherited new and unavoidable responsibilities. It would be foolish to pretend that foreign policy can any longer be made by the executive and the Senate alone; the process of foreign policy determination will have to be organized to take into account the new power relationships stemming from the position of the House.

The participation of the House in foreign policy making intensifies the problem of rationality. Not 96 but 531 people must somehow be kept informed about foreign affairs. Yet discussion and debate are far more limited in the House than in the Senate. The whole membership comes up for election every two years. Turnover is greater. Experience on the House Foreign Affairs Committee tends to be shorter than on the Senate Foreign Relations Committee. And until recently the Foreign Affairs Committee was relatively so unimportant that it accumulated a certain amount of dead wood. The time is nevertheless past when we can think of the Senate as the spokesman for Congress on foreign affairs.

Experience and Inexperience

It would be easy, however, to exaggerate the significance of the fact that the House as an institution is a newcomer to foreign policy. It is the experience of the human beings in the House that counts, not that of the inert organization. And the experience of the institution need not necessarily correlate with that of its members.

The fact is, however, that the typical Congressman, like most other American citizens, has had limited experience with foreign affairs. If he is from a rural area, he may be able to make a shrewd evaluation of a proposed farm policy.

If he is from an urban area, he may have considerable grasp of the implications of a labor-management bill, or a housing program, or federal aid to education. But it is only in rare circumstances that he has had any direct experience in foreign affairs.

Two further facts about the experience of the Congressman, whether Senator or Representative, are highly relevant to the problem of rationality in foreign affairs.

First, the typical Senator or Representative was once trained as a lawyer. Year in and year out, from three-fifths to two-thirds of the Senators and Representatives are people with legal training.[7] In many ways, no background is better calculated to prevent realistic action in international politics. For the tendency of the lawyer is to interpret reality in terms of legality, to determine foreign policy by legal policy. The treaty process, careful analysis of legal obligations, concepts of "rights" in the arena of international politics, emphasis on forms—this is the thrust of the lawyer. The lawyer's view in Congress is strengthened by the dominance that international law and international lawyers have had, until recently, over the study of international politics. It is not too much to say that even the "experts" on foreign affairs for half a century have tended to be experts in the law rather than in the politics of international relations.

But the reality system of the lawyer is often a wholly inappropriate one for an accurate interpretation of international politics. It is as if an infantry observer were so thoroughly trained in the tables of organization of the enemy that he was incapable of reporting simply what he saw—a light machine gun, let us say—but insisted on reporting what he believed he *ought* to have seen—a whole squad, perhaps.

Much of the debate in Congress over important measures of foreign policy—the League, the World Court, neutrality legislation, the Atlantic Pact—has been conducted in lawyers' language and according to lawyers' concepts of what was at stake. As if foreign policy were a contract under examination by a court, debate frequently turns upon the precise meaning of words. To the lawyer, words are decisive; if only the contract is properly drawn up, he likes to believe, one may safely rely upon the court to enforce its terms. Precision in words thus gives the lawyer a sense of security not always shared by the non-lawyer, and not always based upon reality. As a result, debate in Congress over foreign policy is often an inquiry into semantics rather than a debate about whether the proposed action symbolized by the words is or is not an appropriate policy for achieving certain values in a particular context of international relations.[8]

The second important fact about the experience of the Senator or Representative is this: In all probability he will never be held directly accountable, individually or jointly, for administering the policy he proposes or votes upon. If it may be charged against the administrator and sometimes the Secretary of State that he has never had to carry a precinct, it may also be charged against the Congressman that he has never had to carry out a policy he helps enact. Yet to carry out policy is a sobering and enlightening experience. It adds new dimensions to one's concepts of the desirable and the possible, and frequently imparts a kind of realism that cannot be gained merely by discussion and reading.

In this respect as in several others, separation of powers comes off decidedly at a disadvantage in comparison with the parliamentary system. It would be difficult to overestimate the extraordinary significance of the fact that a very great number of those who vote in the House of Commons either have been, are, or hope to be, a part of the Government. Even a supposedly radical cabinet comes into power, as in the case of the Labor party, with a sizable reservoir of experienced ministers.[9] In the House of Commons, members of the Government are numerous enough within the ranks of the parliamentary majority to supply a fuller vision of the problem as seen from the viewpoint of a minister with a department to run. In criticism, proposal, and debate, the leading members of the opposition are, furthermore, guided by their own previous experiences in the various ministries, and their expectation that one day they themselves may have to administer the policies now under debate. Anthony Eden in opposition does not easily forget the experiences of Anthony Eden in power, nor the anticipation of having power and responsibility once again for running the foreign affairs of His Majesty's government.

Contrast this with the United States, where even if members of Congress sometimes become members of the executive branch, they cannot be, under the Constitution, simultaneously members of both, and, more important for the point in question, where a member of the executive branch rarely returns to Congress, like John Quincy Adams, to diffuse the wisdom of his executive experience among his legislative colleagues.

Discovering Reality

Yet it is not merely a question of experience. The Congressman faces a staggering task in attempting to discover the realities of international politics to which policy must be adapted. He is in crying need of reasonably objective information, and all the more so because of his limited experience. To rely on the prime source of information, the executive, arouses his well-founded distrust; to rely on the testimony of special pressure groups is also risky. In the Congressional hearings in 1946 on the organization of Congress, members testified again and again to the inadequacy of their sources of information, not merely on foreign policy but on public policy in general:

Mr. VOORHIS. So when you finally come down to make the decision, the decision is made primarily upon the basis of evidence presented either by an executive department or by a group especially interested in that legislation. What I want is to have that checked against the independent information developed from a congressional source.

Mr. HARE. At present there are many agencies both in the executive branch of our Government, as well as groups on the outside, preparing to submit formulas upon which postwar programs are to be based, but I doubt whether it is possible for these groups or agencies to collect and interpret facts without some bias or be independent of political considerations.

Mr. PRIEST. I think it is important that we have an independent idea about it so we will not be placed in a position of always accepting every estimate or every theory that might originate in an executive agency.

Mr. [Charles] LaFOLLETTE. . . . if a member had a basic idea . . . he knows very well that if he takes that to any existing group either in the Government or to any existing group such as I have mentioned, for statistical information or advice or opinion, he might get a rather biased thing, whereas what I think we want is an unbiased opinion.

The Vice Chairman [Rep. Monroney]. There is need for improvement in committee staffing and experts of our own instead of relying on experts from downtown.

Mr. MICHENER. I think it is conceded, if the Secretary of the Interior determined upon a policy, that his experts working under him would prepare themselves on that side of the case.

> They would be proponents. They would not be judicial. Their objective is to carry out the desires of the head of their department.[10]

Because the Congressman lacks information he trusts, he may turn to whatever other sources he can find. In the end he may select whatever he needs and use it to rationalize his vote.

Policy

But above all, the Congressman lacks expert advice on policy. Even if he possessed an adequate picture of international reality, there would remain the formidable problem of mediating between that reality and the set of preferences he wishes to translate into foreign policy.

One observer has described the despair of many Congressmen when they were faced with the President's request for abolition of the arms embargo in the spring of 1939:

> Most of the Congressmen, appalled by the complexity of the issue and moved as Congressmen seldom are moved, were dancing gingerly on the fence, anxiously observing first the public opinion polls and then their mail, which was approaching flood proportions. Meanwhile, they agitatedly sounded every visitor whose advice they respected. Even the professors of international law had their day—and proceeded to contradict one another with the usual vigor of skilled symbol manipulators. Rumor spread: the House, traditionally more responsive to its constituents than the Senate, was considering a bolt from the President's program. The columnists, heavy supporters of the President on this issue, swung into action, and the Congressmen's mail favoring retention [of the arms embargo] was stigmatized as "inspired propaganda" or the effusion of ignorant hysterics. Congressmen were exhorted to do their duty; the polls were cited as indicating that the tor-

rent of mail favoring retention was obviously unrepresentative.[11]

It is sometimes a case of the blind leading the blind. The Congressman is unable to make up his mind on a question involving a means so inordinately complex. He tries desperately to make out the obscure and distant rumblings of his constituents who presumably are no more able than he to decide rationally on the probable consequences of one set of means or the other. Meanwhile, pressures are applied by the executive and numerous interested groups. Experts are asked to testify, and the experts contradict one another.

So the Congressman, short of information and experience, pressed by time, bedeviled by constituents, pressured on all sides, casts his vote for a policy that in a decade's time may ripen into a million casualties.

X. Reducing the Obstacles

IN a complicated world it is necessary for mere survival to adapt the scope of one's decisions approximately to the level of one's competence. I do not know how to remove an appendix. It is enough for me to know that when I have a persistent pain in the abdomen, I had better see a doctor. It is reported that in the last war a general was killed trying to lead a platoon of men across a field in Normandy in a maneuver that any experienced platoon sergeant would instantly have perceived was suicidal. A general might lead a division; he could not necessarily lead a platoon. Nor, we may assume, could the sergeant have taken over the general's task.

To the extent that Congress attempts to do the sergeant's job, it will, I think, almost certainly fail. Its place is in the ranks of the generals. But, you will say, surely this cannot be true! If Congress does not have the expertness to decide on the details of foreign policy, can it possibly decide intelligently on the major issues? If Congressman Jones does not understand the operation of international exchange, can he vote wisely on the Bretton Woods proposals for an International Bank?

There is one sense, an absolute sense, in which the answer is no. The more one understands all the details of a situation, the more capably, *all other things being equal*, one can decide the basic policies. Ability to lead a platoon in combat might give the general more insight in his decisions as division commander. But to say this is simply to say that human beings could solve their problems better if they were omniscient, if, that is to say, they were not human beings. So long as we do not have the godlike Philosopher-Kings of the *Republic*, we shall have to make our peace, as Plato finally saw, with the human legislators of the *Laws*.

There is a second sense, therefore, a relative sense, in which the answer to our questions is yes. For the important point is that *no one* understands all the details of a complicated policy situation, not even the expert. The most significant characteristic of a judgment on complex public policy is that typically it involves extraordinary interweaving of preferences, interpretations of reality, and plain hunches. In this sense, the broader and more inclusive a public policy decision, the less relevant is the social scientist's familiarity with one limited segment of reality.

More than that, if it is true that the expert can frequently help the policy-maker to clarify his values by spelling out some of the consequences of acting upon those values, his expertness grants him no overwhelming capacity for making the final decisions as to what the values of the society ought to be.[1] At most, he can clarify his own preferences and those of other citizens.

To achieve the fullest competence in this second sense, therefore, Congress needs to move simultaneously toward two objectives: first, to mobilize the highest level of rationality consistent with its function as a popularly elected body; second, to focus its decision-making as nearly as possible on that level of competence. With specific reference to foreign affairs, how might Congress proceed toward these ends?

The Committees

Rational action by Congress would be impossible, almost everyone concedes today, without its standing committees.[2]

We should never be able to assemble a Congress of 531 men, each sufficiently skilled in international politics to make an intelligent judgment on the problem before him, sufficiently wise to exploit the experts in the field, sufficiently free from the claims of his constituents to devote adequate time to foreign policy problems, and sufficiently interested in this *one* among the many fields of major policy to elevate it to the highest priority.

What happens in practice, and perhaps the most that one can expect to happen, is that certain people in Congress specialize in particular aspects of public policy. ". . . after you have been here for a while," one Representative has remarked, "you become sort of a semispecialist with respect to legislation which interests you and the rest 'I trust you' to see that nothing wrong is done." [3] It is by no means true, of course, that all the specialization is confined to members of the relevant standing committees. Some important spokesmen on foreign policy—Representatives Herter and Dirksen are recent examples—have been outside the relevant committees. But the committee is the principal means to specialization, and typically the Congressman will have to rely on one or more of the committee members for his interpretation of policy proposals.

Thus if we think of Congress and its committees as a part of the total process of decision-making on foreign policy, what strikes the eye is that *the range of discretion tends to decrease as the range of detailed knowledge increases*. A highly idealized representation of the operation of this formula in a democratic society might look something like the following diagram. There the horizontal distance represents the *range of discretion* available to those who choose policies at each level, assuming in every case that discretion has been narrowed by choices made at the lower level. The vertical distance represents the *range of detailed knowledge* available to those who make the decisions at each level. Thus (ideally) the members of the State Department would have the most detailed knowledge, and the least discretion in choosing among policy alternatives. The electorate, by contrast, would have the least detailed knowledge but the greatest discretion in choosing among policy alternatives.

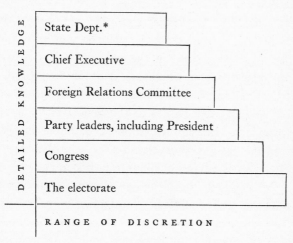

*The attentive student of organization will point out that at some level—usually somewhere below the Secretary's office—the *range* of detailed knowledge begins to decline again, as *specialization* provides greater familiarity with details over increasingly smaller ranges.

Now this kind of relationship between knowledge and power (a relationship that anti-democrats from Plato to the modern totalitarians have looked upon as utter madness) pretty clearly requires a rather complicated meshing of gears to work at all. The system will tend toward *irrationality* whenever people at one level attempt to exercise judgments requiring the detailed knowledge available only to people at the succeeding level. And it will tend toward *irresponsibility* whenever people at one level attempt to exercise their discretion by making policy that runs counter to the preferences of people at the preceding level.

The Congressional committee occupies a key point in this series. For it must act as a kind of transformer between the relatively detailed knowledge of the State Department and the relatively general knowledge of the Congress. Let us take a brief look at these committees.

Perhaps the most important characteristic of the Congressional committee system, from the point of view of rationality, is the fact that experience in the field of policy covered by the committee is not an important criterion for selecting the people who sit on the committee. When Governor Dewey appointed John Foster Dulles to the Senate in 1949, his appointment to the Foreign Relations Committee might have seemed, to the outside observer, a foregone conclusion. Dulles had been Dewey's adviser on foreign policy in two campaigns, had helped work out the bipartisan system on foreign policy from 1944 on, and doubtless would have been Secretary of State had Dewey been elected. He had been a delegate, sometimes with the Secretary of State and the chairman and ranking minority member of the Foreign Relations Committee, to a number of the most important international conferences of the postwar period, including the San Francisco conference on the United Nations charter, the first meeting of the Council of Foreign Ministers in 1945, later meetings of the Council in Moscow and London, the meeting of the Security Council in Paris in 1948, and to various meetings of the United Nations General Assembly and the Trusteeship Council. He was generally regarded as the single most important Republican spokesman on foreign policy, except for Senator Vandenberg himself. Yet he was denied a seat on the Foreign Relations Committee. *This* was in fact the foregone conclusion.

Now it may be argued that Dulles was only filling an interim appointment by gubernatorial selection, and so was scarcely entitled to a seat on an important committee like Foreign Relations. Yet even if he had been elected, the chances are overwhelming that he would have had to stand in line for the Committee behind every other Senator with seniority on the Committee or in the Senate. As a presidential nominee, a Republican Senate would have unhesitatingly confirmed him as Secretary of State; but as a freshman Senator, they would not have granted him the lowest position on the Foreign Relations Committee.

For the primary consideration in committee appointments, both in the Senate and in the House, is the man's seniority, modified somewhat by such factors as the geographical distribution of committee membership, the total population of the man's state, and his personal influence. What the outsider might regard as the most relevant criteria—the man's experience and his willingness to help carry out the party platform—carry the least weight.

Because men with backgrounds in international politics are not deliberately and systematically recruited to the committees, the chances for rationality in the committee rest essentially upon the accidental interplay of three other factors: the prestige of the committee, the kind of people attracted to the committee, and the opportunity offered by the committee for learning by experience.

The prestige of the committee helps determine the number and kinds of applicants for committee positions: the more the prestige, the bigger the field of candidates—and the better the field, because men of ability and experience then exert their influence for positions on the committee. With respect to prestige, the Senate Committee and its House counterpart have, in the past, been poles apart. Assignment to one of the thirteen positions on the Senate Foreign Relations Committee is highly coveted, as two recent pieces of evidence show. After the Republicans took control of Congress in 1946, more Republican Senators put in bids for membership on the Foreign Relations Committee than on any other except the powerful Appropriations Committee. And at the beginning of the Eighty-first Congress, more senior Democratic members sought positions on Foreign Relations than on *any* other committee.[4]

It is easy to see why the Committee should occupy a position of such high prestige. For one thing, the Constitutional functions of the Senate in treaty-making have always tended to give to a member of Foreign Relations a certain aura of statesmanship, influence, and nation-wide recognition. The oldest standing committee in the Senate, Foreign Relations, has had within its ranks an imposing array of great names: Andrew Jackson, Henry Clay, Daniel Webster, Stephen A. Douglas, William H. Seward, Charles Sumner, Elihu Root, Henry Cabot Lodge, William Borah, and a host of others— all men of power and influence in their times. But if the Committee was significant in the past, its importance today has increased a thousandfold.

One would be hard put to discover in Congress a better spot from which to gain political fame, power, future. Surely it is no exaggeration to say that Senator Vandenberg's service on the Committee, together with his dramatic conversion to militant-internationalism, took him out of the chorus and into the spotlight. From a rather ordinary Midwestern politician he emerged with the stature of an international statesman and with an influence at home so imposing that in 1948 the presidential nomination almost fell like a ripe apple into his barely outstretched hands.

As a result, the Committee has attracted to it as able a group as the Senate could provide. Impressions here are probably more relevant than objective data, but the following facts are not without significance. In 1949 the Committee included among its thirteen members four other committee chairmen, including the chairmen of Finance, Armed Services, and Atomic Energy, not to mention the ex-chairman of the latter committee. Among its members were eleven college graduates, including eight LL.B.'s and one Ph.D. It was, to be sure, dominated like the Senate itself by lawyers; nine out of the thirteen members had practiced law. But one could also count two members who had been newspapermen (one of these was the senior Republican member, Senator Vandenberg), a professor of political science, and a onetime university president.

The Foreign Affairs Committee of the House is, by contrast, the poor relation, unloved and unwanted—at any rate until recently, when the Committee has begun to attract attention like Cinderella at the ball. A distinguished Republican House member in the camp of the militant-internationalists referred to the old committee (in a conversation with the writer) as "a dump heap, where service was a chore rather than a privilege." [5] For so long as the House had no real influence in foreign affairs, assignment to the Committee carried too few rewards to attract even such talents as were available in the House.

The Committee has therefore lacked distinguished and powerful leaders, influential in the counsels of their parties and recognized in the nation as important spokesmen. When the President and the majority in the House are of the same party, the Committee chairman is often little more than a spokesman for the White House and State Department; and even when the President represents the opposition party, the chairman and the Committee have had but slight influence on the making of foreign policy.[6]

The importance of the Committee is, to be sure, rising with

the same tide that now brings the House into the midst of foreign affairs, and there is every reason to suppose that this rise in the Committee's prestige and influence will progress much further. It is a sign of the times that in the Eighty-first Congress more members of the House requested seats on this committee than on any other.[7] It will take time, however, for the normal operation of seniority to infuse into the Committee the politically significant leadership it has lacked in the past. When the incumbent in the chair died in 1949, the chairmanship passed by seniority to John Kee, a seventy-four-year-old Representative almost unknown beyond the halls of Congress.

Seniority as a criterion has been systematically attacked by observers outside Congress, and just as steadfastly supported by leaders in Congress. The Congressional spokesman will argue, when pressed, that seniority does in fact lead to competence, for experience on the committee itself educates the committeeman and over the years produces a specialist highly familiar with the committee's problems and with the administrative agencies handling those problems. In the case of the Foreign Relations Committee, there is much to be said for this argument. If we take the twenty-two-year period from 1928 through 1949 as typical of what we may expect in the way of service on the Committee, we can predict with some assurance that any foreign policy proposal is likely to be examined by men who have been serving on the Foreign Relations Committee for about seven and a half years on the average—a rather substantial apprenticeship. These are men, moreover, who probably served in Congress about four years before their appointments to the Committee: men, in other words, who have been in Congress about twelve years. (See Table XIV, Appendix A.) If one examines the tremendous number of hearings the Committee goes through in seven years, one might agree that if only the basic human materials are adequate to begin with, the average Committee member should possess a sizable fund of detailed knowledge about American foreign policy.

By such a test, indeed, even the House Committee does not come off too badly. The turnover is greater in the lower house, of course, and service tends to be shorter. Even so, on the basis of the same two decades of experience, members of the Foreign Affairs Committee at any given moment will have an average of about five years' service on the Committee, and two years of previous service in the House. (See Table XV, Appendix A.)

It is reasonable to argue, moreover, that in neither house need the members depend exclusively upon the experience and knowledge of these two committees. For there are other committees working on problems of a kind that may create intelligent insights into foreign policy, such as Armed Services, Atomic Energy, and Banking and Currency (which handled the Bretton Woods proposals for the International Bank). It is not without significance, indeed, that in the Senate a certain cross-fertilization is provided for by having the chairmen of the first two committees as members of Foreign Relations.

Yet it can scarcely be gainsaid that to give major weight to seniority is to decrease the probabilities that those most talented in foreign affairs will sit on the committees. Five years' service on a committee is all but meaningless if one has little conception of the relevant questions that need to be asked. And at present, when the House Committee needs an immediate injection of new blood, to wait for seniority and the new attractiveness of the Committee to elevate the stature of the Committee is a callous gamble with the future. This is not to say that seniority—or better, one's experience on a committee—is not one valid criterion for selecting members.

But surely the critics are right in saying that seniority ought not to be a dominant criterion.

Congress and the Expert

Through its committees, Congress tends to acquire a body of "policy specialists," as I should like to call them. Just as one function of Congress, taken as a whole, is to mediate between the non-expertness of the citizen and the expertness of the executive-administrative branch, so one function of the Congressional policy specialists is to mediate between the non-experts in Congress and the experts on fact and policy in the executive-administrative. Let us examine the kinds of competence involved in this relationship.

If, suffering from shortness of breath, you go to a doctor, he may tell you that you have a diseased heart. You ask him what you should do. He tells you that if you keep on with your present activities you will probably die in a year or two. If you go to bed, he says, you may live into old age. If you do not take to bed, he tells you, but simply slow down measurably in your activities, you will probably live a good deal longer than your present manner of life would permit you, but probably not so long as if you go to bed.

Now a decision has to be made. If the doctor makes the decision for you, I should call that "expert-authoritarianism," even though you voluntarily abdicate to him the power to make the decision. For you have given over to an expert on medicine the authority to decide a question involving extremely complicated problems of human values concerning which his *scientific* knowledge gives no special competence. If, on the other hand, he makes no suggestion as to the choice you ought to make, I should call that "expert-neutrality." If, thirdly, out of his experience with other patients who have been faced with similar problems in the past, he helps you to explore the various alternatives, calls to your attention consequences you have overlooked, and leaves the final decision to you, I should call that "policy-advice."

If we examine the entire process, at least where expert-authoritarianism is not involved, we shall see that a number of decisions are, in fact, taken. These are: (1) an expert interpretation of reality; (2) an expert formulation of the alternative ways by which your decisions can influence the future, given present reality; (3) your decision to accept the expert's competence on these two points; (4) a clarification of your preferences; (5) a choice among the relevant alternatives, based on your preferences.

The modern epoch, Whitehead has said, is an age of reason based upon faith. The problem of Congress is to discover experts in whom it can place a faith based upon reason. For what Congress desperately needs is access to experts who can interpret reality and formulate alternatives, and yet do so with a neutrality that would permit Congress itself to make the choice among the alternatives.

What Congress has grounds for fearing is the expert who will use his expertness to substitute expert-authoritarianism for expert-neutrality and policy-advice. One long-time Congressional observer has put the fears of many Congressmen this way:

> By and large, back of the war, back in the early days, we found that the executive departments were pretty fair with Congress. They came down and they told the facts. Now, on the basis of those facts the committee could take course A or course B. The department vigorously urged in every way they could to get them to follow course A, but at the same time they told them the troubles and disadvantages, if any, which would occur if they followed that course. . . . In re-

> cent years I think it has been the disposition on the part of some of the executive departments, in their zeal, in their necessity of getting something done, to possibly not come to the committee and explain alternative B as fully as they did alternative A, and the committee has no time to go into the thing and the result is that the department gets its will.[8]

Here is the perennial conflict. On the one side, the executive-administrative is intent on "getting things done" and dubious of Congress' competence for making intelligent policy decisions. On the other, Congress is concerned with the unending difficulty of holding the executive-administrative responsible to it for important policy decisions. At one level the conflict stems from different points of view, what old hands in Washington call the difference between the "executive point of view" and the "Congressional point of view." But at a deeper level, it is clear that a fundamental conflict of values is inevitable whenever the Congress, in order to enforce responsibility on the executive-administrative, must operate at a level requiring detailed knowledge it does not possess.

Given the ever present possibility of a clash between the values of rationality and the values of responsibility in public policy decisions, what may be done? What we must do, I think, is to attack the problem from both directions. On the one side, we must introduce techniques for enforcing responsibility in a way that requires less supervision of details than is presently demanded. This point will be touched upon in the next chapter. On the other side, we must try to raise the level of Congressional competence so that it can enforce responsibility more intelligently. Such a course would require, among other things, a better use of the expert by Congress. There are a number of possible developments in this direction.

First, the committees may specialize within themselves. The House Committee, for example, is already divided into eleven regional subcommittees. There are, however, pretty definite limits to the amount of specialization by Congressmen that is either possible or desirable. Even if it were attainable, I doubt if we should want a national legislature composed of numerous specialists each of whom had to take the opinion of the others entirely on faith.

Second, the committees may employ their own experts. Both committees now do so, as a result of the authorization of committee staffs contained in the Legislative Reorganization Act of 1946. Both have small professional staffs for research and analysis—the House Committee somewhat reluctantly, belatedly, and only as a by-product of Mr. Herter's Select Committee on Foreign Aid.

What ought to be the function of the committee staff? That question will be answered when we decide how large a staff a Congressional committee can properly use. If the staff is extensive, the Congress will face many of the same difficulties in relation to its own experts that it faces in relation to the experts in the State Department and elsewhere. A Congressional committee is ill-adapted to exercising direct supervision over bureaucracy, even its own. And there are slight grounds for arguing that determination of foreign policy by a professional elite in the employ of Congress is any more desirable than determination of foreign policy by a professional elite in the employ of the executive.[9] If the staff is small enough to be controlled, on the other hand, it cannot undertake the kind of detailed research and inquiry possible in the executive-administrative.

Despite this latter consideration, the decision of Congress in the Legislative Reorganization Act of 1946 to fix the professional staff of a committee at four is a wholly sound one. For it is not the function of the staff to compete with the research facilities in the State Department, the Central Intelligence Agency, and elsewhere. On the contrary, the committee professional ought not to be so much an expert research man as an "expert on experts." It should be his function to help the members evaluate the testimony and background of "expert" witnesses from the public and from the executive branch. He should be less the man who answers questions than the man who knows what questions *need* to be answered. He should have a clear understanding of the limitations of expert knowledge and the role of fact and preference in the making of public policy, and he should not hesitate in urging committee members to make the expert stick to his last. He should be another transformer in the flow of information and interpretation between executive-administrative and Congress, a transformer at that crucial point in the line where the "policy specialists" in the Congressional committee and the experts in the executive-administrative branch must be connected.

Whether the professional staffs are, in fact, so employed is an open question. Their function is still far from fixed, and much depends upon the horizon of the chairman. Until committee members themselves have a clear picture of the kind of performance they should exact from their own experts, there is little guarantee that the staffs will be profitably used.[10]

But even assuming the staffs could be used along the lines I have suggested, there will still remain a serious question as to the adequacy of the information available to the committees. There is a distinct limit to the help even the most competent "expert on experts" can give to the committee. For even with his aid the committee must, in the last analysis, still place a heavy reliance upon the information collected and interpreted by experts under the control of the executive-administrative branch.

A third possibility, therefore, is a better relationship between the Central Intelligence Agency and Congress; indeed, almost any relationship at all might constitute an improvement over the present hiatus. The newness of the Central Intelligence Agency (CIA) and the secrecy of its operations make it difficult for an outsider to suggest with confidence what an appropriate relationship might be. But it is highly relevant to our problem that the CIA is intended to be a central governmental agency for the collection, interpretation, and dissemination of information about events throughout the world. Potentially, its information, interpretations, and forecasts may constitute a real check on those of, say, the State Department and the armed services.

If the Central Intelligence Agency should prove to be effective, and yet if its information and interpretations remain inaccessible to Congress, there will be a growing and dangerous disproportion between the rationality and understanding of the executive-administrative and the rationality and understanding of Congress. There will be more and more situations in which Congress must act blindly vis-à-vis the executive, or vis-à-vis the situation—circumstances in which it must either take on faith executive assurances that classified information justifying the policy in question does exist, or act upon its own best hunches in ignorance of the realities of the situation as understood by the executive.

Security of information can only be purchased at the price of some disproportion in knowledge. It would take great naïveté to argue that security of information is not indispensable in the kind of world in which we find ourselves. But as the chairman of the Joint Congressional Committee on Atomic Energy, Senator McMahon, has pointed out, security of information may exact too high a price if it reduces Congressional supervision to a nullity.[11] Precisely because we live in the kind of world we do, Congress—if it is to survive as a meaningful institution—will have to develop some kind of productive relationship with the Central Intelligence Agency.

Such a relationship should be designed to give the Congress a more accurate picture of reality, and to serve as a check on the picture of reality presented by, say, the State Department. The function of this relationship would be to insure "expert-neutrality" with respect to interpretations of reality. It would subvert the purpose of such an agency as CIA to give to it the function of what I referred to as "policy advice." For it is not so much the function of an intelligence agency to analyze the workability of proposed policies as it is to insure that a constant supply of reasonably correct pictures of reality flows up to the policy-makers. Once it is pulled into the business of policy analysis it will be subjected to subtle internal and external pressures to adapt its reporting of reality to the policy analysis, rather than the other way round.

Fourth, then, even if Congress were to have adequate "information," it would need some kind of agency to assist it on policy. The problem at this point changes in character. It ceases to be a question of securing an adequate picture of reality and transforms itself into a question of discovering the best way to mediate between that reality and the preferences of the society or its policy-makers. I have said an agency to *assist* Congress on policy. For surely it is the function of Congress itself to mediate between reality and the preferences of the electorate.

The central function of "policy advice," on the other hand, is to insure that Congress has a full understanding of the alternatives actually available to it and the likely consequences of adopting those alternatives. In foreign policy particularly there is constant danger that the sense of emergency surrounding the conduct of foreign affairs will be exploited to prevent adequate examination of alternatives different from those proposed by the executive.

There is a current line of thought which, building upon the greater expertness of the executive-administrative, erects the argument that Congress should, and in practice can, only accept or reject policies submitted to it by the other branch. Yet the vital point is that Congress cannot even "accept or reject" intelligently unless it understands the alternatives. And as the Congressional observer cited above points out, it is impossible for zealous policy leaders in the executive to present the alternatives as fully as they might when in their own minds they feel quite certain that the only wise policy happens to be the one they espouse.

There are, fortunately, some internal checks within the executive-administrative, like the Budget Bureau, that are intended to provide for a fuller investigation of alternatives within that branch. But these internal checks do not always operate, and even if they do, there is no certainty that Congress will be aware of the alternatives rejected.

As a recent detailed study has shown, the Foreign Service Act of 1946 went through the executive-administrative with no satisfactory examination of the alternatives to the central principle of that act, namely, maintaining the Foreign Service as a distinct professional guild within the State Department. "The particular organization of the Department—formal and informal—and the personalities involved," the study points out, "operated to preclude consideration and review from a vantage point that would have transcended the more immediate interest of the parties concerned." The Bureau of the Budget, in which there was much opposition to the bill, was effectively if not intentionally by-passed during committee hearings. Congress voted upon the bill without realizing that there were alternatives of considerable merit, and many weighty objections to continuing the Foreign Service as a guildlike organization of great influence within the Department. The President signed the bill reluctantly, because the Secretary of State was in Paris and a veto would have been interpreted in the press as a slap at Mr. Byrnes. And yet within three years the Hoover Commission was to recommend, a new Secretary of State was to sponsor, and Congress was to pass a bill giving the Secretary powers to undo the central principle of the 1946 act.[12]

But how is Congress to find out what the alternatives are? Where is it to obtain the policy advice it needs if not from the executive? There are several possibilities, and it is perhaps more important to indicate what these are than to decide among them.

1. Legislative Reference Service

There is, to begin with, the Legislative Reference Service of the Library of Congress. Probably in few federal agencies is there such a clear understanding of the appropriate relationship between expert and Congressman. As the director of the Service testified a few years ago:

> It is not my view that the expert in international relations should advise the Foreign Relations Committee of the Senate or the Foreign Affairs Committee of the House of the attitude it should take on the treatment of post-war Germany; but if the chairman, or the ranking minority member, or the committee asked our expert, "In your opinion, what would happen if a certain course were followed? For example, if there were to be a hard peace . . . ?" he should be a man sufficiently rich on the subject to say, "In my opinion, it would

be thus and so, for the following reasons . . . But, Mr. Chairman, it is only fair to state that the following authorities hold that something else would be the consequence. I find myself in this instance in a minority among the others."

My own view is that, unless Congress specifically directs us, an expert from the Legislative Reference Service ought never to use the word "should" or "ought," or "I recommend." . . . He can give counsel as to the consequences of different courses, but it is then for the committees and for Congress to decide what the policy should be.[13]

Probably few professionals in the public services have made a more admirable statement of the self-denying role of the expert in relationship to the legislative body. So far, however, Congress has not seen fit to develop the Legislative Reference Service as an important staff aide for continuously exploring policy alternatives. The Service is employed primarily as an information-gathering agency. So far, too, Congress has been willing to grant the Service little more than enough funds to supply the committees—as in the case of Foreign Affairs—with their professional staffs.

2. National Institute for Policy Analysis

If it chooses to maintain Legislative Reference as a fact-gathering agency, Congress might proceed to establish its own national institute for policy analysis.[14] Such an institute would provide Congress with analyses of proposed public policies, examine alternative policies, estimate the probable consequences of each alternative, indicate the degree of consensus or disagreement among qualified experts on the probable consequences, and so on. In connection with the Foreign Service Act of 1946, for example, such an institute might have provided Congress with some of the viewpoints on the Foreign Service later contained in the reports of the Hoover Commission, might have pointed out the probable advantages and disadvantages of the guild outlook and methods of the Foreign Service, and might have discussed some alternative solutions and their relative advantages and disadvantages.

3. Party Staffs

A quite different approach to the problem of policy advice lies in the development of party staffs. Party research by its very nature will suffer, like much governmental research, from the powerful tendency to tailor research findings to fit pre-established policy conclusions. There is, nevertheless, much to be said for the development of policy analysis by specialists employed at this level.

For one thing, policy advice and analysis by a party staff would possess such great advantages as immediacy, relevancy, utility, and ease of communication, whereas the physical and scientific detachment of the Legislative Reference Service or an institute for policy analysis may prevent facile communication between policy-makers and policy-experts. And if it is true that some objectivity is almost certain to be lost, a greater amount of party research may significantly raise the level of party debate and discussion. Anyone who will take pains to examine the work of the Fabian Research Bureau in England is likely to conclude, however much one may disagree with the particular point of view shaping the conclusions, that the Bureau was extraordinarily beneficial in bringing modern social science into the analysis of public policy. On foreign affairs, moreover, the problem of distorting policy analyses to fit the party program might prove less intense than on domestic issues, at least so long as there are important differences of view on foreign policy *within* each major party.

Debate and Discussion

The committee member and the expert are but links in a chain. We must not lose sight of the problem to which we are directing ourselves: how to raise the competence of Congress, and through Congress, the competence of the electorate. It is not enough to develop "policy specialists" and experts in and around Congress. For Congressmen who are not specialists on foreign policy ultimately must make a judgment on the proposals coming out of the committees. How can the policy specialists in Congress help the non-specialist to arrive at more rational decisions on foreign policy?

If we re-examine the role of specialization at various levels in the policy-making process from electorate to expert administrator, we shall discover that the relationship between the specialist and non-specialist, or between the less expert and the more expert, is a dual one.

First, people at one level serve as translators who make possible communication between people at preceding and succeeding levels. These translations include both preferences and reality-views. In domestic policy, both may often be translated "upward" from the electorate through Congress to executive-administrative. The farmer, for example, may often possess such a clear picture of his problems that the expert will greatly profit by seeking out the farmer's analysis of his problems and his proposals for dealing with them. In foreign policy, on the contrary, although it is desirable that preferences be translated "upward" (given democratic value-assumptions), it is necessary in most cases, as we have seen, that reality be translated "downward."

Thus the function of the specialist at any point in the line is to define preferences to the more specialized at the "higher" level of competence, and to define reality to the less specialized at the "lower" level. The function of the Foreign Relations Committee is to help define the preferences of Congress to the State Department and President, and to help define reality to the members of Congress. The ordinary Congressman fills a similar role at a "lower" level, by helping the Foreign Relations Committee to understand the preferences of his constituents, and by describing to his constituents the picture of reality he has obtained with the aid of the Foreign Relations Committee. Some such process of "translating" preferences and reality-views at different levels is indispensable to the functioning of most modern organizations. In complicated situations requiring group organization, it is usually the only way by which human purposes can be achieved.

A second aspect of these relationships is that the accuracy of the "translations" often can be verified only within broad limits. To make another use of Whitehead's image, there is a sense in which the whole structure of rationality in a complicated organization depends upon faith, i.e., upon our confidence in "translations" that we cannot verify. Within limits, I can decide by experience whether my confidence is justified or misplaced. If the garage mechanic tells me my car is in good working order, and a few hundred miles later the same old trouble occurs, I will decide that my confidence in him was misplaced. Over a period of time I may find a garage mechanic whose forecasts seem to be verified by my own experience.

In dealing with a doctor, the problem becomes more difficult. I try to assess his competence by his manner, his reputation, the success of his treatments. But my ignorance of medicine is vast and, inevitably, much of my confidence in him rests upon faith. That the appraisal of the layman is often wrong is suggested by the observation, common in the medical profession, that the doctor in whom the lay public expresses great confidence is not infrequently a practitioner for whose competence professional colleagues have but little respect. For the layman has only limited opportunity to verify the "translations" of the doctor. And in a serious case it is of small comfort to me that the verification may—as in foreign policy—permit only my survivors to change to a different doctor.

To understand the function of the policy specialist in Congress, one must grasp the importance of confidence, of faith in the translator. For the relationship between the policy specialists and other Congressmen, and between Congressmen and constituents, will frequently rest on a confidence in "translations" that cannot be entirely verified.[15] A significant example of this kind of faith is the following statement of Senator Brewster:

> I posed the question to the Senator from Michigan [Senator Vandenberg], as one of long experience, to what extent it was practicable for us here in the Senate to participate in the consideration of these matters, recognizing . . . that there must be many matters in which the President and the State Department must proceed without full disclosure, and that there were other matters which they could take up with the Committee on Foreign Relations, but which the Committee on Foreign Relations might not feel it in the public interest to discuss on the floor of the Senate. . . . *if the members of the Committee on Foreign Relations, with their far more intimate knowledge and responsibility at any time indicated that certain matters should not be explored, their judgment would be treated with great respect.*[16]

Because of the limits of time and individual knowledge such a relationship is almost inevitable, whatever dangerous potentialities it may possess.

Are there, however, ways of raising the level of the layman's competence, whether citizen or Congressman, to insure a more careful scrutiny of the "translations"? I think there are.

For one thing, more importance might be attached to the function of Congressional debate as a means of clarifying reality and preferences both to Congress and to the electorate. This is less a problem of the Senate than of the House, where management of legislation scarcely even aims at securing full and orderly debate. As a consequence, both Congress and the electorate are forced to rely almost entirely upon the Senate, operating within a somewhat more august tradition, for intelligent, analytic, and fairly systematic discussion and debate.

The deficiencies of the House reflect the plain fact that Congress is trying to do too much. The House's "efficiency" in the output of bills is secured at the price of debate and discussion on the floor. It is a wholly false conception of function that leads Congress to occupy itself with private bills in a day when there is too little time for adequate debate on major policy. It is not the function of a general to spend all his time cleaning rifles.[17]

In this country, the Congressmen will say, the committees perform the function of educating both the legislature and the electorate which is carried on in England by the full-dress debate. That committee hearings have an indispensable function in supplying the committee members with information and an understanding of alternative policies, the first part of this chapter has sought to demonstrate. And surely it is true that the committee, particularly the investigating committee, may sometimes be a potent force in influencing opinion in and out of Congress, as witness the enormous importance of the Nye Committee in persuading almost a whole generation to the view that the First World War was entirely a product of the munitions industry.

Yet to rely exclusively upon the committee hearings to inform Congress and the public is to misread the committee's role. For one thing, this method of informing Congressmen and citizens rests on the newsworthiness of a particular committee hearing. If the citizen, and to a great extent even the Congressman, does not read the testimony in daily newspapers, the chances are he does not read it at all. In some cases, committee hearings are closed to all but committee members. And even in open hearings, the discussion among committee members preceding a committee decision—in some ways the most vital part of the committee's work—is always closed. During the hearings themselves the committee interrogates for information and policy advice, a procedure that does not provide for a systematic presentation in understandable form of the various alternatives.

Aside from simply having more debate on important measures, and less on unimportant ones, it is necessary to improve both the level of discussion and the effectiveness with which it is communicated.

Some critics of Congress have suggested the need for something like the Question Hour in the House of Commons—a period during which leading members of the executive might appear before the entire Senate or House to answer questions. But in proposing the Question Hour for Congress, critics have sometimes tended to confuse two rather different values: the value of putting questions to members of the executive, and the value of having cabinet-level officials engage in discussion on the floor of Congress.

These are not quite the same thing, for, as many members who discount the Question Hour will point out, the opportunity for Congress to cross-examine members of the executive is adequately provided by the committee system. There is not much evidence that the Question Hour in England is productive of the kind of searching examination that is possible when a Secretary or an Assistant Secretary sits with a committee for several days. In England, the questions must be submitted in advance, in writing. Many of them are merely debating points, or attempts at publicity. The skillful minister may deftly turn them away (although the questioner may pursue the point by precipitating debate a few hours later). On foreign affairs, considerations of state are frequently used to justify a refusal to answer. Professor Jennings, after relating some of the weaknesses of the Question Hour in the House of Commons, concludes: "For the prevention of minor oppressions—often major oppression so far as individuals are concerned—the process of questions is, however, invaluable." [18] It seems likely that Congressional committees accomplish this much and a good deal more.

The other aspect of the proposal—the value of having members of the executive appear on the floor of Congress for debate and discussion—is much more relevant. The important aspect of the English Question Hour is probably not to be found in the questions and answers during the Hour itself but in the debate that may follow in the evening, when the Minister will have to justify himself before the House. Senator Kefauver has only partly recognized this aim in his proposal that the Cabinet member be issued an invitation by the relevant committee to appear before the House and make an oral report, which would be followed by questions from the floor.[19]

There is some doubt as to whether the appearance of Cabinet members before Congress is the way to achieve the kind of debate Congress needs. And certainly adequate debate will not be achieved by a proposal that Cabinet members merely report, and then submit themselves to questions from members of Congress. Professor W. Y. Elliott has argued that the proposal is a "half-way house" toward the parliamentary system, and by itself might only lead to a slackening responsibility within the executive-administrative without any corresponding growth in its effective responsibility to Congress. He said before a Congressional committee:

> It is by choosing Members of Congress to become more and more parts of the policy-forming group of the administration that the transmission of Executive policy back to Congress is actually taking place. In effect, we are getting an addition to the policy-making Cabinet of our Government by drafting both Senators and Representatives into the Executive formulation of policy which is, I think, probably the right way to do it. Then the President's spokesman has the full right of debate and he knows all the wrinkles and he has all the procedures and all the chances of personal contacts . . . which no member of the Executive can ever fully exercise in quite the same way.[20]

Professor Elliott is probably right in arguing that the real need is to build more Congressional links into the chain of responsibility. It is only when leaders in Congress cannot speak with authority on executive policy that there is great need for the Cabinet members themselves to engage in debate. The growth of collaboration between executive and Foreign Relations Committee makes it less urgent for the Secretary of State to appear before the whole Congress to debate those policies *on which there is close collaboration*.

By the same token, however, the development of an executive-Congressional cabinet possessing the confidence of a majority of the Congress would tend to eliminate the possibility that appearance before Congress of the executive members of the team would lead to the slackening of responsibility feared by opponents of the Question Hour. If such a cabinet is ever established in this country—and we shall return to this point in a later chapter—it might be worth while to experiment with the proposal that certain members of the executive be allowed to appear on the floor of each House and participate in debate. The limits of this participation would have to be worked out pragmatically, and there is little point in attempting to work out the details now.

There is also merit in the proposal that Congress broadcast some of its debates over the radio, a technique of public education that has worked with some success in Australia and New Zealand.[21]

In this way local citizen groups for inquiry and discussion, should they ever develop interest and vitality, might participate much more closely in the debates of the moment. One can imagine debate and discussion on a foreign policy proposal in thousands of small assemblies throughout the country following close upon the heels of a debate in Congress. In a small way, the town-meeting aspect of democracy, which to so great an extent has vanished from American life with the advance of the leviathan state, might reappear in the making of national policy.

XI. The Irresponsibles

LIKE father like son. Relations between executive and Congress bear a striking resemblance to those between Crown and Parliament in the eighteenth century. The ever present threat of conflict between executive and legislative; the perpetual problem of getting things done in the midst of this conflict, of discharging the work of the government, of making and administering public policies; the attempt of the executive to reduce conflict and allow government to go forward, by manipulating the legislature through "influence," patronage, and local machines—these aspects of the British constitution were unwittingly copied by the founding fathers into the American political system, at a time when a new and more harmonious relationship was already rendering the old model obsolete in England.

Simply in order to get the work of governing done, the Crown was discovering, it needed ministers who had the confidence of Parliament. By the time the founding fathers assembled in Philadelphia, the practice, if not the theory, of cabinet government based upon the confidence of the legislature had virtually replaced separation of powers in England.

The problem, if not necessarily the solution, of American government in the twentieth century is substantially that of England in the eighteenth. The great weapon of free government has misfired. Separation of powers between President and Congress has proved to be less productive of freedom than of conflict, patronage, inefficiency, and irresponsibility.

To anyone concerned with the conduct of foreign policy, the fruits of the system are unusually bitter.

The By-products of Conflict

Until Jackson's time, it is not unfair to say that there was only one great hierarchy of responsibility among political officials at the national level. Presidential candidates were usually nominated by party caucuses in Congress. The executive branch sought to work in close harmony with the legislative, and for the most part succeeded. Hamilton regarded himself virtually as a Prime Minister. Jefferson had great respect for the legislature as the penultimate source of power and worked in tight accord with the Republican caucus. So close was the collaboration of Madison and Monroe with the legislative branch that they did not so much lead the Congress as they were led by it.

With Adams, collaboration began to break up, and with Jackson a new type of president appeared, the plebiscitary, mass-based executive, operating with his own "mandate" and often fighting fierce battles with the Congress. From that time on, there was never again a President with significant leadership and important policies who did not, sooner or later, come into bitter conflict with the Congress; periods of Congressional supremacy are marked by the nonentities in the White House; equilibrium is rare.

For what has happened since Jackson's time is the splitting of one great political hierarchy in two: the presidential and the Congressional.* The existence of these two great and frequently warring political hierarchies, lodged not in competing parties

---

* Some would add a third: the administrative. At this point, however, I am concerned only with the political leaderships directly removable by elections.

but in two branches of government, generates innumerable difficulties not only for responsibility but for rationality as well. In various places throughout this book, I have discussed these difficulties. Let us bring them together for a moment.

First, many foreign policy proposals are unerringly propelled into the center of a controversy between executive-administrative and Congress. Sometimes the controversy is over basic policy, as with Wilson and the League, Hoover and the Court, Roosevelt and the arms embargo. Sometimes the controvesy is essentially over technical means: the President wanting discretion, the Congress demanding strict definition. Thus arise the initial conflicts over neutrality in the 'thirties and the differences over the method of supplying arms for Europe in 1949. The President wants discretion in order to act intelligently when the future cannot be easily foreseen; the Congress prefers strictness lest foreign policies slip utterly out of its hand. It is a conflict, in our terms, between the need for rationality and the need for responsibility.

Debate and discussion are vital to responsibility if they assist the electorate or their representatives at some "higher" level of policy-making in making intelligent choices. But the second kind of conflict, that over technical means, is precisely the kind of question on which it is most difficult for the citizen to arrive at an intelligent understanding. But even on questions of basic policy—and this is the important point—the electorate is scarcely given the opportunity, in any meaningful sense, to decide the issue. For the electorate could only decide the issue if it could make a choice between the two contestants. But an issue between President and Congress is not always the same thing as an issue between the two great political parties. And the electorate cannot choose President or Congress; it must, perforce, choose President *and* Congress. There is no way out of this circle, unless it be the development of responsible parties between which the electorate might choose.

Second, Congress tends to become preoccupied with the attempt to control details as a method for controlling policy. In a system where the executive rests upon the "confidence" of the legislature, as in England, members of the majority party see less need for controlling details, precisely because they have well-founded expectations that the executive, i.e., the party leadership, is determined to carry out only those policies on which members of the party in the legislature are agreed. But in a system where the executive does not have the "confidence" of the legislature, members will strive to impose detailed controls because of the expectation that, if they do not, the exercise of executive discretion will run counter to their preferences. Yet control over details imposes a heavy burden on the rationality of Congress. It means that Congress is often operating at the very level at which it is least competent. But so long as the executive does not have the confidence of the Congressional majority, Congress will—and from its point of view, must—continue to insist upon supervising details. It is, perhaps, a poor substitute for a relationship based upon confidence. But it is the only substitute Congress is likely to accept.

Third, the conflict generates a mad fluctuation between rigid foreign policy imposed by Congressional legislation and the exercise of a presidential discretion in foreign affairs that would be the envy of a nineteenth-century monarch. To one not familiar with this principle, the contrast between the inflexible neutrality legislation of the late 'thirties and the President's vast discretion over negotiations with Japan would be incomprehensible. The Congress, distrustful of the executive-administrative, shackles that branch as tightly as it can, when it can. But the President, thanks to the vaguely defined "inherent" powers of the office, wriggles loose whenever it is possible to do so and may conduct a vital phase of foreign policy literally for years without Congressional control, as with our foreign policy toward Japan before the last war, toward Russia during the war, and toward China after the war.

The one kind of policy-making leaves slight room for rational adaptation to unforeseen circumstances; the other, slight chance for responsibility—unless one puts one's trust entirely in the presidential conscience. The one policy may tie the hands of the leadership in moments of crisis; the other may lead to policies for which there is inadequate support, as with Wilson, and had not Pearl Harbor intervened, conceivably with Roosevelt.

I do not believe there can be any other solution to this problem except the creation of an executive-administrative branch that rests more nearly upon the "confidence" of Congress. This will require not only responsible parties, but a high degree of collaboration on foreign policy between executive and Congress.

These are the fruits of conflict. In an earlier chapter I alluded to a fourth consequence of the separation between these two great hierarchies: they also tend to be *career* hierarchies, and as a consequence there are substantial deficiencies in the experience of Congressmen for never having been in the executive. In the belief that they were copying an important element in the British constitution, the founding fathers wrote into the Philadelphia document a provision barring members of the legislative branch from serving in the executive branch while still in office. Their action was not merely a huge, if understandable, misinterpretation of the British system as it then stood; it was a blunder of enormous consequence. It is necessary somehow to repair that blunder.

One Extreme: Detailed Congressional Control

Let us take some cases to make these points more concrete. The handling of the State Department budget in Congress is an excellent illustration of Congress attempting to enforce responsibility by controlling details. If severe limitations of time and knowledge beset Congress as a whole, to supervise administration through control of the purse intensifies the problems a thousandfold. If it is difficult enough for the administrator himself to judge the efficiency of his organization, for Congress it is a staggering task. How many Congressmen had the time and inclination to read and digest the 724 pages of testimony on the State Department appropriations for 1949, or the 1068 pages for the 1948 appropriations? Although the Senate committee gave a more cursory examination, its hearings on the Department's appropriations for 1949 ran to 166 pages of testimony.

Once again, we discover, the Congress attempts to specialize. Most Congressmen must rely upon the report of the Appropriations Committee, or, if there is one, on a minority report. But even the committees must break up into subcommittees. And customarily the report of the Appropriations Subcommittee reaches the floor after no more than an hour or two of examination by the full Committee. Such supervision of administration as exists, then, comes from the subcommittee; and within the subcommittee, it is often the chairman who does most of the work. In the hearings before the House subcommittee on State Department funds in the 1948 and 1949 budgets, well over ninety-five per cent of the questioning was conducted by the chairman, Representative Karl Stefan of Nebraska.[1]

Members of the subcommittees face enormous difficulties

in dealing intelligently with the budget before them. Thanks to separation of powers, few of them have had relevant administrative experience. In 1948 the House Appropriations Subcommittee on the State Department had eight members. Four were businessmen, three were lawyers, one was a physician. Not one of them had any experience in foreign affairs or in the State Department other than that gained through the Committee.

The members therefore ranged over an infinity of petty details on which they could scarcely be expected to pass competent judgment: the status of the Philippine abaca crop; the size of the drawing room in the London embassy; the number of bathrooms in that imposing establishment; the development of machinery to crack babassu nuts; and the fearful consequences of an attempt to exhibit abroad, in behalf of better cultural relations, a modern painting entitled "The Circus Girl" (which the legislators with customary Congressional courtesy referred to as "The Circus Lady").

Or the Subcommittee members may wrestle hopelessly with a broad problem. In 1947 they made a relentless and unsuccessful attempt to extract from witnesses, ranging from Secretary Marshall to the Chief of the Publications Division, a statement as to what the American foreign policy was at that time—a search which evidently was wholly satisfied the following year by Marshall's terse statement that the object of our foreign policy "is to promote peace in the world, and to facilitate American business and its relations to all other countries." [2]

Like the legislative committees, the appropriations committees rely on the assistance of technicians. In recent years the House Committee on Appropriations has acquired a staff of accountants and lawyers to study the departments and report to the relevant subcommittees. But the professional staff is too small to perform all the tasks to be done. In 1948 it numbered only seven. Its members suffer from all the handicaps of an outsider in attempting to discover what is *really* happening within a department (a difficulty not even the Bureau of the Budget can entirely overcome); and because they must cover the entire executive structure, they can at best only spot-check a division or a bureau here and there.

Here is a clear case where Congress, in an effort to enforce responsibility, is attempting to act at a level of specialization at which its competence is open to serious question. The levels of political responsibility, one might say, do not coincide with the levels of competence.

That committee interrogations might, nevertheless, perform a service in enforcing responsibility is undeniable. For the administrator knows that he must justify his estimates to a non-specialist holding a modicum of power to curtail activities which the latter or his party dislikes. The threat of an annual review of details before an independent and not wholly sympathetic judge is at least one means of limiting the power impulses of the administrator to purposes approved by the electorate. Such means are all too few. Surely no one can deny that the President's personal supervision must be entirely superficial. Nor do we yet possess any objective test for determining when the marginal utility of a dollar spent in a particular government activity exceeds its utility when spent in private activities or at lower governmental levels. In such a case, who can say better than the Congressman, with all his foibles and shortsightedness, whether a given amount of money is accomplishing objectives in a manner satisfactory to the citizenry? Certainly not the administrator, who is psychologically too close to his work to analyze objectively the utility of his own organization; nor even the members of the Budget Bureau, who, in the derisory and not wholly irrelevant language of the Congressman, "have never had to carry a precinct."

Yet it is not at all certain that Congress, as it now operates, *does* perform this indispensable service. For administrative responsiveness to a subcommittee is by no means the same thing as administrative responsibility to Congress.

In a relatively small department like State, to be sure, "interference" in the details of administration may produce a much more significant response than it does in a large department, where personnel and funds may be reshuffled to meet policy needs, and where Congressional screening is bound to be more fragmentary because of the mass of details. But responsiveness does not create "responsibility" unless the members of the appropriations committees are themselves responsible. The net gain in responsible bureaucracy is negligible, perhaps even negative, if accountability for administrative details is shifted from the executive to one or two members of an appropriations subcommittee who are actually responsible to no one but their own constituents, and who quietly use their appropriations power to nullify policies that have already been established openly by legislation.

Even where the policies rest entirely on executive decision rather than Congressional legislation, it is questionable whether responsibility is increased by any method that does not depend either on open debate of the issues, or on action by Congressional committee members genuinely responsible to Congress. As long as Congress does not act vigorously to make its own committees fully responsible, this weakness in Congressional control over the details of administration is certain to remain.

Why, then, does Congress persist in "interfering" in the details of administration? The criticisms of many administrators and students of public administration come very close to suggesting that the only explanation is the sheer cussedness and perversity of politicians. These critics would have Congress determine only "basic policy" and leave "the details of administration" to the executive-administrative. But if this means anything at all, it means that Congress, like the House of Commons, must for all practical purposes cease using the appropriations process as a device for direct control over administrative details, and must rely almost wholly on its power to determine policy by general legislation.

Yet to say that Congress should, like the House of Commons, give up its control over details, without acquiring some of those aspects of the Commons-Cabinet relationship that make this feasible in England, is to ask Congress what it will never willingly grant. For until the executive comes to possess the confidence of Congress in a way that is not now possible, Congress will fight to control the executive by every lesser means at its disposal, whether by careful statutory definition or, as we have just seen, by review of budgetary details.

The Other Extreme: The Uncontrolled Executive

It is inevitable that the executive will seek to elude detailed Congressional control—particularly on foreign policy, where so much is uncharted and unforeseen and, often enough, unknown to Congress.

The conclusion is unavoidable, for example, that in the years preceding Pearl Harbor, President Roosevelt and his advisers believed that many of their foreign policies could not have secured the support of a majority in Congress.[3] Important foreign policies were made without prior or subsequent Congressional consent. Thus, in the Naval Appropriations Bill of 1940 Congress wrote into law the provision that no item of military matériel could be turned over to a foreign

government without the certification by the Chief of Staff
or the Chief of Naval Operations that it was unnecessary for
the defense of this country—an amendment, as Robert Sherwood puts it, that "was an expression of Congress' profound
distrust of Roosevelt . . ." [4]

Churchill and the Admiralty believed that England, then
in the opening period of the most desperate struggle for
survival their nation had ever faced, had an urgent need for
destroyers. Many leaders in the executive-administrative
branch, including the President, sensed the perilous urgency
of the request. "Various suggestions were made to the President," Sherwood writes, "for new legislation to be asked of
Congress to free his hands—but he was having none of that.
He was determined to find a way to circumvent Congress on
this problem, and he found it." [5] This was the genesis of
the famous destroyers-for-bases deal, which some have con-
demned as political treachery and some have acclaimed as an
act of great statesmanship.

Moral appraisal of the actors in that event is, however,
irrelevant to the purposes of this volume. What is important
here is the relationship between President and Congress expressed in this action: the bitter hostility and distrust that
impels the executive to circumvent the Congress, and the
policy-making institutions that permit him to do so.

A later incident described by Sherwood underlines the
point. At the Atlantic Conference, "whereas Roosevelt was
completely on his own, subject only to the advice of his immediate and self-selected entourage, which advice he could
accept or reject, Churchill was constantly reporting to and
consulting the War Cabinet in London, addressing his communications to the Lord Privy Seal, who was then Clement
Attlee. During three days more than thirty communications

passed between the [battleship] *Prince of Wales* and White-hall, and the speed of communication and of action thereon was astonishing to the Americans." [6]

Put in its most favorable light, what was involved was a profound conflict between rationality, as understood by the President and State Department, and responsibility, as seen by Congress. President and State Department believed they had information, experience, and a grasp of the issues involved that Congress and the electorate lacked. Responsibility to Congress, they evidently believed, would have led to suicidal policies. They therefore chose to avoid Congressional control over certain aspects of foreign policy.

Whether or not the President was more nearly correct than Congress in his appraisal of events, the significance of the actions just described is of grave import. For if the President was more nearly correct in his appraisal, then this is the severest condemnation possible of the arrangements for information and intelligence by which Congress as contrasted with the President possessed such a terrifying incapacity for rationality and understanding of international events in a moment of great national crisis. If the President was more nearly wrong, then we must condemn the entire arrangement by which the President could do so much with so little Congressional control. And whoever was right or wrong, the events show conclusively that the President can and does elude control by Congress over foreign policies of decisive importance.

Those who regard political responsibility as the highest obligation of democratic leadership will argue that the President should have based his foreign policies on Congressional and popular consent, even if this had meant self-destruction of the nation. "In a democracy," it has been said, "the people have a right to go to Hell in their own way."

Those who place highest value on rationality may argue that the President had a "higher" *responsibility* (in a sense different from that employed in this book) to pursue his foreign policies even if these could not be based on popular consent. As Professor Bailey puts the case:

> A president who cannot entrust the people with the truth betrays a certain lack of faith in the basic tenets of democracy. But because the masses are notoriously shortsighted, and generally cannot see danger until it is at their throats, our statesmen are forced to deceive them into an awareness of their own long-run interests. This is clearly what Roosevelt had to do, and who shall say that posterity will not thank him for it? [7]

The problem of the democrat is to reconcile rationality with responsibility. The two must proceed together. That is why it is not enough simply to make Congress politically more responsible, as many political scientists seem to assume. Congress must also possess enough rationality to discharge this responsibility in the most effective way.

But that is also why it is not enough simply to rely on the President. For rationality is instrumental; it is means to ends; it is the design and application of techniques to satisfy preferences. The crucial question is: Whose preferences? [8] Unless the levels of responsibility are so arranged as to insure the uninterrupted upward flow of preferences from electorate to President, there is and can be no guarantee that all the rationality of the executive-administrative will be used for any other purpose than fulfilling in foreign policy the private preferences of the President or members of the State Department. If the rationality of Congress must be increased, so must the responsibility of the executive-administrative to the Congress. The two must go hand in hand.

Party Responsibility

The great gaping hole in the structure of responsibility is the empty place left by the American party system. Without responsible parties, Congress cannot be responsible; and unless Congress is responsible, it has slight claim to enforce responsibility on the President.

The Congressional committee, again, is an illuminating microcosm. In January 1949 Senator Glen Taylor returned to the Senate after a bolt from the Democratic Party to run as a vice-presidential candidate on a party which had as its main impulse a basic attack on the foreign policy of the Democratic Party. Like a prodigal son, Senator Taylor regained from the Senate Democrats all his committee assignments and privileges with no loss of seniority.[9]

Or observe the committee chairman. Let a man be re-elected often enough and he is almost certain to end up as a committee chairman when his party is in the majority, however deeply he may be opposed to the party program on the very subjects covered by his committee.[10] Senator Stone, who became Democratic chairman of the Senate Foreign Relations Committee in 1914 by virtue of his seniority, was completely opposed to Wilson's war policies after 1917. Yet he was never removed, although the majority of the party was pretty clearly behind Wilson. When the elections of 1946 swept the Republicans into power, Mr. Eaton, a strong "internationalist," automatically became the chairman of the House Committee on Foreign Affairs because of his twenty-two years' service. He was then of advanced age. Directly below him on the Republican side were four members who at that time were regarded as leading midwestern "isolationists." Had Mr. Eaton retired or died in 1946, therefore, succession would have gone to a chairman of completely different foreign policy views; and any resulting changes in foreign policy would have come about not because of any party conference, decision, policy, campaign promise, or election result—but because of time, accident, and automatic acceptance of the seniority rule.

Sometimes, to be sure, the party leadership may employ the test of party support, but even then the principle is usually applied in devious and indirect ways. Thus in 1939, Democratic party leaders were deeply concerned with the way in which the Foreign Relations Committee had bottled up President Roosevelt's proposals for modifying neutrality legislation in the spring of that year, despite a Democratic majority on the Committee. So after the 1940 elections they decided to appoint no freshman Senators to the Committee, but instead to add two reliable supporters of the President's program, Senators Glass and Byrnes, both men of great prestige and influence in the Senate. And again, after the war Senator Claude Pepper was for a time kept off the Committee despite his claims of seniority, presumably because he held views on foreign policy hostile to those held by the bulk of the party members in the Senate.

Two arguments are usually advanced to support seniority as a dominant guide in selecting committee members. One is the argument of experience, which we have already examined in connection with the problem of rationality. Such validity as this argument has, however, must apply entirely to the question of rationality, not that of responsibility. For often enough, it may be the old and senior member who is most at odds with the bulk of his party and the platform on which that party was elected to govern the country. By erecting seniority into a principle, committees may be converted, in effect, into associations of members responsible only to their own constituents, not, in any meaningful sense, to the national electorate as a whole.

The other and more relevant argument is that seniority is an impersonal device for selecting membership on the committees; and the use of "party loyalty" as a criterion will, it is contended, precipitate great intra-party conflicts and perhaps even tear the parties apart. This a much more serious contention.

For the criterion of seniority is, after all, not so much a fundamental cause as a consequence of irresponsible parties. It is one thing to suggest techniques by which chairmen and members might be held responsible to the "party." But it is quite another to create *a party* to whom they might be held responsible. In what sense was there a Democratic *party* view on neutrality in 1938 and 1939? Or in what sense has there been in recent years a Republican *party* to enforce responsibility in foreign affairs? Did the Democratic Party in 1938 and 1939 mean Roosevelt and his supporters, or men like James Shanley of Connecticut who was an outstanding Democratic "isolationist" on the Foreign Affairs Committee? Does the Republican Party mean the Vandenberg wing or the Taft wing? Here is the root of the difficulty.

XII. Party Responsibility and Foreign Policy

IN a modern democratic society, competition between political parties is the chief instrument by which political leadership is forced to bow to the preferences of a majority (or a plurality) of the active electorate.* To the extent that the parties themselves are so organized and operated as to evade responsibility, political leadership may nullify the preferences expressed in an election by the majority, or indeed may prevent any clear expression at all. It is a fatuously irresponsible party system under which a party might go before the electorate with a set of pledges based, say, on the views of its spokesmen on the Congressional foreign affairs committees and then fail to carry out such pledges because the party could not enlist the support of its own members on the appropriations committees. And irresponsibility is, if possible, even worse when the party goes before the electorate with both views and wins a "mandate" for each.

* In my use of the word "majority" the reader will understand that I use it as an easy abstract antonym for "minorities." Its meaning includes "pluralalities" and would be more precisely, if more awkwardly, expressed as the "greater number." In actual practice, what we call a decision by "majority rule" in many if not most cases is an extraordinarily complicated process of action dominated by influential minorities. The result probably conforms much more closely to the preferences of the influential minorities than to the preferences of any numerical majority of the adult population. The practical difference between government by "minority rule" and government by "majority rule" lies in the greater probability that the latter method comes closer than the former to closing the gap between public policy and the common preferences of the greater number of adults in the society.

Minorities, Majorities, and Congress

The future of Congress is intimately tied up with the possibility of a more responsible party system. The vast growth in presidential power since Jackson's day is closely related to the fact that in an ironic reversal of the circumstances expected by the founding fathers, the Presidency has become the instrument of majorities, the Congress of minorities. If great masses of the people have turned to the Presidency, it is partly because they have found themselves blocked year after year by the influence of minority groups in Congress. If enormous sections of the electorate seem to countenance and even approve granting vast discretionary powers to the President, if they look on with equanimity as the prestige of Congress declines with the years, if they placidly and even expectantly observe attempts of the executive-administrative to manipulate Congress by all the means at its disposal—it is partly because they have judged Congress to be a citadel of minority interests and the President a tribune of the majority. In the era of mass-democracy, so long as this remains true, prestige, influence, and power must ineluctably flow to the President and away from Congress.

The whole claim of Congress to enforce responsibility on the President rests on an untenable premise, so long as a successful prosecution of its claims can only mean that a great political office vaguely responsive to the preferences of majorities will be transformed into an office directly responsive to the preferences of minorities—and minorities, often enough, whose policies run clearly athwart the preferences of the majority.

What the founding fathers most feared is precisely what every democrat must profoundly hope: that Congress will become an effective spokesman for the preferences of the greater number. And indispensable to such a transformation is the development of government by responsible parties: government, that is to say, through parties capable of formulating a party program binding on President and Congressional members alike, capable of appealing to the electorate for support of that program, and if endorsed by a majority of voters, able and willing to translate the program into legislative and administrative policy.

Three questions suggest themselves. First, is party government desirable in the case of foreign policy? Second, even if one assumes its desirability, is it possible, given the great diversity of views on foreign policy *within* the existing parties? Third, what practical steps may one suggest to achieve it?

As to the first question, there is pretty clearly a potential conflict between the values of party government and the values of making foreign policy under recent arrangements for bipartisan participation. Or to say the same thing in another way, there might be a conflict between techniques for insuring that those who make foreign policy are responsive to the preferences of the "majority" and techniques for securing *agreement* on foreign policy over the widest possible area. This is a complicated conflict of values, and I shall postpone further discussion of it to Chapter XIV. The second and third questions lend themselves to easier treatment.

Foreign Policy and Party Consensus

In the last chapter we witnessed the difficulties of trying to enforce party responsibility on Congressional committees, when, it seems, no "party" exists on issues of foreign policy. That this is a serious problem cannot be denied. People who see eye to eye on domestic issues do not necessarily agree on foreign policy, and vice versa. If the parties polarize around domestic questions, there may be great divergencies around foreign questions. On foreign policy, it has not been uncommon in this country (and elsewhere) for the extreme right and the extreme left to find themselves allied, nor unusual for the left-center and right-center, although in different parties, to find common ground on foreign affairs.

Historically, too, the parties themselves have been little more than great sectional alliances suffering from considerable divergence. The party label has been little more than a ribbon tied around a treaty signed between different sections of the nation for the rather limited purpose of electing a President. In such a situation, it might be argued, there is little promise of party government even on domestic questions, not to mention foreign policy.

These are important objections, but their import is easily exaggerated, as an examination of the table below will show. Any quantitative approach to Congressional voting must be looked upon with a great deal of caution; the most that can be claimed for such an effort is an indication of some very general tendencies. Nevertheless, despite the frequently reiterated assertion that American parties are little more than political versions of Tweedledum and Tweedledee, if we examine the fifteen-year period 1933-48, we find a striking difference in the voting behavior of Republicans and Democrats in Congress on questions of foreign policy.[1] In Table VI, all recorded votes on all issues of foreign policy during the period have been tabulated to show the percentage of the total votes cast by members of each party in support of some particular phase of foreign policy. From 1933-41 in the House, for example, only 40 per cent of the votes cast by Democrats were in support of proposals for neutrality and isolation, as contrasted with 87 per cent of the votes cast by Republicans on these issues.

TABLE VI

PARTY VOTES IN FAVOR OF VARIOUS FOREIGN POLICY PROPOSALS, 1933-48 *

ISSUE	HOUSE		SENATE	
	Dem.†	Rep.†	Dem.†	Rep.†
I. Neutrality and isolation, 1933-41..	40%	87%	48%	74%
Neutrality and isolation (W. Hem.)	1	13	37	44
International organization, 1933-40	78	26	52	26
International organization, 1943-48	95	80	93	71
II. National defense, 1935-39........	77	65	80	61
National defense, 1940-41........	97	75	75	81
National defense, 1946-48........	97	100	100	98
Selective service, economic mobilization, etc.................	80	40	78	56
III. Foreign aid, loans, grants........	89	56	83	55
IV. Regional pacts:				
Latin America, 1947..........	—	—	100	98
Western Europe, 1948 ‡.......	—	—	97	91
V. Tariff reductions, freer imports...	80	29	68	16
Agr. tariff and import protection..	44	54	34	84
Sectional interest protection:				
Minerals....................	—	—	36	55
Shipping....................	24	90	24	45
Wool.......................	—	—	26	69
VI. Strengthening State Dept. by appropriations, etc.............	95	46	71	35

* The reader should be warned not to draw any final conclusions about *party unity* from Tables VI and VII. These tables significantly understate the amount of party unity that actually prevailed because they were designed to show the general orientation of the parties on a number of rather broad issues. Thus, to take a hypothetical case, Democrats might unanimously oppose a strict neutrality bill, and in a later vote unanimously oppose a bill abandoning neutrality altogether. In such a case, the high degree of party agreement (100%) on the position of moderate neutrality would not be revealed by the tables; on the contrary, to average the two votes together under the classification "support for neutrality and isolation" would produce a figure of 50%, representing the votes cast by Democrats for neutrality and isolation. For a table designed to throw light on party unity, see Table IV.

† These figures are averages of percentages for a number of issues in each category. The percentage for each issue was obtained by dividing the Democratic or Republican votes for each issue by the total number of Democrats or Republicans voting on that issue.

‡ Vote on the Vandenberg Resolution.

The pattern of party voting revealed here is more or less internally consistent. The Republicans were, at least until 1943, overwhelmingly the party of "isolation," whereas the persistent tendency of the Democrats was to support "internationalist" efforts. Thus the Republicans strongly supported neutrality in the prewar years, opposed American participation in international organizations, and for military protection counted more heavily than the Democrats on our geographical position: hence their notably slighter support for military appropriations (in the House), domestic economic mobilization, and the draft. They looked upon foreign aid and loans, from lend-lease to ERP, with much more suspicion than their Democratic colleagues. They vigorously opposed tariff reduction, sought to protect agriculture from foreign competition, and generally sought to protect important regional interests— shipowners and wool growers, for example—when these were threatened by a foreign policy proposal.

On virtually all of these positions, the Democrats tended to behave differently: they gave less support to neutrality and more to international organizations; they provided strong backing for military appropriations and distinctly greater support for selective service. They gave overwhelming support to foreign aid proposals, backed the party's traditional low tariff position, and found it less necessary than the Republicans to protect their agricultural constituents through import and tariff restrictions.

Significantly, the Monroe Doctrine provided an area of substantial agreement between the parties, for both tended to distinguish the Western Hemisphere as a region in which isolation was not to apply. One of the significant developments of the postwar period is the growing tendency for both parties to agree about the importance of western Europe to

American security, as they had earlier taken for granted the significance of the Western Hemisphere.

The role of both region and party is suggested in Table VII. In Congressional voting on the question of neutrality toward, and isolation from, international conflict during the period 1933-41, party was a far more significant factor than region. Although the much-touted "isolationist Midwest" is revealed in the votes of the North Central and West Central delegations, members of Congress from the neighboring Central States were no more neutrality-minded than their colleagues from New England, or, in the upper house, than Senators from the Pacific Coast. The party votes, on the other hand, reveal a sizable cleavage *within* delegations from every region, most notably in the Middle Atlantic States where New Deal Democrats were strongly supporting the President's policies and Old Guard Republicans were as strongly opposing them. That the strength of regional attitudes sometimes prevailed over party or executive pressures is, to be sure, evident from the fact that a significantly larger percentage of North Central and West Central Democrats in the House voted for neutrality-isolationist policies than did their party colleagues from other regions.

The South, which of course was entirely represented by Democrats, shows up on this table and on many others as the most "internationalist" of the regions. Although public opinion taken as a whole in the South was probably less isolationist than elsewhere, it seems likely that the "internationalists" have been over-represented in Congress because of the peculiar class character of the Southern Democratic Party. To the question asked in late 1944 and early 1946, "Which of these two things do you think the United States should try to do when the war is over: stay out of world affairs as much as we can, or take an active part in world affairs?" regional

TABLE VII

NEUTRALITY AND "ISOLATION" 1933-41

REGION	HOUSE									SENATE								
	% For			% Against			% Not Voting			% For			% Against			% Not Voting		
	Tot.*	Dem.†	Rep.‡	Tot.	Dem.	Rep.	Tot.	Dem.	Rep.	Tot.	Dem.	Rep.	Tot.	Dem.	Rep.	Tot.	Dem.	Rep.
New England..	64	43	77	28	44	18	8	13	5	58	50	60	37	46	34	5	4	6
Middle Atlantic	58	37	76	35	54	18	7	9	6	42	30	66	44	53	26	14	17	8
Central......	62	41	83	31	51	14	7	8	3	58	45	64	33	47	17	9	8	19
North Central.	79	56	91	16	36	5	5	8	4	47	45	53	31	45	16	22	10	31
West Central..	81	60	88	17	40	10	2	0	2	65	66	68	22	29	17	13	5	15
Mountain §....	50	40	100	39	48	0	11	12	0	49	47	83	40	40	11	11	13	6
Pacific........	58	47	80	36	49	11	6	5	9	59	44	74	26	39	14	15	17	12
Border........	38	34	77	53	57	12	9	9	11	41	41	—	47	47	—	12	12	—
Solid South...	32	32	—	59	59	—	9	9	—	38	38	—	47	47	—	15	15	—
All regions...	54	37	83	39	54	12	7	9	5	48	42	64	39	46	22	13	12	14

Data compiled for the House from 17 votes on 9 issues in 1933, 1937, 1939, 1941; for the Senate from 32 votes on 11 issues in 1935, 1936, 1939, 1940, and 1941.

* Total votes *For*, as per cent of total votes cast.
† Democratic votes *For*, as per cent of Democratic votes cast.
‡ Republican votes *For*, as per cent of Republican votes cast.
§ Throughout this period the Republican delegation from the Mountain States was entirely negligible.

differences in answers were negligible as compared with differences between educational and income groups.[2] Thus in the South and Southwest the percentages of groups classified by education and income supporting the "internationalist" position is shown in Table VIII. The table shows a very great difference

TABLE VIII

SUPPORT OF "INTERNATIONALIST" POSITION IN SOUTH
AND SOUTHWEST

| | | EDUCATION | |
INCOME	College	High School	Grade School
Upper.......	86%	90%	92%
Middle......	84	82	59
Lower.......	86	69	35

in view between those who were in the upper-income group, *or* college educated; and those who were in the lower-income group *and* educated only in grade school. This difference, however, was characteristic not merely of the South, but of every region in the nation. But what makes this significant in the South is the tendency in that region for the high-income and college educated groups to be represented at the expense of the low-income, grade school educated. Had an active two-party system been competing for votes in all strata of the population in the South, there is every reason to suppose that the Congressional delegation would have provided more support than it did for the neutrality-isolationist position. In other words, preferences reflected in the "internationalist" position of the Southern delegation were not entirely those of region but also of class and status groups.

Outside the South, as some recent researches have pretty clearly indicated, class and status are becoming more important than region in determining which of the two major parties one will support.[3]

To be sure, there are and doubtless will continue to be a number of important issues on which regional differences are the most significant: in domestic policy, the status and future of the Negro; and in foreign policy, impacts on certain regional industries, like wool, silver, and cotton. Thus if we examine the Senate vote on a 1947 bill to provide a support price for wool and restrictions on wool imports, we find Democratic Senators from the Mountain States joining their Republican colleagues to pass the bill.

TABLE IX

SENATE VOTING ON PROTECTION OF WOOL GROWERS, 1947

	For		Against	
	Dem.	Rep.	Dem.	Rep.
New England.........	0	3	3	5
Middle Atlantic.......	0	3	2	3
Central...............	0	5	1	0
N. Central...........	X	4	X	4
W. Central..........	X	8	X	0
Mountain...........	7	6	2	0
Pacific...............	2	4	0	0
Border..............	1	3	5	2
Solid South..........	4	X	16	X
Totals..............	14	36	29	14

X—not represented.

The reciprocal trade agreement acts, on the other hand, were much more nearly party measures, supported by Democrats and opposed by Republicans, except for the vote cast in the midst of war in 1943. Even on a party measure such

TABLE X

CONGRESSIONAL VOTING ON RECIPROCAL TRADE AGREEMENT ACTS

| | House | | | | Senate | | | |
| | Dem. | | Rep. | | Dem. | | Rep. | |
	For	Against	For	Against	For	Against	For	Against
1934.......	254	12	10	89	51	5	5	28
1937.......	272	12	10	77	58	9	0	16
1940.......	231	20	13	159	46	19	0	23
1943.......	196	11	148	52	49	8	20	17
1945.......	212	16	35	139	38	6	15	15
1948 *.....	161	6	17	220	43	1	1	49

* House vote: on motion to recommit bill providing for only one-year extension.

Senate vote: on Senator Barkley's amendment to extend for three years instead of one.

as this, however, Mountain State Senators were frequently more influenced by local wool growers than by the party. In 1937, five out of the nine Democratic votes in the Senate in opposition to reciprocal trade came from the Mountain States, and in 1940, ten out of nineteen.

What conclusions may one draw from all this?

First, on a number of foreign policy issues there have been substantial, persistent, and internally consistent differences between the parties as represented in Congress. These differences in some cases flow out of basically conflicting preferences and views of reality. Our argument here is that many such differences are to be expected in a democracy, and ought to be resolved by an attempt to discover the preferences of the greater number in the nation. To resolve differences in this way, there needs to be competition between well-organized parties, capable of not merely presenting their views to the electorate but also of acting decisively upon the mandate given at the polls.

Second, on some issues there have been no substantial differences between the parties. Thus there was a broad consensus within both parties on the Monroe Doctrine; neither party gave much support to a policy of "isolation" from Latin America. It seems likely that this consensus is now being extended to western Europe, and it is altogether possible that the parties will have as little *fundamental* disagreement over the role of Europe in American security in the future, as in the past they have had over the role of the Western Hemisphere. As we shall see in Chapter XIV, such areas of agreement furnish opportunity for bipartisan collaboration and "responsible" opposition.

Third, on very many important issues of foreign policy there is no substantial disagreement within each party as represented in Congress. The reader will recall from Chapter II that on twenty-six highly important issues of foreign policy between 1933 and 1948, about ninety per cent of the Democrats in House and Senate voted the same way, and about eighty per cent of the Republicans likewise voted together. On many such issues a high degree of party responsibility and discipline seems attainable along lines to be discussed in the next section.

Fourth, the tendency toward the development of parties aligned more nearly along lines of class and status may well facilitate the further development of responsibility and discipline within each party. Each party is tending to become representative of different nation-wide class and status groups. Within themselves, these groups will tend to have similar preferences and reality views on many questions of public policy, whatever their geographical location.[4] Because these groups tend to be nation-wide, it will probably be increasingly unprofitable for the parties to give way to local pressure groups at the expense of their nation-wide clienteles.

Fifth, there are, however, some persistent issues relevant to foreign policy that make for intra-party disagreement of a serious kind. Usually these concern either ethnic groups or special industries of great importance and influence in a particular region. A development of more responsible parties would not eliminate the pressures stemming from such ethnic groups or regional industries, nor could responsible parties afford to ignore such pressures. But more responsible and better disciplined parties might have much greater influence on the extent to which nation-wide preferences would give way to purely parochial preferences. Wool growers would, no doubt, still have some influence on the conduct of Senators from the Mountain States. But the party and its national policies might have some influence too—and a good deal more than now.

What I am arguing, in sum, is this: There is nothing in the nature of the issues, the parties, or the party followers that must inevitably prevent the growth of parties capable of organizing themselves and Congress so as to provide much more responsibility toward the electorate on questions of foreign policy than we have at present.

How?

For years, however, political scientists and others have been trying to lecture politicians on the need for responsible parties. One of the most ardent and persuasive of these advocates even became President. If exhortation will not change the party system—and certainly it has not—what will?

The weakness of such appeals in the past is that they have

required a change in the preferences of the politician. He was somehow to be brought around to believe in party responsibility as a prerequisite to effective democracy. Any realistic hope for change, however, must rest on the possibility of a change not in the politician's preferences, but in his view of reality: he must come to the conclusion—a wholly sound one in the opinion of many political scientists—that government by irresponsible parties will no longer pay political dividends.[5]

It seems entirely doubtful that it is any longer of much profit to a party to avoid taking clear-cut responsibility. Political issues are too important to too many voters for ambiguity and evasiveness to pay large dividends today. The parties themselves may find it increasingly in their own interest to appear before the electorate with a rather well-defined program which, upon election, they will carry through without vast concessions to every minor pressure group. Party responsibility seems likely to prove profitable to the politicians themselves. And this, surely, is almost the only guarantee, no matter what political gadgetry could be imported from the English constitution, that American parties will be converted into responsible instruments of the greater number of citizens.

The sanctions potentially available to party leaders are far more important than has commonly been supposed; the absence of a right of dissolution in the American Constitution has served to distract the attention of political scientists from sanctions that may be nearly as effective and infinitely more relevant. There is, of course, the plain self-interest of the member. Today, more than ever before, he is dependent for his election to Congress upon general electoral approval for his *party's* program and its capacity for carrying out that program.[6] But aside from this, there are three other important sanctions: patronage, campaign funds, and committee assignments. The last two of these are now given out, as we have seen, with a curious impartiality; the maverick who votes with the other party on every issue is almost certain to be treated quite as generously by his nominal party as the member who plays on the side of his own team. Even patronage is often disposed with little regard to party loyalty.

Should party leaders begin to employ these sanctions in an effort to create more responsibility, there is little doubt that many members who now feel free to desert the party program whenever it seems to suit their private calculations or the preferences of local pressure groups would be strongly encouraged to work with the party team.

Responsible parties would be headed by a party council. For the majority party in Congress, the party council would normally consist of an executive-Congressional team comprising the President and his major political aides teamed up with Congressional leaders. This team would propose policies and determine party strategy, subject to the approval of the party caucus in Congress and the decisions of the annual or biennial party conference. The minority party would have a similar party council, normally lacking, of course, the Chief Executive. Development of party policy committees in the House, which could join with their opposite numbers in the Senate, would greatly facilitate the creation of such over-all party councils; for it would be a relatively simple matter to combine the accepted repositories of party leadership in each House into a single committee.

If this analysis is correct, a great deal is left to hang upon the capacity of the politician for adjusting his view of reality. A thread of gossamer, some will say. Must responsibility in so vital an area as foreign policy be left thus suspended until the politician plucks it down?

Administrative Politician: The People's Choice?

In an earlier chapter I spoke of the two great political hierarchies created by separation of powers. But the growth of the modern service state has created in the administrative branch a third great hierarchy of political leaders. Probably the discretion and authority wielded by some of these leaders in a single normal day of operation often has greater impact on our society than an entire year of Congressional action during the nineteenth century.

The question may well be asked whether the rise of the service state does not render obsolete the whole scheme of liberal democracy for translating citizens' preferences into public policy. Are there not better ways of securing administrative responsibility than the methods of old-fashioned democracy, such as elections and legislation by Congress? To focus attention on the party system and Congress as instruments for securing administrative responsibility, it may be argued, reflects nothing more than an atavistic urge to rehabilitate the vestigial remnants of primitive democracy. Let us recognize the three hierarchies, and provide each with appropriate techniques for securing the consent of its constituents. Administrative responsibility, it might be contended, does not need to mean responsiveness of the administrator exclusively to the other two political hierarchies—and certainly not to Congress; it simply means responsiveness of the administrator to his own constituents.

Yet to argue along these lines is to beg the essential questions: *How* and *to whom* is the administrator to be responsive? Or in other words, who are his constituents, and how are they to secure responsiveness if not through party competition and elections?

Through consultation? One need not maintain the desirability of cutting the administrative branch loose from Congressional controls altogether to find the argument persuasive that Congressional and presidential controls must be *supplemented* by extensive consultation between administrators and administered, or between policy-makers and citizen advisers.[7] Such consultation may produce a much clearer understanding among administrators of what citizens' preferences and reality-views actually are, and on the part of citizens consulted, a much better view of reality and a sounder appreciation of the administrative problems their preferences may give rise to. Once Congress has arrived at a decision about the basic terms under which crop control and farm subsidies are to be carried on, a great deal is to be said for conducting the administration of those controls and subsidies by means of extensive consultations with farmers. Indeed, without such consultation and even a certain amount of self-administration doubtless the whole effort would collapse in a storm of misunderstanding and hostility.[8]

But has this experience any relevance to foreign affairs? Unfortunately, very little. For one thing, it is impossible to isolate the groups to be consulted in the case of foreign affairs. For on all really important questions of foreign policy the appropriate constituency is the entire electorate. Does the State Department have some way of consulting the electorate more suitable to the expression of preferences than the method of debate between competing parties, elections, and legislation? The Department, to be sure, has maintained for several years a Division of Public Studies for analyzing public opinion on foreign policy as reflected by sample polls, pressure groups, and opinion leaders. But upon examining the limitations at least of the sample polls as guides to policy, surely no one would contend that these can contain much more than a very general and sometimes misleading suggestiveness. And in any case, there is not the least surety that policy-makers will pay attention to these polls, except such surety as may be provided by party competition, elections, and ensuing Congressional and presidential reactions. A public opinion poll without an electoral poll is a weapon with blank cartridges. It may scare but it cannot hurt.

The problem is then, *what* citizen groups should be consulted? How can we provide some guarantees of their representativeness? This is difficult in foreign affairs, where the articulate and educated often have views quite different from the inarticulate and uneducated. Yet in all likelihood the former will be overwhelmingly represented in any consultative organization. And if one were to rely on the spontaneous pressures that develop around policies, there is little guarantee that the unorganized and inarticulate will be represented at all.

But even assuming a more or less representative group, there is a third great difficulty. What is to be done where there are conflicts of opinion between some presumably representative group or groups and that particular representative group known as Congress? To say that Congress should give way to the consultative group is simply to say that some new kind of functional legislature ought to replace the old geographical legislature, or else that the administrative branch ought to be cut loose from both.

Perhaps the most important difficulty of all, however, stems from the fact that there is no significant sociological basis for a consultative group in foreign affairs. In the case of agriculture, there is a genuine social organization on which consultation can be erected. Because living social organizations underlie the consultative groups, consultation is meaningful and important. The Secretary of Agriculture cannot very well afford to by-pass the leadership of the Grange, the Farm Bureau Federation, and the Farmers Union, for these leaders represent real people with real reactions that may be positively and decisively expressed in numerous politically relevant ways. But there is no such basis for a consultative group in foreign affairs.

This last fact gives rise to three probabilities: (1) The consultative groups may simply be ignored. What sanctions can they have to impel consultation? (2) They may be manipulated by the State Department for its own purposes. A consultative organization established to clarify citizen preferences or provide critical appraisals for foreign policy is one thing. But an organization that functions merely as an instrument through which the State Department mobilizes public opinion behind its policies is quite another. It is highly unlikely that a Secretary of Agriculture will convert the Farm Bureau Federation into a pliable agent for the creation of farm support for the Administration's policies (the danger, indeed, is quite the other way around). But it is not at all unlikely that a Secretary of State will do so with any consultative organization he establishes. (3) Through impotence, unuse, misuse, and the sheer difficulty of assembling regularly, the organization may well fall into desuetude not long after being launched with great fanfare and publicity. From the Department's point of view, the publicity will no doubt do the Department much good with the public, and the organization itself no harm. The net effect for increasing responsibility, however, will be negative.

I am not arguing that consultative organizations cannot be of some use in the making of foreign policy. But their utility is limited; they may only provide the form without the substance of power; and unless established under very careful circumstances, they may weaken rather than strengthen control by citizens over administrative policy-makers.

There is, to be sure, a case for consultation under some circumstances. For example, in a world where social developments have propelled working-class leadership and organization into power, there is much to be said for occasional collaboration between State Department and American labor organizations on certain aspects of foreign policy. But at best consultation of this kind is only a supplement to, not a substitute for, penultimate control by the elected representatives of the citizens.

XIII. Responsibility, Confidence, Collaboration

THE stark principle of separation of powers is suspicion: suspicion of the President by Congress, of Congress by the President, of both by the electorate. Because the President suspects the aims and competence of Congress he tries when possible to conduct foreign policy by drawing upon his indefinable reservoir of inherent powers; because Congress suspects the aims and competence of the President, it sews him when it can into a legislative strait-jacket.

The Concept of Confidence

The opposing principle is confidence. In a broad political sense, confidence is my expectation that X will act in a manner suitable to my preferences—combined, perhaps, with the reservation that I will catch him if he does not. If I have great confidence in X, I shall probably grant him great discretion if he seems to need it, for I anticipate that he will act as I would act if I understood the details of the situation as well as he. But I will not have confidence in X if I doubt his competence; this, essentially, is why the executive-administrative distrusts Congress on matters of foreign policy. Nor will I have confidence in X if I doubt that he genuinely accepts my preferences; this, essentially is why Congress distrusts the executive-administrative on matters of foreign policy.

American observers of English political institutions have sometimes misread the nature of "confidence" in the relationship between Cabinet and Commons. They have taken for the essence of the relationship the formal sanctions that may ultimately be employed to bring about a government based on "confidence"—the vote of "no confidence" by Commons, dissolution by the Crown. Some observers, like Thomas K. Finletter, would therefore go so far as to import the right of dissolution into the American Constitution.[1]

But we do not need to import the British constitution in order to develop something approaching a condition of "confidence" in the American political system. To be sure, the British constitution produces the relationship with an automaticity that in all likelihood will never be achieved in this country. Yet even there, it is vital to remember, for over half a century no cabinet that began life with its party in control of the House has fallen because of a vote of no confidence.

The active and vital institutions that have made the fall of a cabinet unlikely are the parties. For the Prime Minister and his colleagues hold their positions only because they are the acknowledged and accepted leaders of their party; because they are elected by the parliamentary party and are responsive to it; and because members of the party in the House of Commons have the well-founded expectation that their party leaders will, as a matter of course, follow the set of preferences defined by the party program and the decisions of the annual party conferences. And when a party leader is not responsive to the parliamentary party or annual conference he will, like Ramsay MacDonald, be scuttled as head of the party.

There are, in my view, three key pre-conditions for developing a relationship of "confidence" between executive and Congress under the American system. Two of these we have discussed in previous chapters; the third has already been experimented with in foreign affairs. The first pre-condition is the development of techniques for improving Congressional competence in foreign affairs. The President is unlikely to forego using his inherent powers so long as he has a profound distrust of Congressional competence in the delicate field of foreign policy. Techniques for raising the level of Congressional competence were examined in Chapter X. The second pre-condition is a greater measure of party responsibility. The President must have the confidence of his own party. He and his party in Congress must work together as a part of a team, enforcing responsibility on the President himself, on the administrative branch, and not least on party members in Congress. These problems were discussed in the preceding chapter.

The third pre-condition is implied by the other two; executive and Congress must collaborate in the formulation of basic foreign policies.[2]

Collaboration: A Case History

As a technique for overcoming the internal stresses produced by the American constitutional system, consultation between policy-makers in the executive and in Congress has been suggested by many a Secretary of State and many a Senator. From time to time Secretaries of State have, like Hay and Root, made a practice of conferring with leading Senators in advance of treaty negotiations. The practice of sending Congressional leaders as delegates to international conferences has been used sporadically since the War of 1812.

But the real development of systematic and extensive collaboration between executive and Congress on foreign policy dates only from 1943. As much as anything, this development was a product of the traumatic experience of Wilson's overwhelming defeat at the hands of Senator Lodge. Franklin

Roosevelt and Cordell Hull, the one in the executive branch at the time, the other in Congress, had witnessed the destruction of what both men enthusiastically believed was a heroic figure and a hope for the world—Wilson and the League. A generation later the potential parallel was too pat to be missed. Was a new League sponsored by the executive to suffer at the hands of the Senate the same fate as the old? It seemed clear that if the Wilson-Lodge battle were not to be repeated, it would be wise for executive and Congress to strike up an alliance. The United Nations charter therefore became the first real testing ground for executive-Congressional collaboration and, at the same time, for bipartisan collaboration.

Sensitized to Congressional attitudes by his long legislative experience and many close friendships with Senators and Representatives, Secretary Hull from the beginning had attempted to maintain good working relations with the Congress. He frequently appeared before Congressional committees, attended group conferences with Congressmen, cautioned his assistants about their sometimes hostile attitudes toward Congress, and occasionally restrained their desires to join in open battle.

In 1943, therefore, when it seemed that time was ripening for action on an international organization, the Secretary and his assistants co-operated cautiously with members of Congress interested in promoting various resolutions favorable to such a policy. In March of that year the Department prepared a brief resolution of its own, and a few days later the Secretary conferred with the Minority Leader, Senator McNary, and a bipartisan group of four men from the Foreign Relations Committee—Senators Connally, George, Vandenberg, and Gillette. Soon thereafter he had a meeting with the so-called B_2H_2 group—Senators Ball, Burton, Hatch, and Hill—which was actively working for American membership in an international organization. In the House, where Representative

Fulbright had introduced a favorable resolution, the Secretary kept in touch with Chairman Bloom of the Foreign Affairs Committee and with the Speaker, who in turn had been negotiating with majority and minority members sympathetic to an "internationalist" policy.

During the summer recess, ten Congressional teams, each consisting of a member of the Senate and the House, took the stump throughout the country and discussed the B_2H_2 resolution. Both the House and the Senate passed favorable resolutions that fall. And not long afterward, immediately following the Moscow conference where agreement had been formally obtained for a postwar international security organization, the Secretary of State, for the first time in history, addressed the two houses in joint session.

Meanwhile, the Department had been making studies and finally tentative drafts of the charter of an international organization to which the United States might adhere. During this preparation and drafting, a number of conferences had been held with leading members of the Senate and House foreign affairs committees, at which their views were carefully solicited and those of the State Department were made known. By March of 1944 preparations had reached a stage where the Secretary and the foreign affairs committees thought it desirable to designate certain members to maintain liaison with the Secretary and the Department. Four Democratic and four Republican members were named to this special subcommittee, which met with the Secretary about once every ten days and exchanged views on the proposed charter. The Secretary also held meetings with House leaders of both parties and with the now widely known B_2H_2 quadrumvirate.

At the Dumbarton Oaks conference in late summer of 1944, the draft thus worked out by consultation was presented to the British, Russians, and Chinese. Although there were no Congressional members in the American delegation, the Congressional leaders knew in advance what the American proposals were to be; moreover, the Secretary continued his conferences throughout this period with the members of the Foreign Relations Committee, the B_2H_2 group, and the House leadership.

After the conference was ended, the meetings were concluded; and apparently Mr. Hull's resignation after the elections led to a decline in collaboration. But following the Yalta conference, on the President's instructions the new Secretary, Mr. Stettinius, appointed Senators Vandenberg and Connally as delegates to the San Francisco Conference which prepared the final draft of the United Nations Charter.[3]

Since that time, the practice of consultation and collaboration has become rather common—Greek-Turkish aid, European recovery, North Atlantic Pact, for example—but by no means customary. Policies regarding German and Japanese occupation, Palestine, and, above all, China have evidently been entirely executive in nature; and there seems to have been no prior consultation with Congressional leaders on the terms of the 1949 bill for sending arms to Europe.

What are some of the lessons of the experiments in consultation so far?

Some Guides for the Future

Despite these beginnings, collaboration need not mean bipartisanship. The one experiment has been so completely enmeshed in the other that it is easy to confuse the two. Yet this is an unfortunate identification. For there are issues of foreign policy on which the parties are bound to take opposing stands; and this should not prevent collaboration between the President and his own party members in Congress.

Collaboration means co-operation in the making of policy between policy-makers in the executive-administrative, and the relevant "policy specialists" in Congress. The range of co-operative activities may extend from intimate collaboration in the detailed formulation of policy to merely informative consultation when the Secretary meets with Congressional policy specialists to exchange information and views. American participation in the United Nations came about as a result of the first, as we have just seen. The second was frequently employed during the "Berlin crisis" in 1948 and 1949, when the Secretary of State consulted with the leaders of the Senate and House foreign affairs committees, informed them of the line the United States was prepared to take, and received their public support. Greek-Turkish aid and the European Recovery Program fell somewhere in between. The North Atlantic Pact was closer to the pattern of collaboration on the United Nations Charter.

Collaboration is vital to "confidence" because it provides Congress with some surety that its preferences will be taken into account. The Congressional policy specialist is an intermediary in whom the Congressman believes he can repose some trust. Thus Congressman Monroney said of the Bretton Woods proposals:

> I think our Banking and Currency Committee has finished one of the hardest bills our committee has ever handled— Bretton Woods. The only thing that saved it and resulted in passage with only eighteen opposition votes against it [in the House] was the fact that Jesse Wolcott, the Republican ranking member, and Mr. Spence [the Democratic committee chairman] had participated in Bretton Woods, and prac-

tically everything had been presented to them as they went along.[4]

There are, however, a number of pitfalls that are not easy to avoid. First, there are all the ordinary problems of people working together, problems magnified in this case by the tradition of separation of powers. Tradition sanctifies the belief that conflict between the executive and Congress is in some mysterious way a genuine benefit. Even such a shrewd participant-observer as Robert Luce succumbed to the *mystique* of separation of powers. Arguing from the dubious axiom of social Darwinism that "wise progress comes from conflict," he urged that on the whole more good than harm issued from "the perpetual struggle between Congress and the President. . . ."[5] In a war in which the executive is the enemy, a man's reputation and influence are at stake if he insists upon looking at the executive as an ally. When Senator Pittman was chairman of the Foreign Relations Committee he opposed active collaboration with the State Department because, he said, it would reduce his effectiveness in the Senate.[6] One cannot serve two masters.

Collaboration, too, is irksome, time-consuming, tiring—which is, presumably, why Secretary Byrnes, even after his lengthy experience in the Senate, began his secretaryship by ignoring his ex-colleagues on the Foreign Relations Committee.[7] And then there are the interminable vexing limitations of human personalities. Jealousies, hatreds, status, protocol—all must be taken into account.

This means that no purely mechanical arrangements will automatically make for effective collaboration. Judgment, tact, and wisdom in the ways of human beings cannot be eliminated as vital elements in the structure of confidence. Precisely for the same reasons that the relationship between a President and his cabinet cannot be fixed by rules, the relationship between the policy specialists on the Foreign Relations Committee, the Secretary of State, and the President cannot be tightly prescribed.

Second, many difficulties are certain to stem from the fact that it is both desirable and yet impossible to distinguish between policy and administration, between collaboration on policy and "interference" in administration. There is a point at which Congressional collaboration might become "interference" of a kind destructive to effective organization, morale, discipline, and action. As Secretary Acheson has said: "We do not want to put the secretaryship of State in a commission." [8]

International events will not conveniently gear themselves to the cogwheel of Congressional routine. Decisions must be made. Day-to-day activities must go on. In case of disagreement, someone must ultimately take the responsibility for decision. Members of the State Department ought not to have to choose between obeying the Secretary or obeying a Congressional leader. Responsibility is possible only if it is clearly understood that internally the Department is responsible only to the Secretary, and that the Secretary in turn is fully responsible for what goes on in the Department.

No one, perhaps, has put the case more strongly than Senator Vandenberg in defining the limits of bipartisan consultation:

> When and where it is possible, in clearly channeled and clearly identified projects, for the legislature, the Executive, and the two major parties to proceed from the beginning to the end of a specific adventure, so that all are consulted in respect to all phases of the undertaking, I think it is a tremendously useful thing . . . But to think that that can be done as an every-day practice in regard to all of the multiple problems of international import which now descend upon the

State Department every day, in my opinion is totally out of the question.[9]

If our analysis is correct, however, the practice of consultation itself—particularly if combined with a responsible party system—will help to keep Congressional action at the level of high policy rather than of departmental details. For Congress will insist on control over details only so long as it lacks confidence in the executive-administrative.* Collaboration and party responsibility will help to create that confidence and will thereby permit Congressional leadership to concentrate on the formulation of basic policy.

The third difficulty is the converse of the second: a façade of collaboration may be set up to conceal the fact that policy is made entirely by the executive-administrative. Unless the Congressional policy specialists are somewhere near the level of competence of the Secretary of State and his top advisers, collaboration may not do much more than provide a disguised transmission belt for carrying State Department policies into Congress. Almost no one outside the Foreign Relations Committee and the Secretary can know when, or whether, this occurs. For the decisive relationship exists in the closed meetings between Secretary and Congressional policy specialists. That is the moment when Secretary and, say, chairman of Foreign Relations meet as equals in a give-and-take relationship, or as unequals in which the Secretary gives and the chairman takes.

Much must necessarily depend upon the personalities and competence of the two men and the men around each, and

---

* I speak here of Congress as a body. Individual Congressmen like Representative May will no doubt seek to influence individual administrators. But party discipline will greatly reduce their power. The administrator will feel more independent of individual Congressmen and more dependent on Congress as a body.

a great variety of relationships must be anticipated. But so far as formal organization may help, despite the personalities involved, a great deal will depend upon the capacity of Congress for securing independent information and policy analysis. So long as Congress lacks these, it is almost inevitable that the Secretary will always be armed with better information and more sophisticated policy analysis, against which the stubbornness or mere common sense of the Congressional policy specialist will not easily prevail.

The Congressman may, of course, urge his superior understanding of Congressional opinion against a proposed policy, and such urgings may well be effective. But it must not be forgotten that the role of the policy specialist in Congress is such that if you persuade him of the correctness of the policy, you persuade a good share of the Congress too. It is not improbable that, since the war, to secure the support of Senators Vandenberg and Connally for a policy was all but to secure the support of a majority of the Senate and House. It is precisely because of the influential position of the policy specialist that the techniques necessary for raising the level of Congressional competence are an indispensable prerequisite to effective Congressional collaboration.

The fourth difficulty is a product of the third. There is always the possibility that when collaboration is combined with bipartisanship, the opposition may have its head lopped off— or its brains blown out. For, in the Senate at least, there is not likely to be anyone in the minority party who will speak with the authority or competence of the ranking minority members of the Foreign Relations Committee. Capture them, and the opposition is likely to be silenced or, worse yet, silly. It is difficult to read the Senate debates on the North Atlantic Treaty without feeling that whatever case the opponents may have had, they seemed quite incapable of making it.

I am not arguing that opposition is in some mysterious way desirable in itself, nor that bipartisanship is for that reason bad. But rational choices cannot be made unless the alternatives are intelligently presented, and bipartisan collaboration may sometimes prevent the intelligent presentation of alternatives. This is a point to be dealt with in the next chapter.

Accountability of Executive Personnel

In the summer of 1949 the question of confidence came up in the Senate in connection with the nomination as Assistant Secretary for Far Eastern Affairs of Mr. W. Walton Butterworth, a Foreign Service officer who had been Director of the Office of Far Eastern Affairs. Mr. Butterworth had been in charge of Far Eastern policy during the period of Nationalist defeat and Communist victory in China. Throughout this period that policy had always been made by a relatively small group.[10] Congressional leaders had not been consulted. The Wedemeyer report, which was known to offer an alternative policy to that of the State Department, had been suppressed by President and State Department. With the crumbling of the Nationalists there was widespread discontent in Congress over our China policy. At one peak of this discontent Mr. Butterworth's nomination was submitted for Senatorial approval.

Although the Foreign Relations Committee gave a favorable report, on the floor of the Senate it came out that Senator Vandenberg, the ranking minority member of the Committee, had simply voted "present." In the indirect Senatorial style he likes to employ, Senator Vandenberg stated his reasons:

> The senior Senator from Michigan did not want to vote against Mr. Butterworth because he considered that he is

one of the most distinguished and able career men in the career service, and that in his relationship to the far eastern question he is not the responsible actor in the drama. . . . On the other hand, the senior Senator from Michigan thought it was a very great mistake in public policy, in the appointment of a new Assistant Secretary in charge of far eastern affairs in general, and in China in particular, not to bring a fresh point of view to the assignment, rather than simply to continue the regime which, for one reason or another, is inevitably connected with a very tragic failure of our policies in the Far East.[11]

Senator Brewster urged that the appointment should perhaps be turned down as a vote of no confidence in the China policy.

Now, observing the evolution of the parliamentary process and observing the functioning of it under the parliamentary system in Britain and in other countries, is it not perhaps appropriate that in the promotion of men in the State Department considerations such as the Senator from Michigan suggests may properly be taken into account, and that, in this instance, with full understanding that we are not reflecting upon the individual, and are not challenging his loyalty or devotion, or even his competency, he is so closely identified with what has seemed to be a tragic failure, that it would not be wise and in the public interest that he should at this time receive recognition of that character?

Unless we are to move in that direction I see no indication that the administration, as now constituted, are likely to give our views here the consideration which seems to me to be essential if their policies are to command the confidence of the country as a whole.[12]

Senator Brewster evidently had in mind the fact that under the parliamentary system in England, it is not unusual for an individual minister to resign when he has lost the confidence of a House of Commons that, however, still retains confidence in the cabinet as a whole.[13] Thus in 1935, when the Hoare-Laval pact on Ethiopia was met with a wave of popular and parliamentary revulsion, the foreign minister, Sir Samuel Hoare, resigned, saying to the House:

> There is the hard ineluctable fact that I have not got the confidence of the great body of opinion in the country, and I feel that it is essential for the Foreign Secretary, more than any other Minister in the country, to have behind him the general approval of his fellow-countrymen. I have not got that general approval behind me to-day, and as soon as I realised that fact ... I asked the Prime Minister to accept my resignation.[14]

Is something like this practice desirable in the United States as an extension of the principle of "confidence"? The answer is decisively in the affirmative. There are occasions on which it might be desirable for Congress to debate a vote of confidence, or no confidence, as a means of indicating to the executive-administrative what Congressional opinion is with respect to some foreign policy or some responsible official. There are, nevertheless, certain vital considerations to be kept in mind.

For one thing, it is desirable to maintain a distinction whenever possible between political officials and professional civil servants. The great difficulty in the Butterworth case, as both Senator Vandenberg and Senator Brewster saw, was that a refusal to confirm the nomination would constitute a decisive blow to a career officer. Yet they were simultaneously frustrated by the absence of any "political" official whom they could hold accountable, and the plain fact that an official at the assistant secretary level is an important policy-maker whose preferences and reality views are bound to shape foreign policy. The position is highly "political" in nature, and yet one requiring the kind of expertness that can normally be expected only from a career official.

Here is another point where the values of rationality seem to conflict with the values of responsibility. To say that the position should be filled by a political appointee is to sacrifice professional competence to political responsibility; but to say that the position should be filled by a career officer who cannot be criticized on political grounds is to sacrifice responsibility to professional competence.

If the claims of competence demand that the opportunities of the career service be expanded upward, the claims of responsibility insist that the accountability and influence of the political official be expanded downward. If the private preferences of career officers are not to establish the nation's foreign policies, a greater role must be allotted to the political official, that is, to the man whose primary task is to see that the appropriate preferences are taken into account. This may well require an increase in the number of political officials operating at the level of the secretary's office. And though in doing so there are very real dangers of creating a top-heavy organization, it seems doubtful that these are as great as the dangers flowing out of our growing enthusiasm for pushing career servants upward to policy-making positions where they are presumed to be above criticism.

Second, a vote of no confidence in an individual ought to be distinguished from a vote of no confidence in a policy. It is possible that Senator Brewster was not only aiming his shot at the wrong target, but he was using the wrong weapon. Unless the issue is clearly a question of confidence in an individual, the appropriate weapon would seem to be a concurrent resolution criticizing or supporting a given policy. It was, after all, the entire China policy that was subject to criticism.

Third, the concurrent resolution expressing a lack of confidence either in an individual or a policy is by no means merely a weapon for Congress *against* the President. When there are signs of Congressional distrust, particularly when these stem from the opposition party, the majority party may find it useful to demonstrate by means of a concurrent resolution that the official or the policy has the backing of Congress. In the spring of 1950 the air might have been cleared by a vote on a resolution of confidence in Secretary Acheson.

Last, and most important, the three major pre-conditions of confidence would, if realized, tend to reduce the significance of the concurrent resolution of no confidence, except perhaps as an occasional device by which the majority party indicates its strength, or, in the unhappy event that President and Congressional majority represent different parties, as a means of staging a debate and making a clear record for the forthcoming elections.

Furthermore, until at least party responsibility has come into existence it is doubtful if the President would, or could, look upon such a vote as much more than the expression of essentially irresponsible minorities. It cannot be said too often that Congress' own claim to enforce responsibility on the executive has little merit until it can enforce responsibility on itself.

XIV. The Problem of Agreement

WITHOUT a substantial measure of basic agreement within the electorate, it has long been recognized, democratic government cannot easily survive. At some incalculable point, disagreement within a nation is an invitation to disruption by civil conflict or conquest by a foreign invader.

The Advantages of Agreement

In the conduct of foreign relations, unity is one of the most important assets leadership can possess, disagreement one of the greatest liabilities. In Europe, where national survival has so greatly depended upon skill in the international game of power, leadership has long recognized the importance of unity; thus Bismarck's extensive social security legislation was motivated in part by a desire to reduce the internal tensions and divisions created by industrialization, that Germany might be better armed for international struggle. In our own lifetime we have come to think (with considerable oversimplification) of the Fall of France as one of the fruits of disagreement and internal tension, and the Battle of Britain as symbolic of the potentialities of a unified nation at bay. Most of us recognize a fundamental difference in our power-potential the day before Pearl Harbor and the day after.

Thus one important reason for trying to base foreign policy upon a broad area of agreement is purely instrumental. The greater the agreement, generally speaking, the more likely is the policy to succeed. This fact has not always been a matter of as great relevance in the United States as it has been in Europe. For more than a century the protective expanses of our oceans insured us greater leeway in our internal bickering. So limitless was the luxury of quarreling among ourselves that we were even permitted a civil war without invasion.

But technological development has rendered as obsolete as the stereopticon slide or the wood-burning locomotive the happy pastime of indulging in great internal disagreements. In the present era, American foreign policy is almost certain to be based upon sacrifice and the potentiality of sacrifice, upon the immediate or potential need for expenditure of money, goods, and men in the cause of national survival. For this kind of policy, widespread agreement is necessary. The days of Polk and the Mexican War are as out-of-date as the Sharpe rifle. A majority can take us into a war. But today a simple majority cannot, unaided, win a war. Nor can we again afford a Pearl Harbor to provide us with enough unity to survive.

On this point there can be so little contention that in itself it constitutes a sufficient justification for the attempt to maximize the amount of agreement underlying our foreign policies. There is also a second argument which, however, rests so fully on assumptions about the kind of political society one prefers, that the reader may well disagree with what I am about to say. Nevertheless, it seems to me that the desirability of undertaking a search for widespread agreement on basic foreign policies is implied by the values contained in the very idea of government based on consent.

To be sure, the concept of political equality seems to imply that public policy ought to correspond with the preferences of the greater number and therefore, where no greater consensus is possible, with the preferences of a plurality or majority. And it may be argued that the citizen living in a democratic society and accepting the rules of the game thereby gives implicit consent to government by the greater number, even though he may happen to be in a "minority."

But the more that political differences occur over conflicting preferences of decisive importance to a considerable number of citizens, the less is an individual in the minority likely to feel that his "consent" has been secured, and the more he is likely to feel frustrated and coerced. Because complete homogeneity in the large nation-state is evidently impossible, an important element of coercion will always exist in a large-scale democracy; government by unanimity is unattainable. But precisely because unanimity is unattainable, it is vital that all avenues of agreement be searched before a decision is taken that has decisive consequences for the preferences of any group of citizens. It would be one thing for a majority of fifty-one per cent to order a minority of forty-nine per cent to drive on the right side of the road rather than the left. But it would be quite another for a majority of fifty-one per cent to ask a minority of forty-nine per cent to offer up their lives to support a foreign policy with which they, the members of the minority, fundamentally disagree.

When all the avenues of agreement have been explored, if there yet remains a basic and irreparable breach between the policy preferences of majority and minority, then, no doubt, it is a question either of the majority coercing, or being coerced by, the minority. On this question, presumably, the democrat will have to say that unless there is some fundamental prerequisite of the democratic order involved, the minority must be coerced or any semblance of democratic rule is impossible.

But such a drastic limitation of the principle of consent is something that any democrat should, I think, bend every effort to avoid in his society, even aside from the purely instrumental considerations suggested earlier.

Case I: The Treaty Process

In its requirement that treaties be approved by a two-thirds vote of the Senate, the treaty process is one of several vital points at which the founding fathers attempted to tie the hands of future majorities. In this case, evidently, it was not so much their transcendent fear of the people that caused them to put into the Constitution a requirement which no other modern democracy has seen fit to adopt; it was simply one of those regional bargains out of which the Constitution was so largely confounded.

The validity of these original grounds—anxieties of New England States over their fishing rights and of Southern States over the future control of the Mississippi River—have long since disappeared. The shift in the basis of American politics from section to class and status, together with the enormous change from the politics of minority rule as espoused and practiced by the Federalists to a mass democracy oriented toward majority rule, increasingly served to make the two-thirds requirement appear anachronistic and anti-democratic. The defeat administered to President Wilson by Senator Lodge and his allies has caused much soul-searching among political scientists and others, and no little condemnation of the rigid two-thirds rule.

Despite the gloomy anticipations of many such observers, who thought in images reflecting the events after the First World War, the treaty power has not been a significant problem in the conduct of American foreign policy since the end of the Second World War. Only one major policy—the North

Atlantic Treaty—has been so effectuated, and that was over-whelmingly approved by the Senate.

That the treaty power has not given rise to any significant conflicts in this period is a result of three factors. First, a significant part of our foreign policy does not require treaties; it rests on executive agreements, informal understandings and consultations, and simple legislation and appropriations. Second, consultation and collaboration with the Senate Foreign Relations Committee have helped to prevent a recurrence of the Wilson-Lodge hostilities. Finally, bipartisan practices have largely cut the ground from under the feet of any Senator who might dream of re-enacting Lodge's role before a new audience.

Are there, nevertheless, sound reasons for eliminating the treaty process entirely, as some observers have proposed, and substituting the executive agreement based on a joint resolution of both houses? The latter evidently has equal legality, and it frees majorities of the irksome two-thirds rule. The answer, it seems to me, *depends on the extent and kind of sacrifices potentially demanded by our commitments.*

For one thing, we must take into account the attitudes of our partners in an international undertaking and those of our potential enemies. Where the commitment represent a serious undertaking of great consequence, insistence on large majorities is desirable precisely because of the weakening effect that bare majorities might have on the evaluation of our intentions and capabilities by both our allies and our enemies. Here is a serious practical ground for preferring the traditional method: partly because it is the traditional method, and resort to the executive agreement might weaken the confidence of foreign nations in the value of the commitment; partly because the very fact that a treaty survives the dangerous battleground of the Senate is living proof that the American government may be able to buttress its words with actions.

But even from our own point of view the treaty process has the virtue of helping us discover whether we have sufficient internal agreement to make it desirable and, realistically speaking, possible for us to embark on a policy of far-reaching consequence. A commitment based on a narrow and fluctuating majority may have much more dangerous consequences than an outright rejection of the commitment. To have accepted the obligations of the North Atlantic Pact on the basis of a bare majority probably would have been a foolhardy and reckless step, a preface to disaster both to ourselves and our allies.[1]

What these considerations seem to imply is that the treaty process ought to be employed *whenever great sacrifices are potentially required under a proposed commitment.* For all lesser matters, the executive agreement supported by a joint resolution of Congress is probably preferable, particularly since it has the advantage of associating the lower house with the undertaking.

It is, to be sure, largely up to the leaders of the majority to decide which of the two techniques to employ. Those who entirely distrust rule by majorities will object even to this concession. But in the last analysis if the majority of the people and their leaders do not have enough good sense to know when a great measure of national agreement is vital and when it is not, mere adherence to the two-thirds rule cannot provide much hope for national survival.

Case II: Bipartisan Foreign Policy

In some ways, perhaps the most significant aspect of the 1948 presidential campaign was the area of controversy that was *not* debated by the two major candidates. On the whole, and despite a campaign on domestic issues of at least normal bitterness and hyperbole, foreign policy was excluded—except, of course, by Mr. Wallace.

There were, to be sure, some breaks in the placid surface of bipartisanship. Mr. Dewey's appeal to Italian voters by taking a public stand on the question of Italy's colonies was a maneuver particularly embarrassing to an administration that was not merely engaging in secret negotiations on the subject, but presumably even putting forth proposals prepared a few years earlier with the collaboration of Mr. Dewey's adviser on foreign policy, John Foster Dulles.[2] But by and large, to anyone accustomed to the uninhibited flamboyance of American campaign behavior, the exclusion of foreign affairs seemed so complete as to indicate nothing less than a major change in the conduct of presidential campaigns.

That the exclusion of debate on foreign policy extended only to the presidential campaign, however, and not entirely to the *Congressional* battle, was only to be expected. For there was in existence no machinery through which the minority of both houses in opposition to the Truman-Vandenberg foreign policies could have been brought into line. Thus in Illinois, where the Republican organization was largely controlled by Colonel Robert McCormick of the Chicago *Tribune*, the Republican candidates for Congress and particularly Senator Brooks, a leader of the militant-isolationist-conservative bloc in Congress, could not be expected to ignore their fundamental differences with such militant-internationalist-reformists as the Senatorial and gubernatorial candidates, Paul Douglas and Adlai Stevenson.

Now the term "bipartisan" as it is currently applied to the politics of foreign relations is used in at least three different senses: (1) *executive consultation* or collaboration with foreign policy leaders of both parties, of which the prime instance is the United Nations Charter; (2) the exclusion of certain policies from *campaign* debate, particularly the presidential campaign; (3) support of certain policies *in Congress* by both parties. Obviously, the three are closely interrelated as a total process. For it is chiefly the issues on which executive-Congressional collaboration has taken place that receive two-party support in Congress and are removed from campaign debate, or at least from the presidential conflict.

The absence during the Congressional campaign of complete bipartisanship in the second sense is directly related to the state of bipartisanship in the third sense. For the former is simply a product of the latter. It is because Congressional members of neither party unanimously support "bipartisan" policies that foreign policy is projected into primary and electoral campaigns. It would probably be safe to predict that so long as American parties remain as decentralized as they are at present, this breach in the solid front of bipartisanship will continue.

Judged by the aims of bipartisanship, the record of bipartisan voting since 1945 is an excellent one. But this does not mean that Congressional opposition was absent or silenced. And on some issues, such as Senator Taft's proposal in 1945 to postpone Senate consideration of the Bretton Woods agreement, bipartisanship, at least in the Senate, virtually broke down. (See Table XI.) Again, in 1948, the House Republican leadership rebelled against the size of the European aid appropriation endorsed by "bipartisan" leaders.* Nevertheless, between 1945 and 1948 on the eleven major bipartisan issues in the House, nearly eighty-four per cent of the votes cast favored the bipartisan stand; and on the fifteen major bipartisan issues in the Senate the figure was almost identical.

---

* This vote was a voice vote, not a record vote, and therefore does not show on Table XI.

TABLE XI

PER CENT OF VOTES CAST FOR BIPARTISAN PROPOSALS, 1945-48

Year	Issue	House Total*	Dem.†	Rep.‡	Senate Total*	Dem.†	Rep.‡
1945	*Bretton Woods*						
	To recommit (H)§ or postpone (S)§.......	67.2%	57.9%	79.7%	64.7%	93.5%	28.6%
	To pass..............	92.5	95.6	88.5	79.2	95.4	52.9
	UNRRA						
	Appropriation.........	94.8	98.0	90.6	—	—	—
	To continue U.S. membership.............	89.0	94.8	81.3	—	—	—
	United Nations						
	To ratify Charter.....	—	—	—	97.8	100.0	93.7
	To appoint delegate...	96.1	99.5	92.6	85.9	95.3	71.4
1946	*UNESCO*						
	H. Joint Res. endorsing	86.6	97.6	74.1	—	—	—
	World Court						
	S. Res. accepting jurisdiction.............	—	—	—	97.8	100.0	94.1
1947	*Greek-Turkish loan bill*						
	Amend. to prohibit military aid §...........	—	—	—	77.1	80.0	74.5
	Motion to lay on the table §.............	—	—	—	76.0	84.4	68.6
	To pass.............	72.0	91.6	57.1	76.0	84.4	68.6
	Interim aid to Europe						
	Amend. to decrease appropriations §.......	—	—	—	66.4	75.6	57.4
	To pass..............	78.7	92.8	69.0	93.7	93.3	94.1
	Italian Peace Treaty						
	To ratify.............	—	—	—	88.5	91.1	86.3
	Inter-American Treaty of Assistance						
	To ratify..........	—	—	—	99.0	100.0	98.0
1948	*European Recovery*						
	To pass authorizing legislation.............	81.8	93.8	73.1	80.0	93.1	68.6
	To adopt conference report...............	80.6	93.0	72.1	—	—	—
	To decrease proposed approp. (H)........	No record vote			—	—	—
	To accept S. Comm. proposal on 12-15 month basis........	—	—	—	74.7	90.9	75.6
	To appropriate........	83.7	94.3	76.0	90.1	95.3	84.2
	Averages................	83.9	91.7	77.4	83.1	91.5	73.8
	Exc. Bretton Woods...	85.6	95.1	77.6	84.7	91.0	78.9

* Total votes for bipartisan proposals, as per cent of total votes cast. All figures exclude minor party votes, and include pairs.

† Democratic votes *For*, as per cent of total Democratic votes cast.

‡ Republican votes *For*, as per cent of total Republican votes cast.

§ I.e., votes *against* the motion, thus *in support of* bipartisan proposal.

The Democrats, as one might expect, had a higher Index of Party Agreement (IPA) on bipartisan issues than the Republicans. In both the House and Senate, just under ninety-two per cent of the Democrats who voted favored the bipartisan stand on the various issues. The Republican IPA in both houses is considerably lower—77.4 per cent in the House and 73.8 per cent in the Senate. If we exclude Bretton Woods, however, the Senate Republican IPA rises significantly, while that of the House Democrats runs over ninety-five per cent.

That Democrats supported bipartisan proposals more wholeheartedly than Republicans undoubtedly stems from two facts. For one thing, from 1945 to 1948 bipartisanship meant supporting a Democratic President. The IPA of the Democratic Party on bipartisan issues might well fall off if a Republican were in the White House. In the second place, the Republican Party has had a much greater number of militant-isolationists in its Congressional ranks. In general, the militant-isolationists have opposed the militant-internationalist policies pursued by the bipartisan leadership.

Bipartisanship is of course much more difficult on certain kinds of issues than on others. Thus, on appropriations the Republican IPA falls off enormously; and in one unrecorded case, that of the House on ERP, party agreement rises, but on opposite sides of the fence, so that the Republicans and Democrats split on more or less typical party lines. On the other hand, in the case of the United Nations Charter and the Chapultepec Treaty, both of which resulted from extensive bipartisan collaboration and neither of which required appropriations, party support on both sides of the Senate was almost unanimous.

It is significant, finally, that the House and Senate do not show up very differently. The IPA of the parties remains at about the same level in both chambers, despite the common assumption that party control in the lower house is more extensive.

Bipartisanship in Congress, in sum, may best be looked upon as a series of concentric circles. In the inner circle, comprising the Foreign Relations and Foreign Affairs Committees, bipartisan support has been virtually unanimous. Thus in the Eightieth Congress, of twenty treaties and agreements submitted by the President and considered by the Foreign Relations Committee, nineteen were approved by a unanimous Committee vote. Of thirty-one bills and resolutions considered by the Committee, all were reported unanimously by the Committee.[3] Indeed, since 1946, on every major problem except the St. Lawrence Waterway and the Anglo-American Oil Agreement, the Committee vote has been unanimous— on something like fifty occasions.[4]

The surrounding circle comprises the "party leadership" of the two houses—floor leaders, policy and steering committees, the Speaker, party whips, and the like. Here unanimity begins to break down. In the Senate, for example, Senator Taft has been something less than an enthusiastic supporter of all the bipartisan policies set forth by his colleagues on the Foreign Relations Committee. Nevertheless, as chairman of the Republican Policy Committee, he is pretty well acknowledged the party leader in the Senate. In the House, Republican leaders have been particularly restless; and they have sometimes come down squarely in opposition to "bipartisan" proposals endorsed by Senator Vandenberg. It was not until the day after Senator Taft had publicly endorsed the larger ERP appropriation in 1948 that Representative Taber and Majority Leader Halleck, in the last hours of the Eightieth Congress, retreated from their opposition to the full appropriation demanded by Senator Vandenberg.

Beyond the party leadership, in the outer circle, lie the

ordinary members of Congress, who are largely free to support or oppose bipartisan legislation as they see fit.

In reality, then, bipartisanship in Congress is a continuum extending from virtually unanimous support by party leaders and members on some issues, to other situations of a more ambiguous sort where some party leaders and members do, and many do not, support the bipartisan proposals emanating from the President and the Senate Foreign Relations Committee.

1. What Price Bipartisanship?

Bipartisanship * combined with the rather slack discipline characteristic of American parties is a way of bringing together an inter-party majority in Congress for a specific and limited purpose. At the same time it permits the *dissenters* in each party, while united temporarily to form a voting minority, *to remain in the party*. Bipartisanship testifies to the inadequacy of a party system to reflect accurately the unities and divergencies within a nation. For what bipartisanship in Congress reflects is the fact that a nation may be divided on domestic issues and at the same time may contain a national majority on foreign policy cutting athwart the interest-group alignments of domestic policy. The conflict of political parties is an awkward mechanism for taking this cross-interest situation into account. Bipartisanship is a means of overcoming the artificiallty of party lines by setting to one side particular issues on which a substantial number of leaders and followers in each party are in agreement.

Throughout this book the advantages of party responsibility have been emphasized. Is there a conflict between bipartisanship as a technique for securing agreement on foreign policy, and

* Used now in Sense (3) above, i.e., support of certain policies in Congress by both parties.

party discipline and coherence as a technique for fixing responsibility? That there is some conflict is undeniable. Is the conflict so great that we cannot have one without foregoing the other?

Let us try to imagine a party system under which party discipline was rigorously enforced *on every important issue.* On an important question of bipartisan foreign policy, Representative Jones refuses to support the party stand as determined in caucus. The leadership therefore denies him his privileges as a party member—his committee seat, support for his private bills, patronage, campaign funds. He is disavowed by the national party. In his primary the party runs a rival candidate committed to the policies of the party.

"If you do not believe in our major policies," the party leaders tell him, "you have no right to represent yourself as one of our party members. You will have to take your chances as an independent, join the other party, or come back with us and accept the party program." What are the likely consequences of combining bipartisanship with such a party system?

First, party discipline might simply break down in the sphere of foreign affairs. It is significant that even the British Labor Party, which not only has grown up within a general tradition of party discipline but has actually written the requirement of regularity into the constitution of its parliamentary party, sometimes encounters difficulty in holding its members together on foreign policy. In several cases (Mr. Platt-Mills in 1948, Mr. Zilliacus in 1949, for example) the party has had to resort to expulsion for a clear breach of the party slant on foreign affairs. But it has not dared to handle so drastically the large group under Mr. Richard Crossman which in several cases actually voted against the party policy.

Assuming, however, that discipline of this kind were actually possible in this policy sector, and with American parties, then the fruits of bipartisanship might be even more undersirable than in the first eventuality. For in the absence of genuine and complete agreement in the community, bipartisanship would create a meretricious unanimity.

The dangers of such a synthetic unanimity are two. First, the leadership may be misled. A Congressional unanimity—or even a large majority—that does not reflect the actual distribution of attitudes among the population may lull leadership into false expectations. Secondly, synthetic unanimity based on disciplined bipartisanship would repress inter-party debate and therefore adequate discussion of minority claims. For the parties are among the chief instruments for getting community conflicts fully examined by the electorate. Even if the façade of monolithic unity were an asset in international politics—a point that is at least open to question—such "unity" would inhibit democratic mechanisms for expressing and exploring different preferences except where (a) the preference structure of the community actually was monolithic and (b) there was complete agreement on the method of attaining those preferences—two very improbable situations in the modern nation-state.

A third possibility is that bipartisanship would break down in a way different from the first: it would tend to splinter the major parties. That this danger exists even under a regime of somewhat loosely disciplined parties is indicated by the Wallace third-party movement, which evidently received a good share of its non-Communist support from people whose opposition to the bipartisan foreign policy of the Truman administration and the Vandenberg wing of the Republican Party led them into the third-party fold. The hypothesis might therefore be set forth that (a) so long as unanimity among the politically active opinion and leadership groups is lacking, and (b) foreign issues are felt with relative *intensity* as compared with domestic issues, a bipartisan alignment on foreign policy will lead to the creation of third-party movements. A fortiori, disciplined parties would accentuate the tendency to splinter.

2. Some Considerations

The fact is, parties disciplined on every important issue in a heterogeneous country like the United States are as unlikely as they are undesirable. It is much more realistic to suppose that there will continue to be a variety of situations, each presenting somewhat different problems both to bipartisanship and party discipline.

First, there are and will be some situations in which there is very substantial agreement *within* each party and disagreement *between* the parties. The question of reciprocal trade agreements largely has been, and may continue to be, this kind of issue. In such circumstances there is every reason why each party, if it wished to do so, should attempt to formulate a reasonably clear-cut party position to which members would be required to adhere. The electorate would then have the opportunity to make a choice between the parties. Bipartisan consultation, of course, would be impossible. This situation might be represented graphically thus:

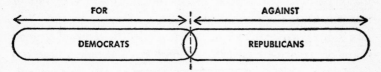

Second, there will be situations in which there is substantial agreement *within* each party, and also agreement *between* the parties. Such a situation would imply a substantial consensus for the policy over the nation as a whole, such as was evidently the case with the Monroe Doctrine in the past. As in the first kind of situation, there is no good reason why the parties should not take a clear-cut stand, to which party members would be required to adhere. It is worth pointing out, however, that in situations where consensus is actually very extensive, deviations from the party position will be so few in comparison with the overwhelming support offered by members of both parties, that probably not much is to be gained by party discipline. Bipartisan consultation in such situations may well be desirable, although it is scarcely urgent. Graphically this condition might be represented as follows:

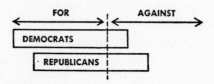

Third, there will be some situations in which there are substantial internal differences on foreign policy within one or both parties, even though the parties are internally united on questions of domestic policy. In such cases the party leadership will have to decide how much it is willing to concede to obtain party unity—and indeed, *can* concede. That there are distinct limits to the use of disciplinary measures seems clear. It is likely, for example, that almost no kind or amount of party organization could have brought all the Senate Republicans into line behind the North Atlantic Treaty. This situation may be represented as:

In situations of this kind, there is every reason for urging bipartisan consultation. For here it is possible to secure a more widespread agreement for a particular foreign policy by bipartisan collaboration and yet, because party unity is impossible, to bring about no net loss in responsibility. If Secretary Acheson, Senator Connally, and Senator Vandenberg in 1949 saw nearly eye to eye on the need for an Atlantic treaty, there was much to lose and nothing to gain by not collaborating with Senator Vandenberg simply because Senator Taft and a minority of Senate Republicans were opposed to the treaty.

Case III: Responsible Opposition

The conditions that gave rise to bipartisan collaboration are the reverse of the conditions that make responsible parties possible. Two unified national parties cannot exist in the absence of certain social pre-conditions, mainly an electorate composed of two great groupings of more or less homogeneous political attitudes. But if these pre-conditions do exist, and unified parties come into being, then bipartisan collaboration becomes a rather academic question. For then all issues would tend to fall into one of the first two categories illustrated above. In the first, bipartisan collaboration is clearly impossible; in the second, although it is not impossible, in many cases it is superfluous. Only because the pre-conditions were, in fact, much closer to the third kind of situation illustrated above, was bipartisan collaboration felt to be necessary.

To the extent that parties come to represent nation-wide class and status groups of considerable homogeneity, and to the extent that responsible, unified parties become possible, the urgency with which bipartisanship has been pressed upon us will doubtless decline.

The real need is the discovery of more situations like the second kind illustrated above. It is possible to imagine the development of responsible parties with leaders who would regard it as much a vital opportunity to discover and explore the areas of common agreement on foreign policy as to take a clear and unambiguous stand on their differences. Leaders of the opposition would regard it as their task to clarify fundamental purposes by discussion and debate, to combine with the majority to "depoliticize" the broad policies on which there was consensus, and yet in these cases to retain their freedom to criticize specific techniques and administrative failures. On the whole, bipartisanship is a mere makeshift to fill the gap made by the absence of a system for intelligent, competent, and responsible opposition.

Is it entirely utopian to imagine this reconciliation of responsibility and the search for common agreement? Unfortunately, it is often difficult not to think so.

On July 27, 1949, Senator McClellan from the agricultural state of Arkansas rose on the floor of the Senate while European recovery appropriations were under consideration and moved an amendment requiring that one and a half billion dollars be set aside exclusively for the purchase of agricultural products. His amendment was a plain attempt to convert foreign policy into a technique for subsidizing American farmers. The Senator was, perhaps, astonished to discover that the vision of the farm lobbyists was considerably less myopic than that of one-third of the Senate. For the three great farm organizations opposed the amendment on the ground that it was a serious blunder to mix American farm policy and American foreign policy. But thirty-two Senators, every one from a predominantly farming state, supported the McClellan amendment.[5]

That one-third of the United States Senate was more pressure-group minded than the pressure groups themselves makes one hesitate to forecast that Congress will ever rise to the challenge of great events.

XV. What Will the Consequences Be?

MUCH ink has been spilled over the manner in which American foreign policy was conducted from 1937 to 1941. To some the history of those years is that of a President personally committed to a policy of intervening in European and Asiatic power struggles, employing deceit and fraud against a national legislature and an electorate committed to staying out of war. To others it is a story of a great statesman who saved a nation in spite of itself, because he saw world events in a wiser perspective than a people and a Congress drugged with self-deceit and the disastrous stereotypes of isolationism.

Whatever one may decide, the conclusion is bound to be an unhappy one for a democratic society. According to one view, the Presidency is an institution of dangerously unlimited power to commit the nation without its consent. According to the other, the electorate is too incompetent to be granted choice over its own destiny. According to a third possible view, both conclusions are sound.

There can be little doubt that we live in an epoch of social techniques and international politics scarcely congenial to the democratic method. Yet this is all the more reason for raising that method to its highest potentialities, given the kind of world in which we find ourselves. That we cannot achieve a Utopia in which competence, responsibility, and agreement are all maximized seems clear. Sometimes one will have to be sacrificed to achieve another. But in the past our political system has needlessly squandered these values.

The real question is: What will be the consequences for the conduct of foreign policy if Congress is brought into collaboration with the executive in the manner indicated in earlier chapters? What kinds of limitations and potentialities does this sort of policy-making structure imply for the conduct of foreign relations, particularly in comparison with executive discretion on the one hand, and, on the other, the methods of dictatorship? The first is relevant because it is an immediately available alternative; the second, because it is the competitor against which our efficiency, and indeed our capacity for survival, evidently will be tested.

Requirements of the Policy Process

If we examine the kind of foreign policy on which we have embarked, we shall see that its success is contingent upon certain requirements. With respect to the general content of our foreign policy, let us simply assume that:

1. A large majority of the people of the United States wishes to prevent external aggression by any major power considered dangerous to the United States. At present, and for the immediately foreseeable future, the only such major power is the U.S.S.R. But the aim also includes preventing a resurgence of the potentiality for aggression by Germany and Japan.

2. The resources of the United States—military, economic, diplomatic, psychological, moral—will be deployed actively, in varying but substantial amounts, to prevent such aggression.

3. The United States will allocate some of its resources to strengthen other powers, primarily nation-states and blocs of states elsewhere, but also some international organizations.

4. An aim of this policy will be to build up, particularly in western Europe and Southeast Asia, a bloc of states capable

of survival, free of both Russian and American domination, yet friendly and in some cases allied to the United States.

What does even such a barebones statement of policy in the modern world imply as to *method?* If the policy is to be effective, certain obvious features must characterize its application.

1. *Prediction and planning.* Those who direct foreign policy must make certain *predictions* as to the kinds of action that may be expected from other powers; and they must predict the conditions under which those actions may or will occur. If the leadership is rational, it will then make *plans* envisaging the creation of the conditions most favorable to its policies. Because the future is not always predictable and plans may go awry, political like military leadership will need alternative plans to meet different sets of expectations.

2. *Flexibility.* International politics has lately witnessed not only a tremendous acceleration of events in time but also a vast broadening in space. Meanwhile, events grow in complexity. A rigid strategy may therefore find itself adapted to the wrong crisis or to the wrong area.

3. *Speed.* The terrifying acceleration of events that Henry Adams foresaw for the twentieth century has nowhere been more evident than in international politics. Since Hitler's advent to power, international crises have followed one another with mounting rapidity. Today, crisis is normal. Periods of apparent calm are really only interludes, like days of quiet on the battlefield, during which forces are being reorganized for the next crisis. A modern policy must therefore be predicated on the expectation of rapidly succeeding crises. Speed of action becomes imperative.

4. *Adequacy.* "Too little and too late," the reverse of Napoleonic strategy, has become a byword for the strategy of democracies faced with internal or external crises. One might almost formulate as a law of politics that democracies will not

act with vigor, mass, and decision until crisis has ripened into disaster. What the great military strategists have always known is today a requirement of political strategy. To commit one's forces piecemeal is an invitation to annihilation; yet to commit an excessive amount on small operations may prove too costly to be long sustained. Let us examine each of these requirements in turn.

Prediction and Planning

Prediction in international politics is a problem largely outside the scope of this book, and I do not mean to deal with it here. Meaningful prediction in international politics by policy-makers depends, first, on the state of knowledge and the condition of the social sciences; second, upon the extent to which experts are recruited into positions where policy-makers have access to them. It would carry us too far afield to attempt an estimate of the consequences of our political structure for the first. As to the second, it is a central part of our argument here that active participation of Congress requires a comprehensive utilization of experts especially by the policy specialists on the committees. It is probably fair to say that the future of Congress as a policy-making institution rests upon its willingness and capacity for attaining and using the knowledge of experts.

But prediction is sterile without planning. The function of prediction, like that of planning, is to give men greater influence over events: to borrow Comte's expression, *savoir pour prévoir, prévoir pour pouvoir.* To employ a military simile, the intelligence officer may be able to describe the capabilities of the enemy. The operations officer may draw up alternative plans for combating or exploiting those capabilities. But the ultimate aim of both is to enable the commander to launch and control the operation that he decides upon in view of enemy actions and capabilities on the one side, and his own objectives and capabilities on the other.

One function of the State Department is to act as the operations officer, or the War Plans Division, for President and Congress. As with prediction, there are problems here of internal organization, recruiting, and expertness which are beyond the scope of this book. But one problem of planning strategies in international politics is entirely relevant to the problem of political structure, and that is the problem of secrecy. Success in international strategy as in war is often contingent upon secrecy (and sometimes on publicity, too, but that is a different, more solvable problem). To draw up plans of action and then to broadcast them through Congressional debate may be, on occasion, as disastrous to one's strategy in international politics as in war; and yet this possibility seems to be implied by our political structure. Because of the importance of the problem of secrecy, it will be discussed separately below.

The real problem, perhaps, is not whether plans can be *created*, but whether they can be *executed*. As prediction is sterile without planning, so planning is sterile unless it is related to potential action. I do not mean to say that successful planning is predicated upon a rigid and undeviating execution of strategies prepared in advance. As any military commander knows, strategy and tactics require a lively, vigorous, and constant reconciliation of means, emerging circumstances, and basic purposes. But the essential difficulty in the case of foreign policy lies with the "commander." Can strategy in international politics be decided on, and subsequently controlled by a team one part of which is a legislative committee?

No one perhaps would argue so in the case of military strategy. It is a universal phenomenon of democracies in war that basic strategy is decided upon by the executive and his military advisers, and it seems doubtful that survival in modern war is otherwise possible. Does not the logic of war carry its dread insistence into that shadowy no man's land between war and peace, the battlefield of international politics? There is much to be said for this point of view. (Perhaps it is worth pointing out, however, that those who have drawn the most complete conclusions from the logic of war are not the advocates of presidential supremacy. They are the modern totalitarians.)

What limits are imposed on the execution of strategy in foreign affairs by the fact that Congress and even its committees are not *expert* bodies? Undoubtedly there are some limits; and the more nearly Congress attempts to fix details rather than broad and basic policy,* the more nearly it concerns itself with tactics rather than strategy, the greater its incompetence and the more likely it is to employ irrational means to the broader objectives agreed on.

But the inverse is also true. For the more closely debate moves toward broad and basic policy, the more competent is the legislative decision likely to be, and correspondingly less competent is the expert. This is not merely because basic policy involves "value" questions which ought to be outside the po-

* The nomenclature of public policy is impossibly inadequate. In this chapter the terms "broad" policy and "basic" policy will be employed with somewhat different connotations. Both are relative terms. A "broad" policy implies more discretion than a "narrow" policy. A policy is "basic" because we think it is so; that is, because it has consequences for a relatively greater *range* of preferences, because it effects *the more highly ranked* preferences, or because it effects preferences in a more *decisive* way than a less basic policy. Policy may be "basic" without being "broad," and vice versa. A statute nationalizing the steel industry might run to two hundred pages and outline the procedure to be followed in such detail as to leave almost no discretion. In the terminology here employed this would not be "broad" policy, but (given existing American preferences) it would unquestionably be "basic."

litical authority of the expert in a democracy. It is also because the judgments of "fact" must include more and more complex variables on which the expert, in the present state of the social sciences, is probably professionally less competent than the intelligent politician.[1] When questions of military strategy broaden into problems of international politics, as they inevitably will at some point, the competence of the general ought to give way to that of the politician, as General Eisenhower so clearly understood in his relations with Churchill and Roosevelt.

At this point, when technical problems swell into basic policy judgments, the limitations of a Congressional committee on foreign affairs are probably not much greater than those of a President. It would be difficult to argue in retrospect, for example, that the basic decisions on war strategy which President Roosevelt had to make as Commander-in-Chief would have been much worse, or much better, had a joint Congressional committee on foreign affairs participated in the decisions.

I am not arguing here that Congress or its committees ought to participate in the making of military strategy. Questions of secrecy and speed, perhaps, make this undesirable. I am simply arguing that what is true of war strategy is true of foreign policy: that at some point it involves complex judgments of value and fact on which the technician has no special competence, and which ought therefore to be made, in a democratic society, by politicians; that there are no very sound grounds for supposing that the politician in the White House is inherently more competent to make these decisions than some politicians on a specialized committee on Capitol Hill; and that the rationality of such a process of foreign policy making is not likely to be less than under a system of widest presidential discretion.

Flexibility

A much more serious problem is that of flexibility. The difficulties imposed on the conduct of foreign policy because certain avenues have been foreclosed by Congressional and public opinion were never, perhaps, of more decisive importance than in the fall of 1941.

> "One problem troubled us very much," Secretary of War Stimson later told a congressional committee investigating the Pearl Harbor fiasco. "If you know that your enemy is going to strike you, it is not usually wise to wait until he gets the jump on you by taking the initiative. In spite of the risk involved, however, in letting the Japanese fire the first shot, *we realized that in order to have the full support of the American people it was desirable to make sure that the Japanese be the ones to do this so that there should remain no doubt in anyone's mind as to who were the aggressors.*" [2]

Plans could have been and perhaps were drawn up, based on the assumption that we could attack first. All questions of public opinion and morale to one side, utilization of these plans might have enabled us to control the situation much more successfully than was possible when we were forced passively to await the enemy attack. But what was possible in an authoritarian regime was not possible in a democratic one, given the state of Congressional and public opinion. In this sense, then, we were very nearly fatally inflexible.

Nor does there appear to be any way by which a substantial measure of inflexibility on broad policy can be avoided in a society where democratic institutions are effectively operating. Secretary Stimson, it is worth pointing out, was testifying about events in a period of extraordinary executive discretion over our relations with Japan. Yet there were limits beyond which the President and his advisers clearly felt Congress and the public would not permit them to go. What was true then is, a fortiori, likely to characterize a decision-making process involving close collaboration between executive and Congress.

The dilemma of the political leadership is this. Only if public opinion is fluid and undecided will the full range of theoretical alternatives be open; to the extent that public opinion hardens, alternatives are foreclosed. But because effectiveness in foreign policy depends finally upon the willingness of a nation to indulge in collective sacrifices, to rely on a fluid and indefinite public opinion is to substitute a reed for a sword. Thus when the American political leadership decided to drop the attempt to collaborate with the U.S.S.R. after the Second World War, an effective policy of containing Russian aggression depended upon stiffening public and Congressional opinion to the point where expected sacrifices might be made. But the very fact that public opinion did congeal tended to foreclose certain alternatives such as "appeasement." I am not arguing that "appeasement" was desirable. The point is, inevitably a certain flexibility was lost.

In contrast, the totalitarian regimes have more elbowroom in foreign affairs simply because the manipulation of public attitudes is more easily accomplished. In 1939 the Politburo presumably was relatively free to decide whether it would align the U.S.S.R. with the democracies or with the Axis—a set of alternatives still open, it is worth noting, despite a lengthy and intensive campaign to work public opinion into a state of hostility against the Axis powers. In 1949 the Politburo was, presumably, still relatively free to decide whether it would appease the West or continue the cold war.

But if at one level effective flexibility may be lost to democratic leadership, at a lower level this need not be so. Whether the leadership can be flexible below the level of basic policy depends primarily upon the extent to which public and Congressional opinion has congealed with respect to certain "means." A fundamental characteristic of the period 1935-41 was the tendency for public and Congressional opinion to fix rigidly on certain stereotyped means, such as neutrality legislation. The attack at Pearl Harbor and the outbreak of war apparently brought widespread disillusionment with this stereotype. The approaching end of the war witnessed a fixation on other means, the United Nations. But as experience with this technique also proved disillusioning, the postwar period came to be marked by a very considerable fluidity in public opinion, a fluidity that made it possible for the leadership to select and "sell" a number of important subpolicies of considerable variety (Greek-Turkish aid, ERP, North Atlantic alliance, Berlin air-lift, etc.). Whether new stereotypes and a more rigid public opinion will emerge, it is still too early to say. Meanwhile, the leadership has retained much more flexibility than has ever been true in the history of American foreign policy.

It is vital to maintain this flexibility as to means. Yet this is possible only in a regime where the leadership rests on the confidence of the electorate; it was, after all, primarily a deepseated distrust of leadership that forced the rigid and inflexible provisions into the neutrality legislation of the prewar period. In this sense, an executive-Congressional team is much more likely to retain the confidence necessary to flexibility than a system under which the President seeks to wield discretionary powers but lacks the confidence of Congress because he is not genuinely responsible to it.

Therefore it is necessary to continue the search for agreement. If responsible parties can discover broad areas of agreement on foreign policy, then many differences over means can be raised to the proper level: as technical questions that sometimes need to be given over to the administrative branch for decision, sometimes need to be discussed in Congress with the aid of experts, sometimes need close consultation between administrators and policy specialists in Congressional committees—but in any case do not need to be converted into party issues for the forthcoming campaign.

By itself, even collaboration between executive and Congress is not enough for the atomic age, when the bankruptcy of peace-maintaining techniques may occur so abruptly that a nation must instantly switch to the more decisive means of war—or fail to survive. A future administration that passively waits for the first shot of the enemy to galvanize public attitudes may be inviting national suicide. Survival itself requires an advance quest for widespread electoral and Congressional agreement on action should war suddenly threaten. We cannot wait for that terrifying event to bring the agreement we need.

This is why the reconstruction of local discussion and inquiry is important, why it is vital that Congressional debates on foreign policy be broadcast, why party leaders should even now begin to work out a bipartisan agreement for that time. Either public opinion in a democracy is capable of the alertness and militance necessary to vigorous and decisive action in foreign affairs, or it is not. If it is not, then democratic institutions are pretty clearly not viable in a world environment transformed by new techniques of violence.

Speed

If flexibility—the capacity for selecting from a wider range of alternatives—is indispensable to survival in an atomic epoch, speed is perhaps even more important. What are the consequences for speed of decision and action implied by the kind of governmental structure described earlier?

In general, it is probably a good deal easier to achieve speed in deciding subsidiary policy, that is, in implementing basic policy, than it is to make quick decisions on basic policy. Because our general policy of withstanding Russian aggression had already been decided by the time the Soviets imposed their blockade on Berlin in the summer of 1948, it was a relatively easy matter for the executive to act quickly in attempting to hold Berlin, and to maintain liaison with Congress while the decision was being made.

The real problem arises when a basic policy must be decided with speed. Here the difficulty is of the same kind that interferes with flexibility. Leadership rests on a measure of public consent, and public opinion often changes much more slowly than international patterns of power. A fundamental step like joining the United Nations required two years of preparation from one point of view, a quarter-century from another. The Marshall Plan occupied a full year from the first public discussion to completed legislative action. Military aid to western Europe was equally delayed. The important point is, however, that without Congressional collaboration these actions might have taken a much longer time, and in the end perhaps would have been endowed with less widespread support. Executive discretion may have the advantage of allowing the executive branch to move with greater speed; but so long as action must ultimately depend on Congressional and public support, the speed of the executive branch may prove to be that of a circus monkey tied to an elephant.

From a Machiavellian point of view, to be sure, there is always inherent in executive discretion the possibility of succeeding with a *fait accompli* where prior consent would not have been forthcoming; this is essentially the late Charles A. Beard's interpretation of President Roosevelt's relation to the bombing of Pearl Harbor, and it is a part of Thomas A. Bailey's justification, as I understand it, for the broadest sort of Presidential authority over the conduct and policy of our foreign relations. But all questions of political morality to one side, the *fait accompli* will work only under certain circumscribed conditions. It is difficult to conceive how it could possibly have been successful in the case of such far-reaching postwar policies as the Marshall Plan and military aid to western Europe. And it is at least an open question whether Machiavellian leadership will not finally defeat itself in a democratic society where legislative institutions survive; for one response to Machiavellianism and *faits accomplis* is to impose upon leadership a set of rigid legislative restrictions narrowly restricting its scope for action.

The *fait accompli* will, nevertheless, remain a persistent temptation to leadership so long as the problem of speed remains unsolved, and it is not clear that the problem *can* be solved. In the atomic age, indeed, lack of speed may well prove to be the Achilles' heel of American democratic institutions. To go to war unquestionably represents a basic policy step, in the sense that the shift from cold war methods to modern techniques of violence is regarded as a decision of tremendous consequence to a great range of highly ranked preferences. And yet if it is true that under our institutional arrangements there tends to be a lag, sometimes a very lengthy one, between changed patterns of international power and our collective decisions reflecting that change, war may well have destroyed us before we have officially declared it to exist.

The way out of this dilemma, if there is a way, is not a

pleasant one. It is nothing less than the advance recognition by Congress of certain contingent circumstances under which the President in consultation with Congressional leaders would be authorized to commence an attack on an aggressor pending a formal declaration of war by Congress. (It is at least conceivable, indeed, that unless civilian defense arrangements are highly developed in advance, Congress and the administrative branch may be seriously disorganized at the very time the vital decision would have to be made.) There is no blinking the fact that such a prior grant of power would place incalculable discretion in the hands of the leadership. At its worst, leadership might manipulate intelligence reports to provide a justification for launching the war, and even at best the leaders might have to act on fragmentary and ambiguous evidence of a coming attack.

What I am suggesting, then, is that the threat of modern air-borne annihilation presents two possible institutional alternatives. Either the whole range of foreign policy and its decisions, including that of war, must be taken out of the hands of Congress and lodged exclusively in the executive, or Congress and its leaders must share intimately in the process of decision-making, and the more so as danger signals begin to go up. As a part of this collaborative process, the Congress can define certain situations under which the executive-Congressional leadership team may launch war pending the overt consent of the Congressional body.

It is doubtful whether Congress will grant the kind of power I am suggesting. But it is doubly doubtful that it will do so unless a structure of leadership and decision-making exists in which it has the highest confidence. Whether the American democracy will in fact cut this Gordian knot is, to say the least, open to serious question.

Adequacy

The problem of adequacy is, to use the language of the economist, a question of securing the optimum allocation of limited resources. A rational society, like a rational person, presumably would wish to get "the most for its money." Whenever the preferences of those people who make the decisions in the society could be served better by employing resources in foreign affairs than in domestic consumption, the rational step would be to shift the needed resources to foreign affairs, and vice versa. Likewise, within the field of foreign affairs itself, a rational society would shift resources from one area of consumption to another whenever the preferences of the society could be better attained by doing so.

However, this is an example of one of those rational pure types, so dear to the economist, which are even less likely to exist in the real world of international politics than in the real world of economic struggle. There are at least three important reasons why the optimum is not likely to be attained in the conduct of American foreign policy, why the rule "neither too little nor too much" will not be followed in practice.

First, the decision-making process is less dynamic than international power relations. Even the economists had to assume that market decisions only *tended* toward equilibrium. The decisions of the market did not necessarily ever catch up with, and therefore perfectly match, the preferences of consumers. Although it would be dangerous to make any predictions for the long run, the international scene as we have known it since the First World War has been one of relatively rapid shifts. The actual power relations tend to outstrip policies based on obsolescent expectations. Sooner or later the change in actual power relations forces a revision of expectations and ultimately a change in policy. Resources are finally reallocated to fit the demands of the new policy. But equilibrium is never quite achieved, for already the international scene has shifted and the new policy is partly obsolete. Policy is always walking down an escalator going up.

All this is in contrast to the relative stability of power relations vis-à-vis the United States in the nineteenth century, when, on the whole, decisions substantially kept pace with changes in the relevant power situations. In that century, moreover, the relative balance between resources expended on foreign affairs and those left over for domestic consumption probably corresponded pretty closely with what would have been the rational preferences of most people in the society.

For American policy in the nineteenth century required relatively slight expenditures on foreign affairs. In practice, the Monroe Doctrine demanded little in the way of collective sacrifice. And it is there that one finds the second important reason why the actual allocation of resources to foreign affairs is not likely to correspond to a rational choice by members of the society: the limited willingness to make the collective sacrifice so often necessary to an adequate and therefore successful policy. This is not to say that, given a clear understanding of all the alternatives and their consequences, citizens might not prefer a present collective sacrifice to the consequences of *not* making that sacrifice. The fact is, however, that most citizens begin with a general predisposition favorable to the production of the relatively more concrete, visible, personalized kind of goods—vacuum cleaners, automobiles, houses, roads, factories. Secondly, they begin with a general predisposition for individual consumption as against collective consumption via the government: for privately owned cars rather than an improved system of public transportation, for private housing rather than public housing. Both attitudes are a natural by-product of an individualist, capitalist cultural milieu; indeed, these preferences simply correspond to the general presuppositions of individualist capitalism. This means that the act of buying the collective benefits of foreign policy through the state has much less social approval than the act of buying private goods on the market.

This is not to say, I repeat, that citizens would necessarily prefer the benefits of the commodities bought on the markets to those "purchased" in foreign affairs through the State, if they had a full understanding of the consequences of each. But the fact is, one kind of action meets with much more resistance than another. In our kind of society, to take a roughly comparable case from another field, it is easier to build a luxurious restaurant (sometimes even a race track) than a public school; and yet it is by no means certain that citizens, given an opportunity for rational choice among these alternatives, would prefer more restaurants over more schools. The point is, the one kind of expenditure is not viewed as a sacrifice of any kind; the other is. The one kind of expenditure is viewed as productive; the other is not.

The tendency of the society to offer relatively great resistance to allocating its resources to foreign affairs is exacerbated by still another set of attitudes. This complex is—to borrow an additional expression of the economist—the high "time preference" of the citizen, his preference for immediate satisfactions over later satisfactions. Yet foreign policy can usually promise only long-run returns, and rather indefinite returns in the bargain. Thus it is easier for policy-makers to secure approval in the society for expenditure of resources on projects promising immediate, visible, and directly consumable returns than on projects promising only long-run, invisible, and jointly consumed benefits.

Because of these three preferences—for concrete benefits as

against the less visible, for individual as against collective consumption, for immediate as against later satisfactions—at any given moment it usually appears to be politically profitable for leadership to economize on the allocation of resources to foreign policy, and by resources here I mean not only economic but human. No more dramatic confirmation of this was ever offered than the one-vote majority in the House for a continuation of selective service during a period of world-wide war into which, not long after, we were to enter.

The difficulty of securing collective sacrifice is in the final analysis unavoidable in a political system where leadership is produced by relatively open competition for public support, that is, in a democracy. Obviously, totalitarian systems may do a good deal more in the way of imposing collective sacrifice, not only because the leadership is much less dependent on public attitudes, but also because the State has a near monopoly of techniques for manipulating those attitudes.

The third major reason why the optimum allocation of resources is unattainable in foreign policy stems from certain characteristics of the democratic political process, particularly as it operates in the United States. In the absence of clear majorities, decisive mandates, and responsible parties, policy is a product of a process of bargaining and compromise. One of the consequences of bargaining and compromise may be ambiguity. Policy may lack the clarity and decisiveness necessary to the occasion precisely because a clear and unambiguous policy would stir up opposition that needs to be placated; yet the very lack of clarity and decisiveness may in the long run prove costly.

A recent instance is the North Atlantic Pact, which during its negotiation created on the floor of the Senate a measure of concern over whether Congress was to be asked to give up its war-making power. In the debate on this point, and under pressure from the more "isolationist" members of the Senate, Senators Connally and Vandenberg were forced to make a number of concessions indicating that this country was in no sense committed to war in the event of Soviet aggression in western Europe.[3] In sum, the statements of Connally and Vandenberg, literally construed, almost nullified the sense of the Pact. In a desire to placate opposition, the Senators converted a relatively clear obligation into a slightly ambiguous one, and as a result the Pact may have lost some of its effect.

This kind of difficulty can only be mitigated by party responsibility, and particularly by the definition of areas of genuine rather than specious agreement. Even so, it would be over-optimistic to assume that the difficulty can be entirely eliminated.

Secrecy versus Publicity

The demand for "open covenants openly arrived at" is one of those slogans of the Wilson period stemming from an enthusiasm for "democratizing" the conduct of foreign policy. A domestic political system resting on the premise that the electorate should decide its own destinies would not, it was argued, live at peace with an international system under which the nation's future was in practice decided by a small group of leaders. That in some countries these leaders were elected by the people was not regarded as sufficient protection against betrayal. International negotiations, it seemed to follow, must be conducted in the full light of day with full opportunity for public debate and discussion.

Subsequent experience has shown this viewpoint to be resting on a serious misapprehension. Full publicity given to the *process of negotiation* itself may be much more of a hindrance to rationality than a guarantee of responsibility. Only a policy of complete intransigence is likely to succeed under the spotlight of public discussion; bargaining becomes almost impossible, for any sign of it is interpreted at home as weakness. Every concession is another Munich. If leadership proposes a bargaining point and gives way to achieve its real aims, abroad and at home it has lost face. Because this is true on all sides of the table, unless the parties discover that they agree at the outset, agreement is almost impossible to obtain. Thus almost the whole point of international negotiation is lost.

To argue that the process of negotiation itself requires full publicity is to argue, in effect, that public opinion must be consulted at every step in foreign policy, even when intricate questions of detail are involved. This argument misses the essential point, which is that the bargaining conference ought to be subsidiary to basic policy. And it is this latter, not the process of negotiation, that ought to be set by open and public debate. If negotiations are merely a part of the process of implementing basic policy, what is vital from the standpoint of values in a democratic order is the method by which the *basic* policy is arrived at.

In point of fact, Congress has largely come to recognize this distinction, particularly since the early postwar meetings of the Council of Foreign Ministers, which were attended by the fullest publicity about daily discussions, turned into little more than set speech-making for international and home consumption.

I am not arguing that negotiations should *necessarily* be secret. All other things being equal, doubtless the advantages of public understanding would throw the balance on the side of public negotiations. But all other things rarely are equal in contemporary international politics; the confidential negotiation may, on occasion, have the clear advantage of leaving the way open for effective bargaining. Under such circumstances it is folly to insist on publicity.

There are, then, two general sets of conditions under which secrecy in negotiations ought to be permissible. These are: first, when basic policy has already been established by public debate and discussion, and second, when the *results* of the negotiations must subsequently be debated and confirmed by some kind of public action. In either case it is difficult to over-estimate the importance of Congressional collaboration both in negotiations and in the decision of the basic policy itself. For if Congressional participation in deciding the basic policy pro-vides some guarantee of open debate on that policy, Congres-sional participation in the negotiations increases the likelihood that secrecy will not be taken as a cloak for policy decisions that have not borne or will not bear the full light of public discussion.

But the distinction between public debate over basic policy and secrecy in negotiations by no means disposes of the whole problem of secrecy. For there are times when *the very fact of public discussion might jeopardize a proposed policy.*

Two kinds of situations come to mind. There are, first of all, situations in which the fact of public discussion would of itself endanger the domestic or international position of one of the parties. A notable instance occurred in our relations with the Tito dictatorship after its break with Moscow in 1948. It is altogether possible that at that time the most effective method of exploiting this breach, assuming this as a desirable policy objective, required some measure of economic aid to the Tito forces. To have decided on such a policy by public debate and discussion might well have forced Tito to reject assistance from a "capitalist-imperialist power."

Assuming for a moment that the case is a sound one, here is a clear conflict between the requirements of rational policy-making and the usual techniques for enforcing responsibility in a democratic order. But it is precisely this kind of problem for which the structure of decision-making outlined earlier is designed. For what is needed is a structure where competence, confidence, and power are appropriately distributed to each level in the policy process. It is doubtful if this need can be reconciled with the American political process except by linking the policy specialists on Congressional committees with the policy-makers in the executive-administrative, and through bipartisan consultation. Under these conditions, if there were broad consensus favorable to the objective, the difficulties of executing the policy would be minimized; if there were not a widespread favorable consensus, the policy ought not, and probably could not, be carried on.

Second, there are circumstances in which the element of surprise is indispensable to the success of the policy. Yet public debate of the proposed action will automatically exclude the possibility of surprise. The decision to go to war may be, under modern conditions, a case of this kind. So potentially important is the element of surprise in a future atomic war that to close off this possibility to ourselves may prove to be a serious handicap, doubly so, because it is unlikely that any enemy we may have will be correspondingly bound by moral inhibition and political institutions. Yet no solution to this dilemma will allow us to possess the best of both worlds, except the arrangement suggested earlier: namely, a Congressional delegation of the *de facto* power to declare war, by legislation permitting the President in consultation with Congressional leadership in certain defined circumstances to begin the military phases without a formal war declaration.

The Problem of Action in a Mass Democracy

Many of the problems referred to here are either caused or accentuated by the conjuncture of two present-day aspects of American society: the enormous increase in the impact of foreign policies on the preferences of many groups and the fact that decisions of foreign policy take place in the social and political milieu of mass democracy.

Mass democracy has a twofold meaning for foreign policy. First, an extraordinarily broad range of groups and strata in society insist upon a consideration of their claims and interests in the making of public policy. Second, and as a result, policy-makers must reckon on the possible effects of a policy decision on all or nearly all strata in the society. By contrast, under nineteenth-century European regimes, both democratic and nondemocratic, foreign policy decisions were made by a relatively small and often quite homogeneous elite with a relatively clear conception of the set of preferences they wished to satisfy and a relatively rational understanding of how to satisfy those preferences in international politics.[4] In the United States, to be sure, foreign policy played a weighty role in public policy during the early years of the republic. But mass democracy is more nearly a phenomenon that dates from about Jackson's day. What is substantially novel in this century is the conjuncture of a post-Jacksonian mass democracy with a tremendous growth in the importance and inclusiveness of foreign policy decisions.

Two problems of fundamental importance flow out of this conjuncture of forces. One is the problem of rationality. It is one thing to formulate and pursue a policy rationally adapted to one's preferences in a democratic or nondemocratic regime where decisions are in fact made by a relatively small and carefully recruited elite with a rather clear comprehension of its goals and the techniques available to it. It is quite another, as many pages of this book have been devoted to showing, to formulate and pursue a rational policy in a society where decisions are arrived at as a result of bargaining among a great variety of different groups, many of whom little comprehend the real world of international politics and, even less, the technical means by which their preferences may best be satisfied in such a world.

The other problem is that of agreement, or to put it in terms of its obverse, the problem of disunity. The importance of unity as a power factor in international politics may be summarized rather abstractly thus:

1. Unity (agreement on means and ends within a society) makes possible:

- (a) full mobilization of the nation in behalf of the policy agreed on, i.e., fuller exploitation of the power-potential of the nation; and
- (b) perseverance and tenacity in policy, i.e., persistent exploitation of the nation's power-potential.

2. Disunity (disagreement on means and ends within a society) results in:

- (a) conflict and compromise, hence only partial mobilization in behalf of prevailing policy, i.e., less than full exploitation of the nation's power-potential; and
- (b) the ever present possibility of a change in prevailing policy if an existing minority becomes a majority, hence the expectation by foreign powers that existing policy may not be persisted in, hence less than full exploitation of the nation's power-potential.

Now the problem of unity is partly a problem of rationality. That is to say, a part of the disagreement (disunity) within society stems from differences over means to ends on which there is agreement. And this kind of disagreement over *means* is often not resolved, because existing scientific knowledge is incomplete and no prediction of high validity can be made about different means, or because existing scientific knowledge is inadequately disseminated or employed, or because political arrangements inhibit the search for agreement.

But partly, the two problems of rationality and unity are separate. Some differences undoubtedly stem from fundamental disagreements over rather basic preferences and attitudes, as, for example, differences over the moral appropriateness of violence as a technique for resolving disputes. In such a case, rationality will, if anything, exacerbate the disagreement; for rational inferences from conflicting preferences may well push the parties into even wider disagreement over the means to be employed by the society in conducting foreign policy.

The existence of some disagreement over ends and means is probably irremovable in modern society, given the existing state of the social sciences on the one hand and the diversity of human personalities on the other. And it is perhaps too much to expect that mass democracy in an epoch of continual crisis will ever achieve the highest level of rationality, whatever that might be. It is therefore important to review the alternative political solutions available to us.

One theoretical alternative is a return to an elite system of decision-making less influenced by mass wants and attitudes. Such a system, obviously, would run counter to the fundamental goals set forth as criteria at the beginning of this book. What is more, such a system probably may be ruled out as a relevant alternative in the modern world. For if anything seems clear, it is that the old-fashioned kind of elite rule is impossible in an age of total war. Total war implies an extraordinarily broad distribution of sacrifice. Leadership, whether democratic or dictatorial, must be mass-oriented in order to evoke the loyalty and discipline necessary for the society to carry through under the severe trials of a war that is experienced in every stratum of the nation. Realistically speaking, then, there are really only three alternatives.

The first is a frank dictatorship of the modern type: one based upon mass support and employing every technique of manipulating attitudes and personalities of the mass so as to achieve a society unified around a small range of common purposes, including war. *Provided it has leadership of a high degree of rationality* (as with the Politburo, for example) the dictatorship is a formidable enemy in international politics. For it then combines with its relatively high competence in selecting means a large measure of unity over ends and a very considerable capacity for intensive mobilization in behalf of a given policy.

The second alternative is a "democratic" regime with extensive executive discretion. One thinks here of the Weimar Republic in its final stages, of the proposals of General de Gaulle's followers for reforming the constitution of the Fourth Republic, and so on. In the United States, this solution would imply the broadest sort of presidential control over foreign policy.

The third alternative is a democratic regime under which executive policy rests upon the confidence of the legislative branch. In the United States this would imply a high degree of collaboration between executive and Congress in the formulation and conduct of foreign policy.

It is the recurrent theme of this book that the second of these alternatives—presidential supremacy—inevitably runs afoul of a number of difficulties that are eliminated or mitigated by executive-Congressional collaboration. And to the extent that the executive is capable of solving its problems without accepting Congressional collaboration, it must inescapably become more and more the democratic shadow of that first grim alternative.

Notes

CHAPTER I

1. L. E. Gleeck, who studied rather carefully the influences on ninety-six Congressmen during the special 1939 session to repeal the arms embargo, asks: "Even without quibbling, can it be said that the Congressman really *knows* what factors have determined his vote? . . . it was difficult for them [the Congressmen] to state precisely, without benefit of rhetoric, the part played by the various factors that influenced their decisions." ("96 Congressmen Make Up Their Minds," *Public Opinion Quarterly*, March 1940, p. 7.)

2. Perhaps the most thorough examination of the relationship between these factors and political behavior is to be found in the works of Harold Lasswell, particularly *Power and Personality* (Norton, 1948).

3. Committee on Public Administration Cases, *The Foreign Service Act of 1946*, Washington, D. C. (mimeo.), 1949, p. 112.

4. Paul H. Douglas, "Report from a Freshman Senator," New York *Times Magazine*, March 20, 1949, p. 74.

5. Gleeck, *loc. cit.* The importance of the symbol of "independence" to the Congressman is confirmed by my own interviews. I was struck by the large number of Congressmen, of varying influence, who wished to emphasize that they had arrived at their decisions on the basis of their own "independent" judgment. Even party leaders tried to emphasize this quality in their own party—although not necessarily in the opposition. "Independence" is easily the most socially acceptable explanation of one's political decisions in the American milieu.

6. *Public Opinion*, Macmillan, 1930. This volume is still in many ways the best introduction to the problem of rationality in public policy-making.

7. Cf., however, Lasswell, *op. cit.*, chap. vi.

CHAPTER II

1. *The Memoirs of Cordell Hull*, Macmillan, 1948, I, 563.

2. *Speaking Frankly*, Harper, 1947, pp. 8-9.

3. *Congressional Record*, March 8, 1948, p. 2285.

4. Hull, *op. cit.*, I, 650. Although there has been some question about the story, it is corroborated by Alben W. Barkley, a witness to the statement, in

"President *and*—Not *vs.*—Congress," New York *Times Magazine*, June 20, 1948, p. 26.

5. No implications are intended at this point about individual responsibility versus party responsibility. The statement holds under either view of responsibility, although techniques for enforcing responsibility would differ.

6. These assumptions are not quite the same as either Professor Schumpeter's "classical doctrine of democracy" or his "new theory of democracy," although the theory as stated here seems to me to be more nearly in accord with reality than his. See J. A. Schumpeter, *Capitalism, Socialism, and Democracy*, 2d ed., Harper, 1947, chaps. xxi-xxii.

7. *Organization of Congress: Hearings before the Joint Committee*, 79th Cong., 1st sess., p. 281. See also Rep. Ramspeck's testimony on the same point, p. 295. The Legislative Reorganization Act of 1946 provided for adjournment by the end of July. In 1948 a special session was called. In 1949 the session ran, despite the Act, through the summer and early fall.

8. Gleeck, "96 Congressmen Make Up Their Minds," pp. 14-15.

9. The American Institute of Public Opinion (AIPO), Nov. 2, 1939. An AIPO poll with slightly different wording reported on Oct. 22, 1939 that 60 per cent of the sample favored repeal and 40 per cent opposed it.

10. Rowena Wyant, "Voting Via the Senate Mailbag," *Public Opinion Quarterly*, Fall 1941, pp. 359-82, and Winter 1941, pp. 590-624. See especially pp. 360, 372-73.

11. American Institute of Public Opinion, Sept. 24, 1949. To the question, "Have you ever written or wired your Congressman or Senator in Washington?" the response was:

	Yes	No
By occupation		
Prof. and business	33%	67%
White collar	20	80
Farmers	17	83
Manual workers	12	88
By education		
College	39	61
High school	21	79
Grammar school	11	89

12. On Congressional attitudes toward mail on neutrality legislation, see Gleeck, *loc. cit.*, p. 14. For one Congressman's general attitude toward letter-writers, see Jerry Voorhis, *Confessions of a Congressman*, Doubleday, 1948, chap. v.

13. These figures may be compared with the results of a mail questionnaire in 1940 to all U.S. Senators and two hundred Representatives, to which thirty-three Senators and eighty-four Representatives replied. To the question, "Do the results of public opinion polls aid you in deciding upon the desires of your constituents?" 71 per cent replied "no." When, however,

the question was changed to read, "Do you think public opinion polls aid other men in public life in deciding their policies about or stands on various subjects or issues?" the results changed significantly. Only 21 per cent denied that *others* were influenced by polls. (George F. Lewis, Jr., "The Congressmen Look at the Polls," *Public Opinion Quarterly*, June 1940, pp. 229-31.)

Some further indirect light is thrown on the influence of polls by responses of fifty-eight New York State legislators to a mail questionnaire in 1942. They were asked: "When circumstances prevent you from making an independent analysis of some issue that does not directly affect the welfare of your constituents, do you vote the way the majority of the public voted in the sample poll?" Seven per cent replied "always," and 70 per cent said "frequently." (G. W. Hartmann, "Judgments of State Legislators Concerning Public Opinion," *Journal of Social Psychology*, February 1945, pp. 105-14.)

14. For Congressional attitudes on accuracy of polls see Martin Kriesberg, "What Congressmen and Administrators Think of the Polls," *Public Opinion Quarterly*, Fall 1945, pp. 333-57.

15. Leonard W. Doob, *Public Opinion and Propaganda*, Holt, 1948, p. 51.

16. *Ibid.*, pp. 153-56.

17. Among other reasons, the practice of electing Senators by State legislatures was doubtless influential; legislatures frequently gave rather specific injunctions to their Senators. Allen Johnson has an interesting and amusing account of how Stephen Douglas once carried out the letter, if not quite the spirit, of instructions from the legislature of Illinois, with which he disagreed. (*Stephen A. Douglas: A Study in American Politics*, Macmillan, 1908, p. 140.)

18. The replies of fifty-eight New York State legislators are probably not too dissimilar from those of Congressmen. When asked, "Do you consider it your public duty as a 'representative' to reflect in official voting whatever preponderant sentiment your district displays on every issue, even if this is contrary to your personal conception of community welfare?" only 39 per cent replied "yes," and 57 per cent answered "no." (Hartmann, *loc. cit.*)

CHAPTER III

1. Cf. James M. Burns, *Congress on Trial*, Harper, 1949, chaps. ii and iii.

2. This is of course an arbitrary criterion, but given American party organization almost any other criterion is equally so. If one were to take as the criterion the way in which two-thirds or more of the party members voted, or the position taken in Congressional debates by party leaders, the results on these issues would be almost identical with those given.

3. This quotation is drawn, as is all other information in this section, from interviews with Congressmen and Congressional employees.

4. *The Autobiography of Sol Bloom*, Putnam, 1948, p. 130.

5. Hull, *Memoirs*, I, 389. Repetition of this technique today might be less successful. Congressmen are perhaps more suspicious of such campaigns.

CHAPTER IV

1. Wilfred E. Binkley, *President and Congress*, Knopf, 1947. Roy Franklin Nichols has recently documented in detail some of the fateful consequences of Buchanan's incapacity. Cf. *The Disruption of American Democracy*, Macmillan, 1948.

2. Cf. Blair Bolles, "President, Congress, and Foreign Policy," *American Perspective*, March 1949.

3. Cf. Tables, Appendix B. Edward S. Corwin lists the discretionary actions of the President leading up to World War II in *The President: Office and Powers* (rev. 3d ed., New York University Press, 1948, pp. 246-48).

4. When, as has been recounted earlier, Representative Ludlow of Indiana obtained the necessary signatures (218) on his petition to discharge the Judiciary Committee from consideration of his proposed constitutional amendment for a war referendum, the Administration leapt into action. According to Secretary Hull, "Postmaster General James A. Farley, who was also chairman of the Democratic National Committee, personally telephoned all the Democratic Members of the House who were available at the other end of the telephone, to enlist their support." (*Memoirs*, I, 564.)

CHAPTER V

1. The public opinion data in this discussion are from *American Opinion on World Affairs in the Atomic Age*, Leonard S. Cottrell, Jr., and Sylvia Eberhart, Princeton University Press, 1948. See also *Public Reaction to the Atomic Bomb and World Affairs*, Cornell University (mimeo.), April 1947.

2. Cottrell and Eberhart, *op. cit.*, p. 14.

3. Harold Lasswell, *World Politics and Personal Insecurity*, McGraw-Hill, 1935, esp. pp. 75, 246, 247.

4. At the 1948 Republican Convention, Senator Henry Cabot Lodge, Jr., chairman of the subcommitee to draft the Republican platform, candidly declared that the party's 1948 platform was "broad enough for all Republicans—or all Americans for that matter—to stand on." (New York *Herald Tribune*, June 21, 1948, p. 1.)

Of the 1940 Democratic plank on foreign policy, which pledged aid to the democracies but no participation in "foreign" wars, "except in case of attack," Anne O'Hare McCormick reported in the New York *Times*, "The Roosevelt supporters will now be satisfied, it is said, with a generalized declaration that will enable the head of the ticket to interpret it as he pleases or as circumstances dictate. . . ." (Quoted in Charles A. Beard, *American Foreign Policy in the Making, 1932-1940*, Yale University Press, 1946, p. 289.)

5. New York *Herald Tribune,* Sept. 22, 1948, p. 19.

6. For the basic data from which these percentages were computed, I am indebted to Joseph A. Kilbourn, who prepared a senior essay on this subject in Yale College in 1949.

7. Thus on public opinion polls, people will often respond favorably to a generalized proposal for action, but will oppose a specific and concrete step to implement it. The second, unlike the first, better indicates the sacrifices. In an American Institute of Public Opinion poll released July 1947, when asked, "Would you favor or oppose giving European countries credit of about $5 billion a year so that they could buy the things they need in this country?" of the 49% of the sample who had heard of the Marshall Plan, 55% responded favorably and only 35% unfavorably. But when asked, "Would you be willing to pay more taxes, if necessary, to raise this money?" only 41% of the same group replied in the affirmative and 50% replied "no." See also the comments in Cottrell and Eberhart, *op. cit.,* p. 54.

8. *Human Nature and Conduct,* Holt, 1922, p. 262. An excellent statement of the means-end relation and its bearing on rational behavior in the field of administration is contained in Herbert Simon, *Administrative Behavior* (Macmillan, 1947).

9. The figures are Senator Langer's. *Congressional Record,* June 15, 1948, pp. 8320, 8316.

10. Charles Beard has assembled portions of many of the speeches and documents in his *American Foreign Policy in the Making.* A second line of argument that later became popular turned on the question, *"But if war comes?"*—with both groups predicting advantages for their policies.

11. *Congressional Record,* June 4, 1948, pp. 7168-70. The same argument was employed by Representative Wigglesworth a few minutes later, pp. 7172-73.

12. *Ibid.,* June 15, 1948, p. 8318.

13. Even so, questions of "fact" subject to empirical verification by relatively advanced scientific techniques can become "politicized" and subject to dispute. Thus in 1944, western governors and the Bureau of Reclamation in the upper Missouri Valley disagreed vociferously and publicly with Army engineers over the question of whether a deepening of the Missouri River channel from six to nine feet from Sioux City to St. Louis would, or would not, significantly reduce the water available to upstream farmers. Cf. the article on the Missouri Basin by Robert W. Glasgow, New York *Herald Tribune,* Aug. 22, 1949, p. 2.

14. *Congressional Record,* June 15, 1948, pp. 8308-9.

15. *Science News Letter,* Nov. 11, 1949, p. 317. It is only fair to say that these social scientists were not necessarily "experts" in international politics. But even so, they constituted, on the whole, a much better informed group than the general public, and all other things being equal, one would have expected a better performance.

CHAPTER VI

1. A case in point occurred when leading government economists, who had been steeped in the atmosphere of depression economy and who were influenced by the slow rate of conversion from peace to war, failed to predict the rapid postwar transition to full employment and inflation.

2. Karl Mannheim, *Diagnosis of our Time*, London, 1943, pp. 3-5.

3. Cf. Hannah Arendt's analysis, "The Concentration Camps," *Partisan Review*, July 1948.

4. Paul F. Lazarsfeld, Bernard Berelson, and Hazel Gaudet, *The People's Choice*, Columbia University Press, 1948, Preface to the Second Edition.

5. This is not the place to compare the relative success of that program with the failure (in the opinion of this writer) of the discussion and "orientation" program in the American Army. Several factors may be mentioned: (1) Immediate, often highly personalized events made British soldiers and leadership aware of the crisis they were facing; most Americans were psychologically isolated from the political and social meaning of the crisis. (2) The discussion system was adopted and ordered in the American Army late in the war. (3) The program was rarely taken seriously by the leadership. (4) The discussions were normally under the control of the unit leaders who were (a) ill-trained in discussion, and (b) endowed with an authority irrelevant to the discussion but influential in suppressing spontaneity. (5) The emphasis, whether intended or not, was "orientation" in a coercive sense; American soldiers, already highly sensitized by the unfamiliar coercions of military life, were suspicious that the program was one more attempt at coercion, this time by "propaganda." These are, I believe, difficulties highly relevant to the problem of stimulating citizen discussion groups.

For a recent but somewhat limited critique, see *Information and Education in the Armed Forces*, a Report to the President by the President's Committee on Religion and Welfare in the Armed Forces, Washington, D. C. (mimeo.), Dec. 1, 1949.

6. David Riesman, "Government Education for Democracy," *Public Opinion Quarterly*, June 1941, p. 204.

7. A notable exception is Robert S. Lynd, *Knowledge for What? The Place of Social Science in American Culture*, Princeton University Press, 1939.

For the view of a Swedish social scientist, see Gunnar Myrdal, *An American Dilemma*, Harper, 1944, Vol. II, Appendix 2, "A Methodological Note on Facts and Valuations in Social Science."

And cf. Edward Shils, *The Present State of American Sociology*, Free Press, 1948.

CHAPTER VII

1. Joseph Barthélemy, *Démocratie et politique étrangère*, Paris, 1917, p. 141.

2. Woodrow Wilson, *Constitutional Government in the United States*, Columbia University Press, 1908, pp. 77-78. For his remarkably prescient prescription of how he could have later dealt with the Senate, but did not, see pp. 139-40.

3. The case for executive supremacy in foreign affairs, and even downright deceit of the electorate where the President regards this as necessary to national survival, has recently been set forth by Thomas A. Bailey, in *The Man in the Street* (Macmillan, 1948). Cf. the criticisms of his viewpoint in the symposium "Can American Foreign Policy be Democratic?", by Bertrand Russell, Mulford Q. Sibley, Nathaniel Peffer, Max Kampelman and C. Hartley Grattan, in *American Perspective*, September 1948. Cf. also Professor Bailey's rejoinder, "The Dilemma of Democracy," *American Perspective*, October 1948.

4. Samuel Flagg Bemis, *A Diplomatic History of the United States*, 2d ed., Holt, 1942, p. 229.

5. One of these, Henry L. Stimson, later regarded his support for Harding as "a blunder." He had signed the Statement of Thirty-one Republicans urging Harding's election as the best way into the League. "Events soon proved that these men were deceived and their hopes unfounded."—Henry L. Stimson and McGeorge Bundy, *On Active Service in Peace and War*, Harper, 1948, p. 105.

6. Robert Sherwood writes: "Of all the political battles in which he had been involved, this campaign of 1940 is, I believe, the one that Roosevelt liked least to remember. It was no clean-cut issue between two philosophies or ideologies, nor even between two contrasted personalities. It had the atmosphere of a dreadful masquerade, in which the principal contestants felt compelled to wear false faces, and thereby disguised the fact that, in their hearts, they agreed with one another on all the basic issues."—*Roosevelt and Hopkins*, Harper, 1948, p. 200. Cf. also pp. 189, 190-91.

7. *Memoirs*, I, 194.

CHAPTER VIII

1. William L. Neumann, "How to Merchandise Foreign Policy," *American Perspective*, September and October, 1949, pp. 183-93, 235-50. See also Homer Bigart, "State Department's News Policy," New York *Herald Tribune*, Jan. 10, 1950, p. 22.

2. Witness the following encomiums by Democratic and Republican members of the House Appropriations Subcommittee:

"Mr. O'BRIEN. Mr. Chairman, I should like to say for Mrs. Shipley [Chief of the Passport Division] that she is the most accommodating person, man or woman, in Government service, has been certainly to Members of Congress; and I am willing to vote anything Mrs. Shipley says she needs for her office.

"Mr. STEFAN. I think we all agree with Mr. O'Brien's comment concerning Mrs. Shipley."

(*Department of State Appropriation Bill for 1949: Hearings before the Subcommittee of the Committee on Appropriations*, House of Representatives, 80th Cong., 2d sess., pp. 155-56.)

3. Representative Karl Stefan, chairman of the House Appropriations Subcommittee on the State Department, stated in the 1948 hearings: "In my forty-five-odd years of traveling around the world, I have had the pleasure of meeting a great many of our employees who represent the Government in various capacities, especially Foreign Service officers. . . . it is a great inspiration to get into a little bit of American land in foreign countries, and there meet an American who has his finger on the pulse of the country in which he is serving us as our representative. . . . To see these Americans typify America, the American way of life, and transmit it to these foreign people was a great inspiration to me." (*Dept. of State Approp. Bill for 1949, Hearings*, pp. 314-15.) Representative Stefan's enthusiasm did not, however, prevent a cut in the Foreign Service appropriation for that year.

4. Congressman Ramspeck, at that time majority whip in the House, testified in 1945 on the basis of his intimate observation of Congress since 1911: ". . . actually the executive branch of the Government has come to wield more and more influence over the legislative branch, because we have undertaken to do things for our constituents which put us under obligation to the executive branch of the Government. It is fine to talk about not being influenced by those sorts of things, but if you go down to a department and get them to do something for one of your constituents and then they come back up here on an appropriation, human nature being what it is, there is going to be an influence there passing back and forth. . . . I have seen it happen many, many times in my experience here, and I know it does happen all the time." (*Organization of Congress: Hearings before the Joint Committee*, 79th Cong., 1st sess., p. 297.)

5. Conversation with the writer. For evidence of a contrary view, see Representative Stefan's comments, footnote 3; and the remarks on the Foreign Service, pp. 112 ff.

6. Committee on Public Administration Cases, *The Foreign Service Act of 1946*, pp. 112-13.

7. Thus in connection with the Foreign Service Act of 1946, Mr. Vorys, the chairman of the Congressional subcommittee, asked if the Board of Foreign Service Examiners "were not the cornerstone of the whole Foreign Service personnel system, and was told [by members of the Foreign Service] that it was. On learning this, he said, 'put it in the book,' [i.e., the statute] and the others agreed." Yet the Bureau of the Budget had serious doubts that the board should be given statutory status, and would have challenged the statement that it was in any sense the "cornerstone" of the system. (*Ibid.*, p. 112.)

8. William L. Neumann (*loc. cit.*) gives a critical evaluation of the De-

partment's use of various "sales techniques" in selling Congress on Administration foreign policy in the postwar years.

9. For a discussion of some of the social and political consequences of a "disproportionate development of human faculties," see Karl Mannheim, *Man and Society in an Age of Reconstruction*, London, 1940, p. 42.

10. Both as a member of the administrative branch and as an outside observer, the author has been impressed time and again by the extent to which conscientious and socially minded experts can develop unconscious hostilities to democratic politics as a result of their experience in the administrative branch. Deeply devoted to democracy at the verbal level, after a few years in the administrative branch they come to distrust the political processes of democracy and particularly the legislative process, because of the unremitting threat offered by "politics" to the prosecution of "right" policies allegedly beneficial to the electorate.

CHAPTER IX

1. Byrnes, *Speaking Frankly*, p. 239.

2. The average age of its members is also high. "In 1944, for example, the average age of United States Senators was 59, and the median age of Representatives was 52, while the average adult was only 43 years old." (George B. Galloway, *Congress at the Crossroads*, Crowell, 1946, p. 28.)

3. See the colloquy on the Standing Rules of the Senate in *Evaluation of Legislative Reorganization Act of 1946: Hearings before the Committee on Expenditures in the Executive Departments*, Senate, 80th Cong., 2d sess., pp. 52-53.

4. Voorhis, *Confessions of a Congressman*, pp. 31-32.

5. *Eval. of Leg. Reorg. Act of 1946, Hearings*, pp. 171-72.

6. For these quotations see *Organization of Congress: Hearings before the Joint Committee*, 79th Cong., 1st sess., pp. 25, 297-98, 340, 58.

7. Cf. Galloway, *op. cit.*, Table III, p. 348, for data on the 54th and 79th Congresses; Madge M. McKinney, "The Personnel of the Seventy-seventh Congress," *American Political Science Review*, February 1942, p. 67; *New Leader*, May 7, 1949, p. 7, for data on the 81st Congress.

8. A case in point is the speech by Senator Donnell, a lawyer, on the North Atlantic Pact, *Congressional Record* (daily edition), July 7, 1949, pp. 9211-20.

9. A point emphasized recently by Bertrand de Jouvenel, *Problèmes de L'Angleterre Socialiste*, Paris, 1947.

10. *Org. of Congress, Hearings*, pp. 33, 286, 157, 114, 118, 426.

11. Gleeck, "96 Congressmen Make Up Their Minds," p. 6. For a recollection of the doubts and hesitations of one Congressman, see Voorhis, *op. cit.*, pp. 235-39. Voorhis said to the House at that time: "Were I to have to cast these votes again [on the arms embargo and the Neutrality Act of 1939] I know I should have to go through the same inward struggles all

over again. All I do know is that there is nothing I seek so much as a clear and certain answer to the question: What ought a member of the House of Representatives to do to protect the peace of his own country and to promote the peace of the world?" (p. 236).

CHAPTER X

1. Willmoore Kendall has argued this point with great cogency in his article, "The Majority Principle and the Scientific Elite," *Southern Review,* Winter 1939, pp. 463-73.

2. It is highly significant that some careful students of the British Parliament have come to the same conclusion about the House of Commons, where standing committees with more or less fixed membership have not been regarded with favor. Thus W. Ivor Jennings, after arguing the need for standing committees, writes:

"But standing committees will not be effective unless they are capable of acting as committees. This implies a limited membership. Committees of more than twenty members are rarely efficient. The maximum should certainly be thirty, and the quorum ten. . . . Indeed, if it is possible so to arrange, it is desirable that other expert opinions may be obtained in order that the committee may decide between the experts in the same way as a court of justice or a private Bill committee. Moreover, the committee must be as specialist in character as a committee of members of Parliament can ever be. One of the major defects of the present standing committees is that Bills are allocated to them, not in accordance with the knowledge of the members, but according to their relative freedom from other work (except in the case of Scottish Bills).

"The first reform, therefore, is to make the standing committees more expert in character. . . .

"It seems desirable, from the point of view of legislative procedure alone (other arguments will lead to the same conclusion), that each Department which legislates frequently should have a special standing committee."

(*Parliamentary Reform,* London, 1934, pp. 83-85.)

3. Statement of Representative Plumley, *Organization of Congress: Hearings before the Joint Committee,* 79th Cong., 1st sess., p. 340.

4. New York *Times,* Dec. 9, 1946. *Congressional Record,* Jan. 5, 1949, p. 62.

5. One long-standing and intimate observer of Congress—not a Congressman—observed to the writer that the Committee was sought by the socially ambitious, because membership gave social prerogatives and possibilities not available to most other House committees.

6. Albert Westphal, *The House Committee on Foreign Affairs,* Columbia University Press, 1942, pp. 102-3.

7. James Reston, New York *Times*, Mar. 10, 1949, p. 13.

8. Statement of Middleton Beaman, legislative counsel of the House, *Org. of Cong., Hearings*, p. 427.

Prof. Walton Hamilton later testified: "From my very inadequate experience, the thing that impresses me most in attending hearings is that the representative of the department knows intimately the subject which he is discussing and, if I may say so, I do not think that the Senators and the Congressmen are anything like as fully informed. This is not a question of ability. . . . Recently, I was present at a session in which a Senator was questioning the head of a department. There was no question whatsoever about the Senator's ability. There was no question about his devotion to the public interest, but he did not know fully the affairs of the department about which he was inquiring. The result was that the administrative officer, who was in an impossible position, managed to protect himself very nicely against all those thrusts." *Ibid.*, pp. 707-8.

9. I do not believe the argument of "duplication" is a serious one. If it were only a question of duplication in staffs, this would be a slight price to pay for a more competent Congress.

10. There is evidence that some of the committees have not known how to make use of their professional staffs. Cf., for example, the testimony of Congressman Monroney, *Evaluation of Legislative Reorganization Act of 1946: Hearings before the Committee on Expenditures in the Executive Departments*, Senate, 80th Cong., 2d sess., p. 84.

11. *Congressional Record*, Appendix, Feb. 3, 1949, pp. A505-7.

12. Committee on Public Administration, *The Foreign Service Act of 1946*. The quotation appears on p. 65. For the Hoover Commission reports, see The Commission on Organization of the Executive Branch of the Government, *Foreign Affairs: A Report to the Congress*, February 1949, Government Printing Office. Also *Task Force Report on Foreign Affairs* (Appendix H), prepared for The Commission on Organization of the Executive Branch of the Government, January 1949, Government Printing Office.

13. *Org. of Cong., Hearings*, pp. 445-46.

14. In *Public Opinion*, Walter Lippmann proposed an "intelligence bureau" for each Federal Department, substantially independent of both Congress and the executive, but with full access to information available in the departments. His objective was more nearly that of improving the Congressman's picture of reality than in giving him "policy advice" in the sense in which I have used the term. The proposals, nevertheless, are parallel.

15. Cf. Carl J. Friedrich, "Public Policy and the Nature of Administrative Responsibility," in *Public Policy*, ed. by C. J. Friedrich and Edward S. Mason, Harvard University Press, 1940, pp. 3ff. See also Herman Finer's attack on that position as a misreading of the nature of the democratic process, "Administrative Responsibility in Democratic Government," *Public Administration Review*, Summer 1941, p. 335. Both writers are, I think,

essentially right. But each is, in my view, concentrating on a different aspect of the problem—Friedrich on rationality, Finer on responsibility.

16. *Congressional Record*, June 24, 1949, p. 8298. Italics added.

17. It is all but incomprehensible that Congress has not even adopted such modern time-saving devices as the electrical recorder for roll calls and votes. George Galloway has calculated that in the 78th Congress, "had the halls of Congress been equipped with automatic voting devices, two calendar months would have been saved. . . ." *Congress at the Crossroads*, p. 80.

18. W. Ivor Jennings, *Parliament* (Macmillan, 1940, pp. 89-95) contains an excellent description of the Question Hour. For some observations on interpolations and questions in the Assembly of the Third Republic, and the significance of these for the conduct of foreign policy, cf. Joseph Barthélemy, *Démocratie et politique étrangère*, pp. 132-35.

19. *Org. of Cong., Hearings*, p. 78. Cf. Estes Kefauver and Jack Levin, *A Twentieth Century Congress*, Duell, Sloan and Pearce, 1947, chap. vi. George B. Galloway has proposed that the whole Question Hour proposal might well be dealt with on an experimental basis (*op. cit.*, p. 218).

20. *Org. of Cong., Hearings*, p. 960.

21. *Eval. of Leg. Reorg. Act of 1946, Hearings*, pp. 223-50.

CHAPTER XI

1. The predominance of the chairman is somewhat less characteristic of the Senate subcommittee.

2. *Department of State Appropriation Bill for 1949: Hearings before the Subcommittee of the Committee on Appropriations*, House of Representatives, 80th Cong., 2d sess., p. 10.

3. Most writers now agree on this point, although differing violently in their interpretation of its significance. Cf. Sherwood, *Roosevelt and Hopkins*, pp. 136-37, 174-76; *The Autobiography of Sol Bloom*, pp. 245-46; Hull, *Memoirs*, I, 177. Perhaps the most extreme statement is that of Bailey, *The Man in the Street*, p. 12. For an interpretation hostile to Roosevelt cf. Charles A. Beard, *President Roosevelt and the Coming of the War 1941*, Yale University Press, 1948.

4. Sherwood, *op. cit.*, p. 175.

5. *Ibid.*, p. 175.

6. *Ibid.*, p. 361.

7. Bailey, *op. cit.*, p. 13.

8. This point has been almost entirely missed by Joseph Barthélemy in *Le Problème de la Compétence dans la Démocratie* (Paris, 1918, cf. especially pp. 24-25).

9. In the same Congress, Representative John Rankin, a "Dixiecrat" during the preceding presidential campaign, was "punished" by his removal from the Un-American Affairs Committee. But he was allowed to retain his chairmanship of Veterans' Affairs, from which he subsequently launched sev-

eral pension bills of grave embarrassment to the Democrats and the Administration.

10. The parties, indeed, go to incredible lengths to exhaust all "objective" criteria for recruitment without having to resort to party loyalty as a test. The Republican conference in the Senate, for example, will consider the following factors, roughly in the order given: seniority, previous political stature, age, popular votes, professional qualifications. In 1948, Senator William Langer of North Dakota had precisely the same seniority as another contestant for the chairmanship of the Committee on Civil Service. Despite the fact that Senator Langer had long been a thorn in the flesh of the Republican Party because of his refusal to support the party program, any attempt to consider this factor was swept aside. He was made chairman because of his superior rating under the second criterion; he had been Governor of the State of North Dakota.

CHAPTER XII

1. Since these tables were compiled I have had an opportunity to read a dissertation by George L. Grasmuck, "Congressional Politics in Foreign Affairs," Johns Hopkins University. Grasmuck has made a detailed statistical analysis of Congressional voting on foreign policy, with particular attention to party, section, and type of issue. He also concludes that party is a highly important influence, particularly on some issues.

2. This was substantially true on eight other questions about foreign policy. Cf. F. W. Williams, "Regional Attitudes on International Cooperation," *Public Opinion Quarterly*, Spring 1945, pp. 38-50.

3. Lazarsfeld, Berelson, and Gaudet, *The People's Choice.* Cf. also the results of Elmo Roper's post-election studies of voting behavior, New York *Herald Tribune*, June 19, 1949, p. 1. These studies are based on an analysis of voting in every ward of seven large cities. Roper cites Boston as typical of the trend:

	1944 Rep.	1948 Rep.
Prosperous	57.4%	61.6%
Upper middle	50.4	45.4
Lower middle	35.4	27.3
Poor	32.2	7.3

4. Thus in answer to the question cited earlier whether the United States should take an active part in world affairs, an upper-income college graduate in any region in 1944 and 1945 was likely to have views much more nearly like those of upper-income college graduates in other regions, than those of lower-income grade school graduates in his own or any other region.

5. For the analysis in these paragraphs I am indebted to Professor E. E. Schattschneider. Cf. his "Outline of a Proposed Program for Party Responsi-

bility," a preliminary draft for discussion, prepared for the Committee on National Political Parties and Elections of the American Political Science Association (mimeo., 1948).

6. Cf. the study of Connecticut voting cited in chap. v, footnote 6.

7. *Task Force Report on Foreign Affairs* (Appendix H), prepared for The Commission on Organization of the Executive Branch of the Government, recommends a consultative organization "to counsel the Planning Adviser." Its purpose, however, is to provide expertness—not to state preferences. (Government Printing Office, January 1949, p. 27.)

8. In a recent volume, Paul Appleby has forcefully called attention to the importance of what he calls "the eighth political process," namely, direct mediation between citizens and administration. As he points out, however, the State Department and the defense establishments are relatively isolated from this kind of control. (*Policy and Administration*, University of Alabama Press, 1949, chap. ii, and pp. 91, 103.)

CHAPTER XIII

1. *Can Representative Government Do the Job?*, Reynal & Hitchcock, 1945.

2. Cf. Corwin, *The President: Office and Powers*, pp. 270-71.

3. For these details, see Hull, *Memoirs*, I, 214-15; II, 1312-14, 1657-98; Lawrence H. Chamberlain and Richard C. Snyder, *American Foreign Policy*, Rinehart, 1948, p. 113; Byrnes, *Speaking Frankly*, p. 234.

4. *Organization of Congress: Hearings before the Joint Committee*, 79th Cong., 1st sess., Part V, p. 1169.

5. *Legislative Problems*, Houghton Mifflin, 1935, p. 239.

6. Hull, *op. cit.*, I, 216.

7. Joseph and Stewart Alsop, "Chairman Vandenberg of the Senate Foreign Relations Committee" in Chamberlain and Snyder, *op. cit.*, p. 131.

8. *Org. of Cong., Hearings*, p. 509.

9. *Congressional Record*, June 11, 1948, p. 7800.

10. Joseph Alsop (New York *Herald Tribune*, May 23, 1949, p. 21) describes the principal actors in some detail.

11. *Congressional Record*, June 24, 1949, p. 8292.

12. *Ibid.*, p. 8293.

13. Instances are cited in W. Ivor Jennings, *Cabinet Government*, rev. ed., Cambridge University Press, 1950, pp. 461-63.

14. Quoted in Jennings, *op. cit.*, p. 444.

CHAPTER XIV

1. Some House members of the Foreign Affairs Committee wanted the President to employ the executive agreement with a joint Congrssional reso-

lution. He refused, insisting on a treaty. (New York *Herald Tribune*, Feb. 7, 1949, p. 1.)

2. New York *Times*, Aug. 18, 1948, p. 1; Aug. 19, 1948, p. 1.

3. Senator Vandenberg, New York *Herald Tribune*, Oct. 5, 1948, p. 8.

4. Senator Vandenberg, *Congressional Record*, June 24, 1949, p. 8294; Jan. 5, 1949, p. 61.

5. *Congressional Record* (daily edition), July 27, 1949, pp. 10462 ff.; Aug. 3, 1949, pp. 10872 ff. Technically the vote was on a ruling by the Vice President that the McClellan amendment was legislation on an appropriations measure, and therefore barred by the rules of the Senate. A direct vote on the question itself might have considerably increasd the vote for the amendment.

CHAPTER XV

1. Cf. Appleby, *Policy and Administration*, p. 62.

2. Quoted in Beard, *President Roosevelt and the Coming of the War 1941*, p. 519.

3. *Congressional Record*, Feb. 14, 1949, pp. 1164-69. Among others, Senator Connally, speaking as chairman of the Senate Foreign Relations Committee, stated, "I certainly would not desire the adoption of any language which would morally commit us to fight." And later, "Of course we are interested in the peace of the world. But that does not mean that we shall blindfold ourselves and make a commitment now to enter every war that may occur in the next 10 years, and send our boys and resources to Europe to fight." "I do not believe in giving carte blanche assurance to these people, 'Do everything you want to do, you need not worry, as soon as anything happens, we will come over and fight your quarrel for you. In the meantime you may have a good time, and bask in the sunshine of leadership which you do not deserve.'" These words, produced under the skillful prodding of Senator Donnell of Missouri, a neo-isolationist, presumably referred to people with whom the State Department was then negotiating as our future allies.

4. Karl Polanyi has effectively demonstrated this point in *The Great Transformation* (Rinehart, 1944, chap. i, "The Hundred Years' Peace").

Appendix A

TABLE XII

PUBLIC OPINION AND CONGRESSIONAL VOTING *

ISSUE AND YEAR	PUBLIC OPINION POLLS				CONGRESSIONAL VOTES	
	% of the Total Sample			% of Those with Opinions	% of House	% of Senate
	For	Vs.	Not informed, no opinion, or "don't know"	For	For	For
Reciprocal Trade Program †						
1937...............	48	27	25	64	74	71
1940...............	27	20	53	57	57	52
1945...............	61	8	31	88	63	72
Strict Neutrality Law rather than Presidential Discretion						
1937...............	65	30	5	68	97	91
Repeal of Arms Embargo						
June-July 1939......	—	—	—	—	45	No vote
Sept. 1939.........	42.5	42.5	15	50	—	—
Oct. 1939..........	52	39	9	57	58	63
Allow American Ships to Enter War Zones						
Dec. 1940..........	34	52	14	40	—	—
Sept. 1941..........	46	40	14	53	—	—
Nov. 1941..........	—	—	—	—	52	57

TABLE XII (*Continued*)

PUBLIC OPINION AND CONGRESSIONAL VOTING *

ISSUE AND YEAR	PUBLIC OPINION POLLS				CONGRESSIONAL VOTES	
	% of the Total Sample			% of Those with Opinions	% of House	% of Senate
	For	Vs.	Not informed, no opinion, or "don't know"	For	For	For
Lend-Lease						
Jan. 1941	52	32	11 ‡	62	—	—
Feb. 1941	50	18	22 §	74	—	—
Mar. 1941	—	—	—	—	63	67
Joining United Nations						
1945	66	3	31	96	96 ‖	98
British Loan						
Jan. 1946	46	37	17	55	—	—
Feb. 1946	27	40	33	40	59	60
Greek-Turkish Aid						
1947: Greece	42	25	33	63 ⎫	72	76
1947: Turkey	37	28	35	57 ⎭		
Marshall Plan						
Early Aug. 1947	27	4	68 ⚹	87	—	—
Late Aug. 1947	38	10	49 **	79	—	—
Nov. 1947	29	9	62	76	—	—
Dec. 1947	36	11	53	77	—	—
Mar. 1948	45	14	41	76	—	—
Mar.-April 1948: Law	—	—	—	—	82	80
June 1948: Appropriation	—	—	—	—	82 ††	90

TABLE XII (*Continued*)

PUBLIC OPINION AND CONGRESSIONAL VOTING *

Polling data were based on responses to the following questions:

Reciprocal Trade Program

Jan. 1937	AIPO	"Should Congress renew the President's power to make trade agreements abroad?"
Jan. 1940	AIPO	"Do you think Congress should give Secretary Hull the power to make more reciprocal trade treaties?"
June 1945	Roper	"Do you think it is a good idea or not such a good idea to have reciprocal trade agreements with foreign countries?"

Strict Neutrality Law rather than Presidential Discretion

Sept. 1937	AIPO	"Which of these plans for keeping out of war do you have more faith in: Have Congress pass stricter neutrality laws? Leave the job to the President?"

Repeal of Arms Embargo

Sept. 1939	AIPO	"Should Congress change the present Neutrality Law so that the U.S. could sell war materials to England and France?"
Oct. 1939	AIPO	"Should Congress change the present Neutrality Law so that England and France could buy war supplies here?"

Allowing American Ships to Enter War Zones

Dec. 1940	AIPO	"Should the Neutrality Law be changed so that American ships can carry war supplies to England?"
Sept. 1941	AIPO	Same as above.

Lend-Lease

Jan. 1941	OPOR	"This Lend-Lease Bill would permit the President to have the U.S. government pay for war materials made in this country for England or any other country which the President thinks would help our national defense. Do you favor or oppose this part of the bill?"
Feb. 1941	AIPO	"Do you think Congress should pass the President's Lend-Lease Bill?"

TABLE XII (*Continued*)

PUBLIC OPINION AND CONGRESSIONAL VOTING *

Joining United Nations

| July 1945 | AIPO | "Should the United States approve the United Nations charter for a world organization as adopted at the San Francisco Conference?" |

British Loan

Jan. 1946 NORC — The sample was given a statement explaining the purposes and advantages of the loan and was then asked: "Do you think Congress should or should not approve it?"

Feb. 1946 NORC — The sample was given *no* statement of explanation about the loan; the respondents were merely asked whether they approved or disapproved of the loan.

Greek-Turkish Aid

Mar. 1947: Greece AIPO — "Do you approve or disapprove of the bill asking for 250 million dollars to aid Greece?"

Mar. 1947: Turkey AIPO — "Do you approve or disapprove of the bill asking for 150 million dollars to aid Turkey?"

Marshall Plan

1947-48 AIPO — "What is your opinion of the Marshall Plan?" or similar question.

* There is an arbitrary element in the comparison between opinion of polling samples and Congressional voting because opinion polls are not available on all Congressional issues and because there are very few relevant polls before 1937.

† Public opinion data is lacking for other years in which Reciprocal Trade Program was voted on in Congress.

‡ Five per cent of the total sample gave qualified answers.

§ Ten per cent of the total sample gave qualified answers.

‖ No House vote on membership. Vote given is on bill providing for appointment of representatives to U.N. and probably overstates actual support in House for joining.

⅌ One per cent gave qualified answers.

** Three per cent gave qualified answers.

†† No record vote was taken on original appropriation bill, which cut appropriation below Senate figure. Figure here is vote on conference report "compromise."

TABLE XIII

PARTY VOTING ON FOREIGN POLICY, 1933-48

Type of Issue	No. of Roll Calls	No. of Issues	Percentage of Total Issues on Which Party Agreement Was				
			90-100%	80-89%	70-79%	60-69%	Less than 60%
I. *Neutrality and Isolation: 1933-41*							
HOUSE	17	9					
Democrats			55	45			
Republicans			45	33	11	11	
SENATE	32	13					
Democrats			38	31	7	17	7
Republicans			23	23	31	15	8
Neutrality and Isolation, Western Hemisphere: 1939-47							
HOUSE	3	3					
Democrats			100				
Republicans			67		33		
SENATE	7	7					
Democrats			57	29	14		
Republicans			86			14	
International Organization: 1933-40							
HOUSE	5	5					
Democrats			40	20		40	
Republicans				80	20		
SENATE	9	2					
Democrats					50		50
Republicans			50			50	
International Organization: 1943-48							
HOUSE	9	9					
Democrats			89		11		
Republicans			11	45	33		11
SENATE	10	10					
Democrats			80	20			
Republicans			30		60		10

TABLE XIII (*Continued*)

PARTY VOTING ON FOREIGN POLICY, 1933-48

Type of Issue	No. of Roll Calls	No. of Issues	Percentage of Total Issues on Which Party Agreement Was				
			90-100%	80-89%	70-79%	60-69%	Less than 60%
II. *National Defense: 1933-39*							
HOUSE	15	14					
Democrats			36	36	7	7	14
Republicans			21	36	21	15	7
SENATE	14	11					
Democrats			18	27	28		27
Republicans				36	9	37	18
National Defense: 1940-41							
HOUSE	10	10					
Democrats			100				
Republicans			60		10	20	10
SENATE	7	7					
Democrats			58	14	14		14
Republicans			44	14	14	14	14
National Defense: 1946-48							
HOUSE	3	3					
Democrats			100				
Republicans			100				
SENATE	1	1					
Democrats			100				
Republicans			100				
Selective Service, etc.							
HOUSE	10	4					
Democrats				75	25		
Republicans				25	25	25	25
SENATE	22	22					
Democrats			32	18	32	14	4
Republicans				4	4	55	37
III. *Foreign Aid, Loans, Grants*							
HOUSE	32	15					
Democrats			80	14	6		
Republicans			37	25	13	17	8

TABLE XIII (*Continued*)

PARTY VOTING ON FOREIGN POLICY, 1933-48

Type of Issue	No. of Roll Calls	No. of Issues	90-100%	80-89%	70-79%	60-69%	Less than 60%
SENATE............	42	27					
Democrats.......			37	37	18	4	4
Republicans......			46	11	18	14	11
IV. *Regional Pacts*							
HOUSE.............	—	—					
SENATE............	3	3					
Democrats.......			100				
Republicans......			100				
V. *Tariff Reductions, Freer Imports*							
HOUSE.............	16	16					
Democrats.......			82	6	6	6	
Republicans......			50	32	12	6	
SENATE............	48	16					
Democrats.......			25	32	25	18	
Republicans......			43	25	13	13	6
Agr. Tariff and Imports							
HOUSE.............	3	3					
Democrats.......			34		33	33	
Republicans......			33		67		
SENATE............	10	7					
Democrats.......			29		29	42	
Republicans......			71		29		
Sectional Interest Protection							
HOUSE.............	1	1					
Democrats.......						100	
Republicans......				100			
SENATE............	7	7					
Democrats.......				14	43	14	29
Republicans......			29	14	29	14	14

TABLE XIII (*Continued*)

PARTY VOTING ON FOREIGN POLICY, 1933-48

Type of Issue	No. of Roll Calls	No. of Issues	Percentage of Total Issues on Which Party Agreement Was				
			90-100%	*80-89%*	*70-79%*	*60-69%*	*Less than 60%*
VI. *Conduct of Foreign Relations*							
HOUSE............. 11		11					
Democrats.......			73		9	18	
Republicans......			37	18	18	9	18
SENATE............ 24		14					
Democrats.......			21	50	21	8	
Republicans......			13	13	27	20	27
TOTALS							
HOUSE.......... 133		103					
Democrats....			68	15	7	8	2
Republicans...			36	28	19	10	7
SENATE......... 236		147					
Democrats....			36	26	21	10	7
Republicans...			33	12	19	21	15

TABLE XIV

AVERAGE AGE AND SERVICE OF MEMBERS OF SENATE COMMITTEE ON FOREIGN RELATIONS, 1928-49

Year	Congress	Average Age of Committee Members (Years)	Average Length of Service in Senate Prior to Membership on Committee (Years)	Average Length of Service on Committee (Years)	Average Length of Service in Senate (Years)
1928.......	70th	60.11	2.51	5.06	7.57
1929.......	70th *	60.28	2.85	5.72	8.57
1929.......	71st	56.15	4.38	4.75	9.13
1930.......	71st	56.84	4.35	5.50	9.85
1931.......	71st *	57.84	4.35	6.50	10.85
1932.......	72d	57.27	4.41	6.45	10.86
1933.......	72d *	54.47	4.41	7.45	11.86
1933.......	73d	55.87	3.41	5.45	8.86
1934.......	73d	56.45	3.44	6.17	9.61
1935.......	74th	57.09	3.07	6.68	9.75
1936.......	74th	58.09	2.97	7.27	10.24
1937.......	75th	59.09	2.94	8.17	11.11
1938.......	75th	59.05	3.13	7.87	11.00
1939.......	76th	60.89	3.43	8.22	11.65
1940.......	76th	61.04	4.47	7.09	11.56
1941.......	77th	61.14	4.58	8.09	12.67
1942.......	77th	62.65	4.04	8.35	12.39
1943.......	78th	64.18	4.37	9.30	13.67
1944.......	78th	65.30	4.93	9.83	14.76
1945.......	79th	63.95	6.24	9.09	15.33
1946.......	79th	63.23	6.46	8.91	15.37
1947.......	80th	64.77	4.62	9.69	14.31
1948.......	80th	65.77	4.62	10.69	15.31
1949.......	81st	60.08	6.96	7.77	14.73
Average..		60.07	4.21	7.50	11.71

* Lame-duck session.

TABLE XV

AVERAGE AGE AND SERVICE OF MEMBERS OF HOUSE OF REPRESENTATIVES COMMITTEE ON FOREIGN AFFAIRS, 1928-49

Year	Congress	Average Age of Committee Members (Years)	Average Length of Service in House Prior to Membership on Committee (Years)	Average Length of Service on Committee (Years)	Average Length of Service in House (Years)
1928.......	70th	56.45	3.23	7.29	10.52
1929.......	70th *	57.45	3.23	8.29	11.52
1929.......	71st †	(55.68)	(3.54)	(6.00)	(9.54)
1930.......	71st	56.68	3.54	7.00	10.54
1931.......	71st *	55.95	2.35	7.65	10.00
1932.......	72d	53.47	0.92	5.52	6.44
1933.......	72d *	54.47	0.82	5.46	6.28
1933.......	73d	52.87	2.48	1.80	4.28
1934.......	73d	53.05	2.32	2.76	5.08
1935.......	74th	51.72	2.16	3.44	5.60
1936.......	74th	52.72	2.16	4.44	6.60
1937.......	75th	50.42	2.12	4.52	6.64
1938.......	75th	51.84	2.32	5.36	7.68
1939.......	76th	51.43	1.08	5.20	6.28
1940.......	76th	51.88	1.12	5.52	6.64
1941.......	77th	52.11	1.96	4.92	6.88
1942.......	77th	53.11	1.96	5.92	7.88
1943.......	78th	52.64	2.00	4.84	6.84
1944.......	78th	55.58	1.80	5.83	7.63
1945.......	79th	55.04	1.65	5.77	7.42
1946.......	79th	54.65	1.57	6.54	8.11
1947.......	80th	53.16	1.41	6.25	7.66
1948.......	80th	54.00	1.40	6.96	8.36
1949.......	81st	50.44	0.96	6.48	7.44
Average..		53.62	1.96	5.57	7.58

* Lame-duck session.

† No data were available on the standing committees in the House during the first session of the 71st Congress. The figures given in parentheses are based on the assumption that both the 1st and 2d sessions of the 71st Congress had the same men on the Committee on Foreign Affairs. Five changes in membership on the Committee were made between the lame-duck sessions of 1929 and 1931.

Appendix B

The Decision-Making Power in Foreign Relations, 1933-1948

TABLE XVI

EXECUTIVE POLICY DECISIONS: NO CONGRESSIONAL PARTICIPATION

1933	Disarmament policy proposed to Disarmament Conference.
	Policy proposals at London Economic Conference. (The delegation, however, included the chairman and a Republican member of the Senate Foreign Relations Committee, and the chairman of the House committee. Implementation of the policy would have required Congressional action.)
	Recognition of the U.S.S.R.
	Declaration of Good Neighbor Policy.
1934	Moral embargo on arms shipments to Germany.
1935	Moral embargo on shipments to belligerents in Italo-Ethiopian War.
1936	Moral embargo on shipments to Spain (i.e., prior to legislation extending the Neutrality Act).
1937	Refusal to apply Neutrality Act to Sino-Japanese conflict.
1939	The Declaration of Panama establishing a neutral Western Hemisphere zone, 300-1000 miles out from coast, to be patrolled by American republics for information and reporting.
	Moral embargo on airplanes to Japan.

TABLE XVI (*Continued*)

EXECUTIVE POLICY DECISIONS: NO CONGRESSIONAL PARTICIPATION

1939	Moral embargo on airplanes to Russia.
	Moral embargo on all exports of plans, plants, etc., for manufacture of aviation gasoline (directed at Japan).
1939-41	All relations and negotiations with Japan prior to Pearl Harbor.
1940 and after	All relations and negotiations with Vichy France and French resistance leaders.
1940	Transfer of destroyers to England in exchange for bases. (This was purely an executive action. Provisions in the National Defense Act of June 28, 1940, which provided technical legal justification, apparently were intended more to prevent than to facilitate such actions.)
1941	Occupation of Iceland.
	Atlantic Conference and Charter.
	Active armed patrol in Atlantic.
	Declaration by United Nations.
	All military decisions with consequences for international politics (e.g., cross-channel invasion vs. Balkan invasion).
1941 and after	Economic and political relations with Spain and other neutrals.
1942 and after	Argentine policy.
1942	Casablanca Conference.
1943	Moscow and Teheran Conferences.
1943 and after	Policy toward a defeated Germany.
1944	Yalta Agreement.
1945	Potsdam Agreement.
1945 and after	Policy toward China.
	Policy toward Japan.

TABLE XVII

POLICY DECISIONS PRIMARILY EXECUTIVE IN ORIGIN AND LEADERSHIP BUT REQUIRING CONGRESSIONAL ACTION

YEAR	LEGISLATION	HOUSE Total Votes For	Vs.	HOUSE Party Votes DEM. For	Vs.	HOUSE Party Votes REP. For	Vs.	SENATE Total Votes For	Vs.	SENATE Party Votes DEM. For	Vs.	SENATE Party Votes REP. For	Vs.
	Passed by Congress												
1934	Arms embargo (Chaco War)......	No record vote						No record vote					
1934	Trade Agreements Act......	72%	28%	95%	5%	10%	90%	63%	37%	91%	9%	15%	85%
1937	Trade Agreements Act......	73	27	93	7	11	89	70	30	87	13	—	100
1940	Trade Agreements Act......	57	43	92	8	5	95	52	48	70	30	—	100
1943	Trade Agreements Act......	85	15	95	5	74	26	73	27	86	14	53	47
1945	Trade Agreements Act......	62	38	93	7	20	80	72	28	86	14	50	50
1948	Trade Agreements Act......	61*	39*	11*	89*	98*	2*						
1937	Arms embargo (Spain)......	99.8	00.2†	100	—	100	—	100	—	100	—	100	—
1939 (Sept.-Oct.)	Arms embargo repeal ‡......	58	42	87	13	13	87	66	34	79	21	30	70
1941	Lend-lease......	64	36	91	9	19	81	67	33	80	20	36	64
1941	Repeal of prohibitions on arming merchant ships entering war areas	53	47	78	22	14	86	57	43	72	28	21	79

Year	Measure											Notes
1944	UNRRA..........................	86	14	96	4	77	23	81	19	71	29	
1946	British loan....................	59	41	84	16	33	67	40	68	32	49 51	

Defeated by Congress

	Measure											Notes
	President's power to embargo arms to aggressors	68	32	92	8	92	8	77	23	77	60	Substantive amendment eliminating executive discretion passed by unanimous vote. House refused to concur. Bill died.
	Adherence to World Court......	—		—								
	Pittman-McReynolds Neutrality Bill (executive discretion)	—		—				61§	39	70	30	39 61	Killed in Senate Committee on Foreign Relations.
	Repeal of arms embargo ‖........	45	55	73	27	5	95	95				Killed in Senate Committee on Foreign Relations by 12-11 vote.

* Voting *for* extension for only one year; those who voted *against* wanted longer extension.

† One negative vote cast by Rep. Marcantonio, American Labor Party.

‡ Vote on Vorys' amendment prohibiting all arms shipments; votes against amendment counted as votes for repeal of embargo.

§ Less than the necessary two-thirds majority.

‖ Vote on Vorys' amendment to Bloom Neutrality Bill. Amendment provided modified arms embargo. Votes *for* amendment counted as *against* repeal of embargo.

TABLE XVIII

POLICY DECISIONS PRIMARILY CONGRESSIONAL IN ORIGIN AND LEADERSHIP

Year	Legislation	House						Senate					
		Total Votes		Party Votes				Total Votes		Party Votes			
				DEM.		REP.				DEM.		REP.	
		For	Vs.	For	Vs.	For	Vs.	For	Vs.	For	Vs.	For	Vs.
	Without strong executive opposition												
1936	Neutrality Act..............	94%	6%	96%	4%	90%	10%	No record vote					
1937	Neutrality Act..............	96	4	98	2	89	11	No record vote					
	With moderate executive opposition												
1935	Neutrality Act (absence of discretionary power opposed by President)................	No record vote						98%	2%	97%	3%	100%	—
	With strong executive opposition												
1937	War Referendum Proposal........	45	55	38	62	76	24	—	—	—	—	—	—

TABLE XIX

POLICY DECISIONS WITH EXECUTIVE-CONGRESSIONAL COLLABORATION

Year	Legislation	House Total Votes		House Party Votes Dem.		House Party Votes Rep.		Senate Total Votes		Senate Party Votes Dem.		Senate Party Votes Rep.	
		For	Vs.	For	Vs.	For	Vs.	For	Vs.	For	Vs.	For	Vs.
	Requiring legislation												
1943	Res. favoring U.S. entry into post-war international organization...	91%	9%	98%	2%	85%	15%	95%	5%	97%	3%	90%	10%
1945	Membership in U.N....	—	—	—	—	—	—	98	2	100	—	94	6
1945	Bretton Woods Agreement....	93	7	96	4	89	11	79	21	95	5	53	47
1946	Adherence to World Court....	—	—	—	—	—	—	98	2	100	—	94	6
1946	Greek-Turkish aid....	72	28	92	8	57	43	76	24	84	16	69	31
1947	Peace Treaty with Italy....	—	—	—	—	—	—	89	11	91	9	86	14
1948	Inter-American Treaty of Reciprocal Assistance....	—	—	—	—	—	—	99	1	100	—	98	2
1948	ERP: Authorization....	82	18	94	6	73	27	80	20	93	7	69	31
	Appropriation....	84	16	94	6	76	24	90	10	95	5	84	16
1948	"Vandenberg Resolution" on Regional Defense Pacts....	92	8	98	2	95	5	—	—	—	—	—	—

Consultation only: no legislation required

1946 and after	Policy for U.S.S.R												
1948	Berlin crisis												

Index

A

Acheson, Dean, 104, 213, 220, 237
Acheson-Lilienthal report, 74
Adams, John Quincy, 136
Adequacy, 241, 253-57
Administrative branch, definition of, 26. *See also* Executive-administrative
Administrative responsibility. *See* Responsibility
Agreement, 4, 9, 23, 44, 63, 125, 257, 262; advantages of, 221-24. *See also* Presidential supremacy, Political leadership
Alsop, Joseph, 278 *n.*
Alsop, Stewart, 278 *n.*
Alternatives, formulation of, 63, 156-58, 164, 216
American Institute of Public Opinion, 266 *n.*, 269 *n.*
Appleby, Paul, 278 *n.*, 279 *n.*
Appropriations. *See* European recovery
Appropriations committees, 174, 175
Arendt, Hannah, 270 *n.*
Arms embargo, 14, 18, 33-34, 81, 98, 138, 171, 265 *n.*, 273 *n.*
Arms for Europe. *See* Europe
Army, American, 270 *n.*
Atomic bomb, 249, 252
Atomic energy, 72, 74-75, 86
Atomic Energy, Joint Congressional Committee on, 155

B

B_2H_2 group, 208-10
Bailey, Thomas A., 181, 251, 271 *n.*, 276 *n.*
Baker, Newton D., 101
Ball, Joseph H., 208
Barkley, Alben W., 265 *n.*
Barthélemy, Joseph, 270 *n.*, 276 *n.*
Beaman, Middleton, 275 *n.*
Beard, Charles A., 83, 251, 268 *n.*, 269 *n.*, 276 *n.*, 279 *n.*
Bemis, Samuel Flagg, 271 *n.*
Berelson, Bernard, 270 *n.*, 277 *n.*
Berlin crisis, 102, 211, 248, 250
Bigart, Homer, 271 *n.*
Binkley, Wilfred E., 268 *n.*
Bipartisan: consultation, 213, 236-37, 260; definition of, 227-28; foreign policy, 144, 187, 226-37, 249; voting, 228-29
Bipartisanship, 126, 208, 210, 215-16, 225, 227-37
Bloom, Sol, 49, 209, 267 *n.*, 276 *n.*
Bolles, Blair, 268 *n.*
Borah, William E., 26
Boston, 277 *n.*
Bretton Woods, 72, 140, 149, 211, 228, 230
Brewster, Owen, 163, 217-19
Bridges, Styles, 33, 83
British Labor Party, 233
British loan, 55, 72, 75
British Parliament, 169, 274 *n. See also* House of Commons